On Account of Sex

An Annotated Bibliography on the Status of Women in Librarianship, 1998–2002

Edited by
Betsy Kruger
Catherine Larson

The Scarecrow Press, Inc.
Lanham, Maryland • Toronto • Oxford
2006

SCARECROW PRESS, INC.

Published in the United States of America
by Scarecrow Press, Inc.
A wholly owned subsidiary of
The Rowman & Littlefield Publishing Group, Inc.
4501 Forbes Boulevard, Suite 200, Lanham, Maryland 20706
www.scarecrowpress.com

PO Box 317
Oxford
OX2 9RU, UK

British Library Cataloguing in Publication Information Available

Library of Congress Cataloging-in-Publication Data

On account of sex : an annotated bibliography on the status of women in librarianship, 1998–2002 / edited by Betsy Kruger, Catherine Larson.
p. cm.
Includes bibliographical references and indexes.
ISBN-13: 978-0-8108-5227-3 (pbk. : alk. paper)
ISBN-10: 0-8108-5227-6
1. Women in library science—United States—Bibliography. 2. Women in information science—United States—Bibliography. 3. Sex discrimination against women—United States—Bibliography. 4. Sex discrimination in employment—United States—Bibliography. I. Kruger, Betsy, 1954– . II. Larson, Catherine A., 1958– .
Z682.4.W65O54 2006
016.02082—dc22 2005033333

∞ ™ The paper used in this publication meets the minimum requirements of American National Standard for Information Sciences—Permanence of Paper for Printed Library Materials, ANSI/NISO Z39.48-1992.
Manufactured in the United States of America.

Contents

Acronyms and Abbreviations

AASL	American Association of School Librarians
ACRL	Association of College and Research Libraries
ALA	American Library Association
ALISE	Association of Library and Information Science Educators
ARL	Association of Research Libraries
AZLA	Arizona Library Association
BS	Bachelor of Science
CAYAS	Children's and Young Adult Services Interest Group
CHRC	Canadian Human Rights Commission
CLA	Canadian Library Association
CONSER	Cooperative Online Serials
COSWL	Committee on the Status of Women in Librarianship (ALA)
CSLA	California State Library Association
DC	District of Columbia
DLS	Doctor of Library Science
FTF	Feminist Task Force (ALA)
GLBTRT	Gay, Lesbian, Bisexual, Transgendered Round Table (ALA)
IFLA	International Federation of Library Associations and Institutions
ILS	Illinois Library Association
IMLS	Institute of Museums and Library Services
IT	Information technology
JAL	*Journal of Academic Librarianship*
LA	Library Association (UK)
LAMA	Library Administration and Management Association
LAPL	Los Angeles Public Library

LC	Library of Congress
LHRT	Library History Round Table
LIASA	Library and Information Association of South Africa
LIS	Library and information science
MA	Master of Arts
MLIS	Master of Library and Information Science
MLS	Master of Library Science
NAACP	National Association for the Advancement of Colored People
NASIG	North American Serials Interest Group
NCLIS	National Commission on Libraries and Information Science
NY	New York
NYPL	New York Public Library
OPAC	Online public access catalog
Ph.D.	Doctor of Philosophy
RBMS	Rare Book and Manuscripts Section
RTWI	Round Table on Women's Issues (IFLA)
SLA	Special Libraries Association
SLJ	School Library Journal
SOLINET	Southeastern Library Network, Inc.
TRL	Timberland Regional Library
UCLA	University of California at Los Angeles
UK	United Kingdom
US	United States
WLA	Washington Library Association
WOMBL	Women in British Libraries
WSS	Women's Studies Section (ACRL)

Preface

Women's status in librarianship continues to garner significant attention in library and information science (LIS) literature. With the publication of this volume of *On Account of Sex: An Annotated Bibliography on the Status of Women in Librarianship*, the American Library Association's Committee on the Status of Women in Librarianship (COSWL) Bibliography Task Force offers an index to LIS literature concerning the status of women in librarianship and information science published from 1998 to 2002. The 1998–2002 compilation is a continuation of the four previous compilations, which together index the relevant literature from 1977 through 1997. For this volume, as for its predecessors, numerous dedicated contributors monitored library and information science journals, monographic publications, government publications, conference proceedings, theses and dissertations, electronic publications, websites, and ERIC documents, as well as publications outside the library and information science field.

From 1998 to 2002, a number of topics appeared to be of particular interest for a profession that is often considered to be at a crossroads. Career development and satisfaction for all aspects of librarianship was an area of focus, including career development outside the field, with corresponding and continuing attention to salaries as well as pay equity. Career advice is offered, such as that found in "Climb High: High Altitude Mountaineering Lessons for Librarians," by G. Briscoe in *Law Library Journal*, and a smattering of articles examine the personality traits of librarians. Diversity issues in libraries continued to be a matter well-considered in the literature. This bibliography also indexes, as have previous bibliographies, the histories, biographies, and autobiographical stories of the many interesting, accomplished, diverse, and exciting women in the LIS field today. Librarians of all types, from academic to children's to special librarians, are represented. Kathleen de la Peña McCook's *Women of Color in Librarianship: An Oral History* offers the stories of eight women of color leaders in LIS, including their encounters with bias and discrimination. A number of articles offer first-person reflections on their narrator's accomplishments, struggles, and progressions.

Information technology also continued to be a subject of great interest, particularly the subtopics of access to information and women working in information technology. *Women, Work and Computerization: Charting a Course to the Future*, edited by Ellen Balka and Richard Smith, examined the effect of information technology on work and society and included papers by several renowned LIS writers. In *Artificial Knowing: Gender and the Thinking Machine*, author Alison Adam drew on feminist theory to examine the social aspects of artificial intelligence and the effect of technological innovations on women. H. Austin Booth explored the literature on women and "cyberculture" in her article "Women, Gender, and Cyberculture" (*Choice*, July/August 2000).

LIS associations continued to reflect the status of women in librarianship, and this bibliography points to a number of interesting activities, programs, and publications. The Association of Research Libraries continued its annual salary survey and its programs in leadership and career development. The library associations of both the United States and the United Kingdom continued to offer their members a voice in the development of the profession and the status accorded to women. Most articles pertaining to association activities can be found in the section, "Library Associations."

HOW THIS BOOK IS ORGANIZED

The format of this edition of the bibliography continues that which began with the 1992–1997 bibliography. Each entry is numbered and assigned to one of thirteen broad subject areas, such as biography and autobiography, career development and satisfaction, leadership and management, and library history. Each subject area forms a separate section in the bibliography; each section is arranged alphabetically by author, continues the entry numbering from the previous section, and begins with a scope note. The scope note is intended to guide the user as to what types of entries are included in or excluded from that section, as well as to suggest terms in the subject index that can be used to locate related entries. For example, the scope note for the section on library associations informs the user that this section encompasses publications detailing the current and past activities of library organizations and to refer to the biography and autobiography section for publications focusing on individuals within an organization, and to the library history section for women from the past.

While this arrangement allows a user to browse entries within a broad subject area, many of the publications indexed could have been placed appropriately in more than one of the sections listed in the table of contents. We tried to be as consistent as possible in our placement, but because topics may be viewed from several different aspects, the best way to find entries is to look in the subject index at the back of the volume. One example is "diversity," which may have been examined as an issue in a particular woman's story (in which case it would be in the section on biography and autobiography), as the focus of an association's programs (in which case it would appear in the section on library associations), or as an employment issue (in which case it would appear in the section of employment issues). Each entry in the bibliography has been assigned at least one entry term.

Additional finding aids at the back of the volume include author and geographic indexes. The geographic index is arranged by country name. When pertinent, entries for the United States are also indexed by state. Not all entries are indexed geographically, however.

Please note that the numbers referenced in all the indexes refer to citation numbers, not page numbers.

Acknowledgments

We would like to extend our sincere gratitude once again to the great staff members of the Library and Information Science Library and Interlibrary Borrowing Office at the University of Illinois at Urbana-Champaign. Their assistance over these last several years while compiling the bibliography has been invaluable. We also appreciate the helpful staff members of the many interlibrary loan offices at our contributors' "home" libraries. Without their willing assistance, this volume could not have been completed. Two graduate students from the University of Illinois Graduate School of Library and Information Science, Jessica Moorman and Rachel Rohlf, maintained the Procite database that we used to collect, sort, and index the annotations that are brought together in this volume. Finally, we would also like to thank Hope A. Olson and Amber Ritchie for their thoughtful introduction, which follows.

Introduction: Gentility, Technicality, and Salary: Women in the Literature of Librarianship

Hope A. Olson, University of Wisconsin, Milwaukee
Amber Ritchie, University of Alberta

The literature of librarianship has addressed the status of women in the field for at least a hundred years. In 1904, Salome Cutler Fairchild confronted women's secondary position as she presented the findings of her research in *Library Journal*. Fairchild's study (discussed further in this introduction) established three themes that mark the history of librarianship as a female-intensive profession. The first theme is the transfer of feminine gifts from the private to the public women's sphere—gifts such as service to others and ability with children. The second revolves around women's clerical abilities, especially our perceived acceptance of routine and attention to detail. The third theme is that of women's lower salaries and their consistently lower positions within the library system. This essay will survey some of the historical and research literature documenting these themes in the past and reflect on the constancies and changes exhibited by the literature of the last few years as listed in this volume.

HISTORY

Melvil Dewey's recruiting speech to "college-bred women" in 1886 established a pattern that might be considered either exploitative or enabling

(103). The speech was characterized by flattery, missionary zeal, and excuses, all aimed at attracting the graduates of women's colleges who were attaining degrees at a rising rate and looking for fulfilling and socially acceptable careers. Dewey's flattery was not subtle: Women going into librarianship were a "picked class selected from the best," with their undergraduate degrees giving them the advantage of knowledge and ability. He stirred missionary zeal with claims that librarians give people the best books to read every day throughout their lives and are, thus, even more influential than teachers or clergy. In spite of this glorious picture of women in librarianship, Dewey had to make excuses for the low salaries offered, implying that the fulfillment to be found in a library career far outweighed the monetary aspects.

Justin Winsor's infamous quote (London, 1877) carries much the same message and tone: "In the Boston Public Library two-thirds of the librarians are women. In American libraries we set a high value on women's work. They soften our atmosphere, they lighten our labour, they are equal to our work, and for the money they cost—if we must gauge such labour by such rules—they are infinitely better than equivalent salaries will produce of the other sex."

Such pronouncements have been irresistible fodder for feminist interpretations of the history of librarianship as a female-intensive profession. Historian Dee Garrison (1979) suggests that librarianship as a female-intensive profession was feminized to enforce a late-nineteenth-century version of gentility, and that public librarianship, as a profession and as an institution, has suffered ever since. Garrison claims that in the late nineteenth century, the organization of librarianship replaced the rural sense of community in the United States that had traditionally drawn people together. Even the newly developed "domestic science" was an institutionalization of community. Efforts to maintain genteel values were part of the establishment of librarianship as a profession.

Most early leaders, such as Justin Winsor, William Poole, and Charles Cutter, were of the "gentry." Women were recruited to the field partly to maintain this gentility. They were seen as "standard bearers of the genteel value system" in both the public and private spheres, and the library was used to maintain the idea of the well bred in the face of mass culture, feminism, economic change, and threats to Victorian sexual mores. Education, especially of the weaker sex, was viewed as an antidote to most social ills. When late Victorian American women flocked to popular fiction, library leaders took a moral stand against it. Much was written, in a very prescriptive manner, on what and what not to read. Fiction was viewed as a moral threat, especially to the genteel woman. The sensual heroines who flouted convention and ended up happy—and often independent—threatened authority and, therefore, the genteel status quo that the library was trying to maintain. Thus, according to Garrison, the combination of the expansion of public libraries and the increased availability of college-educated women resulted in librarianship becoming a genteel occupation reinforcing genteel values.

Garrison posits that the low status of librarianship stems from its being established as women's work. In her view, Annie Godfrey Dewey's "activity in establishing professional careers for women in librarianship and home economics was chiefly a glorification of women's service roles in society" (1979, 119). Garrison states that women were preferred for the "tedious" job of cataloging. She sees the clericalization of librarianship as a result of this supposed preference for supposedly tedious work combined with Dewey's standardization of the profession. In 1923, the Williamson report on education for librarianship blamed the technical nature of such education for the profession's low status and lack of men. Also, librarianship, like social work, was part of the white, middle class woman's efforts at reform aimed to realize the ideal of white, middle class women. The development of services to urban children and to immigrants further followed these missionary-like sentiments. As education became more accessible, however, the role of the public library waned. Around the time of World War I, women left libraries for better-paying clerical jobs as they realized that they weren't making a difference in social reform. Garrison concludes that the feminization of public librarianship stunted the growth of the public library as an institution by creating an image of a "homey" place with "helpful" staff. Such a feminization inhibited leadership and the cause of intellectual freedom. Garrison believes that we are now trying to remedy this by being more "scientific," making the librarian an "indispensable expert in knowledge retrieval" as a reaction to the evils of gentility (1979, 241).

Written in the 1970s, when a feminist reevaluation of traditionally feminine traits was only beginning to be popularized, Garrison's analysis is limited by a climate of liberal feminism. She is stuck in the "great man" method of history—she includes little about the everyday lives of librarians except to characterize them as the "genteel library hostess." Garrison's thesis in *Apostles of Culture* is that the purpose of the public library movement was social control and maintenance of the status quo, that its failure to achieve social control was the result of the predominance of women and that, in addition, close affiliation with women's roles prevented the development of librarianship into a "real" profession.

Suzanne Hildenbrand (1983), on the other hand, observes that Garrison uses a very conservative definition of a profession, employs a double standard in her interpretation of male and female historical sources in terms of the validity she gives to their remarks, takes rhetoric at face value, and minimizes women entering the workforce as an extension of women's sphere. Hildenbrand illustrates that Garrison's sources could just as easily be interpreted in reverse, that the public library's low status as an institution allowed women in and then dragged them down. Women entered the profession as pioneers and developed children's work as part of the Progressive Era's emphasis on children, but still found themselves in dead-end jobs, like Dewey's Wellesley half-dozen who were left behind with the routine tasks when Dewey moved on to greater things. Hildenbrand suggests it was the institution itself that lacked vision, not the women who became librarians.

Hildenbrand (1985) develops her own interpretation of the historical evolution of librarianship as a female-intensive profession. She looks at librarianship in the context of the rise of progressivism after the close of the frontier in the 1890s. This progressivism eventually led to the welfare state, and government intervention was justified as curtailing unfair competition and protecting the individual. The progressive model of the state required large numbers of professionals to support it, providing advancement opportunities for middle class youth, especially young women. The system was developed to make professionals legitimators of the progressive state, especially in the "women's professions" meant to make the state seem just and acceptable while providing worthwhile services. Women in these professions tended to work for government in the public sector and to have little autonomy over their work.

At the same time, the Victorian gender system was eroding. Men's jobs were less independent and more bureaucratic. The New Woman was emerging. Men felt threatened, building a "masculine cult" to replace Victorian gender distinctions. One result was job segregation, both hierarchical and territorial. Both types of segregation are seen within librarianship where women in upper-level library jobs peaked in the 1920s and internal segregation by specialization is still a factor. The cult of individualism tended to blame victims for their own status. Women did not realize that their low status was from social causes. The lack of feminist movement allowed individual women to be blamed for their lack of success. That women in librarianship really did achieve positive social gains is clear but is not always linked to a discussion of professional status. For example, the efficacy of summer reading programs promoting success in school for urban children has been well documented. This kind of women's work is often called "social housekeeping," but it is actually community building. When valued it exhibits the transfer of so-called private traits to the public sphere as important contributions to the fabric of modern society.

EMPIRICAL RESEARCH

A series of empirical studies conducted over the course of the twentieth century statistically documents and validates the three themes of librarianship—women's work sphere, women's clerical tasks, women's low status and pay—that those looking from the historical view had noticed.

Salome Cutler Fairchild was the first to empirically document that men are in charge, especially in large libraries, and that they earn higher salaries than do women. She also documented the types of attitudes that hold women back from greater success. Sponsored by the American Library Association (ALA) and published in 1904, Fairchild's research explores the status of women in American librarianship at the beginning of the twentieth century. Her methodology included sending a questionnaire consisting of four questions to one hundred representative libraries, which included fifty-four public, six reference, three government, three proprietary, and four subscription libraries.

Out of a total of 2,958 employees in the 94 libraries that responded to the questionnaire, 2,024 were women; however, it was men who were in charge in all types of libraries except small public libraries and libraries in women's colleges. The hierarchical status of women was apparent: The lower the position levels, the fewer men and more women were likely to hold them. This divide was also visible in levels of remuneration. Fairchild looked at salaries in public libraries and reported that for administrative positions in large libraries men received between $3,000 and $7,000, while women received up to $2,100. Salaries came closer together when considering all librarian positions in small libraries, with men averaging $2,118 and women $1,429.

Fairchild's open-ended questions received comments largely suggesting that women are willing to accept lower salaries and are not as businesslike or ambitious, are handicapped by a more delicate physique, are not original, do not experiment, cope well with routine, are gracious and hospitable, and are good with the public. Fairchild's conclusion is that men and women are suited to different tasks and can complement each other, but that women's advancement is subject to the barriers of conservatism and prejudice.

Published nearly fifty years later in 1952, Alice I. Bryan's major study of public libraries in the United States included site visits, questionnaires, and interviews of sixty libraries and more than two thousand librarians, 92 percent of who were women. She found that men held higher positions, were more likely to be married, did less domestic work, brought home higher salaries, and were more satisfied than women. Both men and women often believed that their sex had an effect on their careers.

Bryan's research studied the characteristics of personnel in public libraries in general. Sex was one of her major variables, so this report is an excellent source of information on the role of women in public librarianship. Bryan visited 60 libraries from a population of 7,408 "to exemplify various types of library service available to a variety of population-sized groups, in various geographic locations" (1952, 13). The sample was skewed toward libraries serving larger populations. The questionnaire was sent to three main groups. Individual professional librarians were asked to fill out a fifty-two-page questionnaire, including a personality inventory and a vocational interest blank. Eighty-four percent responded, including 85 percent of the women and 69 percent of the men to whom the questionnaires were sent. Library directors were asked to fill out a fifty-six-page questionnaire, including sections on personnel administration policies and practices. A questionnaire was also sent to the thirty-four American accredited library schools.

The results most relevant to women in librarianship came from the professional librarians' responses. Of 2,395 librarians, 92 percent were women, but there were a considerably higher percentage of men in high-level positions; 4 percent of the women and 15 percent of the men were head librarians or "first-line assistants." One quarter of the professional women and two-thirds of the professional men were married. "The professional men receive more help from their mates than do the professional women" (1952, 37); men averaged 8.8 hours and women 14.2 hours per week of domestic work. As a group both men and women were lower in self-confidence than other people of similar education; men and women both had very similar psychological profiles in general. In 1947 one woman had a salary of $10,000, as did 102 men; in all areas men's salaries were higher. Sixty percent of the men and 38 percent of the women felt that the sexes were treated equally. Men often felt that being male benefited their careers, and women felt disadvantaged by being female. Top administrators of both sexes were more satisfied than they expected with librarianship; however, 42 percent of female middle managers found it very disappointing. Overall, Bryan's results show little change from Fairchild's study over forty years earlier.

In the early 1970s, Anita Schiller (1974) surveyed and summarized the available empirical data from 1878 to 1972. She found the expected pattern of discrimination: Women held lower positions, received lower salaries, and were blamed for the lower status of the profession. She addressed some myths, pointing out that women were less likely to be married and did not have greater turnover or lower mobility than men. She also noted the beginnings of interest in women's issues in librarianship in 1969 as a source of optimism.

Schiller reanalyzed data on the status of women in librarianship as it appeared in reports, surveys, and articles from 1878 to 1972. She included scholarly, popular, and official works done both in the field and outside of it. From this data Schiller draws certain generalizations. The latest study to that date specifically on women in librarianship was Fairchild's in 1904, and other data on the topic is fragmentary and drawn from a variety of sources. Sex is not always a variable in research about the profession, thus hiding discrimination. The gendered salary differential is ubiquitous, and women are consistently underrepresented in upper-level positions, especially in larger libraries. Women in high positions peaked in 1920 or earlier, with the 1960s being worse than previous years. "The evidence is overwhelming," wrote Schiller. "Women are being systematically eliminated from leadership positions in an occupation in which they constitute four-fifths of the membership" (1974, 121).

Kathleen Heim's (Kathleen de la Peña McCook) 1982 review of newer data followed up on Schiller's report. Again, salaries and positions for women were lower, but Heim found the salary gap at the entry level closing. Heim reviewed statistical data on librarians mainly from large empirical studies but also included some dissertations on the subject. The time period she covered was 1938 to 1981 with an emphasis on 1970 to 1981, the period following Schiller's analysis. Most of the surveys she included were done by or were about specific associations and institutions.

Heim draws certain generalizations from the data. In education for library and information studies, the higher the degree the fewer the women, although she notes an increase in the number of women obtaining doctorates. At the time of her study, entry-level salaries were converging quite close together for women and men. Among American Society for Information Science members the lowest-paid specializations have the highest percentage of women. Large public libraries have a predominance of male directors who are paid more than women, while smaller public libraries have more women. Heim's cautious conclusion is "Whether women are rising up the ladder of librarianship at an accelerated rate is still an open question. A decade of activism on the part of women has resulted in no clear improvement of status. There have been some gains and some losses. A closure of the starting salary differential (up to 1979) is outweighed by a continuing divergence of salaries in relationship to time spent in library work" (42).

Kathleen Heim and Leigh Estabrook (1983) examined career profiles of librarians to evaluate the status of women in librarianship. They sent a seven-page questionnaire to a random sample of three thousand American Library Association librarian members, receiving nearly two thousand usable responses. The questionnaire consisted of thirty-seven questions on overall career pattern, current or most recent job description, educational background, professional involvement, and personal data. The results indicated that 78.3 percent of the sample was female and 93.7 percent was white. More men (66 percent) than women (49 percent) were married. Women's salaries were lower than men's, at a median of almost $5,000 less, with women's job classifications less prestigious. The greater the percentage of men in a specific type of library the greater the differential in salary between men and women, as demonstrated by the survey's 46.2 percent men and 29.6 percent women who worked in academic libraries and the 17 percent women and 3.4 percent men who were in school libraries. Again, fewer women than men held administrative positions.

This study by Heim and Estabrook was inspired by a similar study in Britain (Margaret Slater, 1979) and by a Canadian study. It is interesting to look at the Canadian study after considering the situation in the United States because of the generally accepted influence of U.S. culture on Canada. The study was funded by the Canada Council; it was performed by two University of Waterloo (Ontario) sociologists, Linda Fischer and Mary Ann Wasylycia-Coe, and two Toronto librarians, Phyllis Yaffe and Sherrill Cheda. Although a full report of the study was never published, its methods and findings were summarized by Cheda (1978; Cheda et al. 1978) and by Elizabeth Futas (1983).

The Canadian study looked at causal relationships between the variables of discrimination and motivation for female librarians. The researchers developed a model with various links between variables including current job status, rate of advancement, continuity of work, number of job changes and promotions, motivations and aspirations, the perceived roles of compatibility and conflict, and perceived opportunities. Gender, age, and family status were also included. A two-stage questionnaire was sent to a stratified cluster random sample of 667 Canadian librarians, two-thirds of whom were female. Stage one consisted of a short demographic questionnaire; stage two included longer questions on more subjective topics. From the reports of the research, the following results may be gleaned. Females had higher representation at lower salary levels, males at higher levels, with the same differential noted for all levels of positions. Large libraries were more likely to have male directors, and female directors earned less than male directors even when library size was taken into consideration. Also, men's salaries were higher even when education levels were considered. "Motivation and aspirations were measured and no difference between the sexes was found in this sample, but it is of particular importance that over 60 percent of all librarians had little or no expressed ambition to move on to a more prestigious position" (Cheda 1978, 27).

Cheda concludes that "if a woman does all the 'right' things, i.e., becomes Chief Librarian . . . , adds an M.A. to her library degree . . . , and takes no breaks in her career, she will be most heavily financially penalized for her gender" (1978, 27). Cheda also suggests that lack of motivation is not the issue but rather that the further women go in education and status the more discrimination they encounter. While the study's links between job changes and promotions, motivation and aspirations, and current job status may be seen as tenuous, the demographic data reported by Cheda still echoes the U.S. data gathered by Schiller and Heim and Estabrook.

Another culture heavily influenced by the United States is Taiwan, where Chang Su-chüan did a similar study in 1991. Surveying 242 female academic library staff in Taiwan, Chang found that women were younger than their male colleagues, were paid less, held lower positions in the hierarchy, were better educated, and were more likely to be in technical services or automation. The last factor is the only quality different from women in North American libraries. Chang's findings were based on a questionnaire sent to a random sampling of sixteen public and private universities and colleges. A total of 188 (75.6 percent) questionnaires were returned, 165 (87.77 percent) from women and 23 (12.23 percent) from men. The results conclude that female library employees were mainly between the ages of thirty and thirty-nine, they were university graduates with salaries mostly in the range of 20,000 to 25,000 Taiwan dollars per month (approximately US$800 to $1000), and the majority were married with up to two children. They were well represented in administration, but not in the higher positions, while a higher percentage than men worked in technical services and automation. Chang's conclusions are very similar to conclusions in North American studies, except for the preponderance of women in the technology area.

All of these studies bear out the three themes mentioned at the outset of this essay: women's transfer of the gentility of the private sphere to the public sphere, women's adeptness at clerical tasks, and especially a general devaluation of women's work in relation to salary and position.

THE PAST FIVE YEARS

The five years of library literature reflected in this volume offer interesting variations and extensions on these three themes. The following discussion explores each of the three themes as they are or are not represented in the past five years and highlights.

Image, the ubiquitous lament about librarians' stereotypical portrayal, is the issue most closely related to the notion of gentility as a characteristic of librarians. The anything-but-glamorous vision of sensible shoes, glasses, and a bun is the professional equivalent of the spinster aunt of domesticity transferred to the public sphere. This concern about image continues to attract considerable attention in our literature inspiring titles like "Leaders of the Stacks" (Garrison 1999) and "Wear Lipstick, Have a Tattoo, Belly-dance, Then Get Naked" (Brewerton 1999). Specific attention has been given to the image of youth librarians (Feehan and Buie 1998) and library media specialists (Turock 1998), recalling that the traits of the private sphere have fostered women's predominance in librarianship for children and young adults.

Curiously, little has been written about women and cataloging or other technical or perceived clerical specializations. A series of interviews with librarians prominent in cataloging in *Cataloging & Classification Quarterly* was less than open about gender issues except for Elaine Svenonius, interviewed by Dorothy McGarry (2000), who expressed her dismay at the gender split between librarianship and information science. However, a parallel situation has arisen in information technology. As Roma Harris (1999) explains, the technology gender gap makes control a largely masculine endeavor and takes control away from those who actually use the technology for everyday work, a predominantly female workforce. Technology first entered librarianship via applications in technical services and has developed in the field to parallel gender roles in cataloging with clerical tasks deemed "women's work."

The theme of these three that has gained the most force is that of the gender gap in salary. Reports on librarians' salaries from *The Bowker Annual Library and Book Trade Almanac*, *Library Journal*, the Special Library Association, the Association of Research Libraries (ARL), and others show a continuing discrepancy based on sex. Optimistic data for 1998/1999 did not continue, although predictions regarding the slow advances toward parity are somewhat justified by the data. Female special librarians and ARL directors seem to have the most equitable remuneration. However, comprehensive analysis of all data considering all major relevant variables (sex, position, salary, experience, and education) could be illuminating.

In this same vein, a number of significant pay equity cases have occurred in California, Canada, and New South Wales (Australia), the last linked to the profile of librarianship as human service work (Cortis 2000). Pay equity concerns connect the issue of low salary much more closely to gender. The year 2000 saw John N. Berry's campaign in *Library Journal* and the tempest spawned by James LaRue in *American Libraries* draw attention to librarians' low salaries and set the stage for Mitch Friedman's ALA presidency's focus on salaries and ALA's support for Equal Pay Day.

The literature of librarianship also presents evidence of strong themes that have been emerging for some time and are now well established. Most of the topics that expand the work of earlier researchers are related to inclusion. They focus either on diversity in terms of sexuality, race, or ethnicity or on the increasing awareness of international and cross-cultural issues in a global world. Literature addressing the concerns of lesbian librarians and information seekers, minority women librarians, and the information needs of specific groups such as older women continues to be welcome and is growing into a significant corpus. International women's concerns have been highlighted by articles such as Suzanne Hildenbrand's (1998) during Barbara J. Ford's ALA presidency which focused on "global reach, local touch." Specific literature highlighted in this volume comes from India, Taiwan, Germany, South Africa, Nigeria, France, Australia, the United Kingdom, and elsewhere.

CONCLUSION

Women's status within librarianship has consistently been lower than men's in terms of position and salary. Whether the status of the profession allowed women in or whether the preponderance of women lowered the profession's status is not clear. Librarians, for the most part, continue to be preoccupied with the intangible concern of image and the all too tangible concerns regarding salary. Technology and gender persist in having a complex concatenation of access, technical, and power issues. The themes of gentility, technicality, and salary still haunt us though in updated guise.

Where can we go from here? How can future enquiry address persistent inequities and misperceptions? Persistence must be answered with persistence. Persistence is needed in linking the stereotypes of librarians to the stereotypes of women and the devaluation of service professions in the public sphere to the trivializing of domesticity in the private sphere. Failure to make these connections, even in efforts to raise the professional profile of librarians, distracts our efforts to understand the issues and to address them effectively. Persistence is required in understanding the changes to gender roles as the profession evolves as the result of technological change. Research could fruitfully look at the synthesis of cataloging and technology in our growing standardization and application of metadata. Who is controlling the development of metadata and who is applying it on an everyday basis? Are the gender roles of cataloging and of technology being replicated or are new and more equitable roles possible in this new context? Persistence is essential in documenting and fully analyzing salary and status data as a basis for addressing these issues. A full meta-analysis of salary and position data in relation to gender similar to Kathleen Heim's 1982 study would be an excellent starting point for further work on pay equity. More consideration of status and salary in comparison to other female-intensive professions and to male-intensive professions would also form a foundation for action. Persistence is crucial in pursuing all types of inclusion. Exploring our differences is as important as establishing our unifying bonds.

Equity for women has yet to be attained in librarianship. We have to keep raising women's issues in our literature to increase our understanding and to provide a foundation for continuing improvement. Equity is a long-term struggle that requires persistence.

BIBLIOGRAPHY

Bryan, Alice I. *The Public Librarian: A Report of the Public Library Inquiry*. New York: Columbia University Press, 1952.

Chang Su-chüan. "Wo Kuo ta hsüeh t'u shu kuan nü hsing kuan yüan kung tso lei hsing chih yen chiu." T'ai-pei shih: Han Mei t'u shu yu hsien kung ssu, 1991.

Cheda, Sherrill. "Women and Management in Libraries." *The Bertha Bessam Lecture in Librarianship*, vol. 5. Toronto: University of Toronto Faculty of Library Science, 1978, 20–30.

Cheda, Sherrill, et al. "Salary Differentials for Female and Male Librarians in Canada." *Emergency Librarian* 5, no. 3 (1978): 3.

Cortis, Natasha. "Pay Equity and Human Service Work: A New South Wales Case Study." *Australian Journal of Political Science* 35, no. 1 (2000): 49–62.

Dewey, Melvil. "Librarianship as a Profession for College-Bred Women: An Address Delivered before the Association of Collegiate Alumni on March 13, 1886." *Melvil Dewey: His Enduring Presence in Librarianship*. Edited by Sarah K. Vann. Littleton, CO: Libraries Unlimited, 1978.

Fairchild, Salome Cutler. "Women in American Libraries." *Library Journal* 19 (1904): 157–62.

Futas, Elizabeth. "An Analysis of the Study 'Career Paths of Male and Female Librarians in Canada.'" In *The Status of Women in Librarianship: Historical, Sociological and Economic Issues*, ed. Kathleen Heim, 393–423. New York: Neal-Schuman, 1983.

Garrison, Dee. *Apostles of Culture: The Public Librarian and American Society, 1876-1920*. New York: Free Press, 1979.

Harris, Roma. "Gender and Technology Relations in Librarianship." *Journal of Education for Library and Information Science* 40, no. 4 (Fall 1999): 232–46.

Heim, Kathleen. "The Demographic and Economic Status of Librarians in the 1970s, with Special Reference to Women." *Advances in Librarianship* 12 (1982): 1–45.

Heim, Kathleen, and Leigh Estabrook. *Career Profiles and Sex Discrimination in the Library Profession*. Chicago: ALA, 1983.

Hildenbrand, Suzanne. "Ambiguous Authority and Aborted Ambition: Gender, Professionalism, and the Rise and Fall of the Welfare State." *Library Trends* (1985): 195–98.

Hildenbrand, Suzanne. "Revision Versus Reality: Women in the History of the Public Library Movement." *The Status of Women in Librarianship: Historical, Sociological and Economic Issues*, ed. Kathleen Heim, 7–27. New York: Neal-Schuman, 1983.

Hildenbrand, Suzanne, and Mary Biblo. "International Library Women: Identifying Problems, Seeking Solutions." In *Libraries: Global Reach—Local Touch*, ed. Katherine de la Pena McCook, Barbara J. Ford, and Kate Lippincott, 187–94. Chicago, IL: American Library Association, 1998.

McGarry, Dorothy. "An Interview with Elaine Svenonius." *Cataloging & Classification Quarterly* 29, no. 4 (2000): 5–17.

Schiller, Anita. "Women in Librarianship." *Advances in Librarianship* 4 (1974): 103–47.

1

Biography and Autobiography

This chapter includes profiles of contemporary, individual women in library and information science; honors and awards; notices of women appointed to important professional offices and positions. Profiles of women from the past are recorded in the chapter "Library History." For women in history, see the chapter "Library History." For related entries, refer to the subject index under type of librarian, e.g., "Academic librarians," "African American librarians," etc.

GENERAL

1. "ALA Announces New Head of D.C. Office." ***ALA Washington News*** **51, no. 9 (September 1999): 1–2.**

Announces appointment of Emily Sheketoff on September 17, 1999, as associate executive director for the American Library Association. Ms. Sheketoff's previous experience includes a variety of positions in federal government and broadcasting.

2. "ALA Washington Office Associate Director Anne Heanue Retires." ***ALA Washington News*** **51, no. 1 (January 1999): 8.**

Announcement of the December 26, 1998, retirement of Anne Heanue, associate director of the ALA Washington office. Heanue's accomplishments included increasing public access to government information, building coalitions between ALA and other organizations, and helping to gain increased federal funding for American libraries.

3. "ALA Washington Office Associate Director Anne Heanue to Retire." ***ALAWON*** **7, no. 152 (11 December 1998).**

Describes Ms. Heanue's contributions as a representative of ALA to Congress, federal officials, national organizations, and ALA units.

4. "Augusta Baker." ***Voices of Youth Advocates*** **21, no. 2 (June 1998): 95.**

Obituary of Augusta Baker, an influential pioneer in young adult librarianship. Her bibliography, *Books about Negro Life for Children*, published in 1948, became a standard work for collection development worldwide. ALA's Grolier Award was one of the many awards she received during her career. In 1961 she was the first person of color to become the coordinator of children's services at the New York Public Library.

5. "Augusta Baker, a Librarian and Storyteller, Dies at 86." ***Library Journal*** **123, no. 5 (15 March 1998): 11.**

Obituary for Augusta Baker, who spent most of her career at the New York Public Library in children's services and who was a pioneer in producing reading lists and bibliographies of materials promoting positive images of African Americans. After retiring from NYPL, she relocated to the University of South Carolina's College of Library and Information Science where she assumed the newly created position of storyteller in residence until her second retirement in 1994. An annual storytelling festival is held in her honor in Columbia, South Carolina.

6. "Bush, Laura." ***Current Biography Yearbook*** **(2001): 64–67.**

Biographical profile of First Lady Laura Bush, former teacher and librarian. Outlines her education, childhood and family life, and political and social agenda.

7. "Carol French Johnson ILA President 2000." ***Catalyst*** **54, no. 2 (2000): 6.**

Profiles Johnson, the Iowa Library Association president for 2000 and director of both the Waterloo and Cedar Falls Public Libraries. Johnson's unique career path is noted, as well as her thoughts about the changing profession. Johnson cites computers and demographics as the two major differences in libraries since she began her career thirty-one years ago.

8. "Diane Frankel, Director of the Institute of Museum and Library Services to Step Down." ***ALAWON*** **8, no. 17 (18 February 1999).**

A press release that describes Diane Frankel's leadership as director of the Institute of Museum and Library Services. In her post she testified before Congress and traveled throughout the United States to meet with library and museum leaders and advocate for the public benefits of strong museums and libraries.

10. "Gay Liberation: From Task Force to Round Table: Interview with Barbara Gittings." ***American Libraries*** **30, no. 11 (December 1999): 74–76.**

This is an interview by *American Libraries* editor Leonard Kniffel with Barbara Gittings. Gittings, though not a librarian, is a prominent gay activist and library advocate who was instrumental in founding the ALA Gay, Lesbian, and Bisexual Round Table. She talks about other challenges concerning gay rights for libraries throughout the years.

11. "Georgetown's Martin to Step Down." ***Library Journal Academic News Wire*** **(12 December 2000).**

Susan K. Martin, Georgetown University librarian, announced that she would step down from her position on August 1, 2001. Martin's accomplishments at Georgetown included restructuring the library organization and overseeing extensive renovations. She has also been credited with instituting the library's collection development policy and many other accomplishments. Prior to leaving her position, Martin hoped to realize a few more objectives, particularly in regard to fund-raising and the completion of Georgetown's Gelardin New Media Center, named for Jacques Gelardin in honor of his substantial gift to the library. Martin said she planned to stay involved in the library profession through consulting and teaching and would serve as coeditor of the library journal *PORTAL*. Martin's educational background includes a doctorate from the University of California at Berkeley. Previous positions include a stint at Johns Hopkins. Martin is also known for her decision to leave her editorial position at the *Journal of Academic Librarianship* when it was taken over by publishing giant Elsevier.

12. "A Globetrotter Librarian Discusses Her Role in a Changing World." ***American Libraries*** **31, no. 9 (October 2000): 48–50.**

Marianna Tax Choldin describes her experiences as the director of the C. Walter and Gerda B. Mortenson Center for International Library Programs at the University of Illinois at Urbana-Champaign. Choldin was awarded Russia's Pushkin Medal for "extraordinary contributions to Russia in the sphere of culture and education." Choldin discusses her activities with libraries throughout the world.

13. "Henderson to Retire from ALA-WO." ***ALA Washington News*** **51, no. 4 (April 1999): 1.**

Announces Carol Henderson's retirement from the post of executive director of the American Library Association's Washington office. Her accomplishments include the expansion of ALA's Washington office, establishment of an Office for Information Technology Policy, enactment of the Library Services and Technology Act in 1996, revisions to copyright legislation, and enactment of telecommunications discounts for libraries and schools.

14. "Mary Helen Mahar 1913–98." ***Knowledge Quest*** **26, no. 4 (May 1998–30 June 1998): 71.**

Reports the death of Mary Helen Mahar, executive director of American Association of School Librarians from 1954–1956. Summarizes Mahar's career from 1956 until her retirement in 1978. Notes that she was responsible for the development and implementation of rules and regulations for Title II of the Elementary and Secondary Education Act; the definitions she developed are still in use. In 1981, Mahar received the AASL President's Award for distinguished service to the school library profession.

15. "New ALA Publication Showcases Outstanding 'Women of Color in Librarianship.'" ***Library Personnel News*** **13, no. 1/2 (Spring 2000–Summer 2000): 8.**

Announcement of the publication of *Women of Librarianship: An Oral History*, which began as a project of ALA's Committee on the Status of Women in Librarianship and was funded by a 1988 World Book-ALA Goal award. Edited by Kathleen de la Peña McCook and introduced by Suzanne Hildebrand, the book features interviews with eight librarians representing African Americans, Native Americans, Latinas, and Chinese Americans.

16. "Nigeria: How Mariam Abacha Haunted Her Rivals." ***Africa News*****, (27 January 1999): 1–5.**

Article relates the story of Hadiza Shittu Fawiba's ousting as director of Katsina State Library by Nigeria's first lady, Mrs. Mariam Abacha. This move was the culmination of Mrs. Abacha's jealous rage against Ms. Fawiba, who had once been the love interest of Sani Abacha and continued to hold the favor of his mother. Before being forcibly removed, Fawiba had risen in Nigeria's civil service ranks from college lecturer to president of the Nigerian Association of Librarians to the directorship of the state library. Ms. Fawiba, who had initially planned to take the First Lady to court, has dropped her suit and "left everything to God."

17. "Peggy Barber: Reminiscences and Hopes for the Future." ***American Libraries*** **30, no. 6 (June 1999–31 July 1999): 8–9.**

This interview is a dialogue with Peggy Barber about her service in the American Library Association. She was employed at ALA for over thirty years and was an associate executive director of communications since 1984. In the interview she discusses the library profession from the 1960s to the present and the challenges of the future. Barber was responsible for creating the "Read" poster campaign.

18. "Profiles in Diversity." ***Illinois Library Association Reporter*** **17, no. 4 (August 1999): 5–8.**

Five profiles of "individuals making a difference in Illinois' libraries and communities" are intended to "put a human face" on the abstract concept of diversity. Included (along with two men) are Lian Ruan (Illinois Fire Service Institute, University of Illinois at Urbana-Champaign), Vandella Brown (East St. Louis Public Library), and Kuntala Sathaye (Itasca Community Library). Each writes about what influenced her to become a librarian, her professional accomplishments, and how the library profession can recruit a more diverse workforce.

19. Allen, Christina. "Ching-Chih Chen." In ***Women of Color in Librarianship: An Oral History,*** **ed. Kathleen de la Peña McCook. Chicago: American Library Association, 1998.**

Dr. Chen was born and raised in China but received her graduate degrees in the United States. Before becoming a professor of library and information science, Dr. Chen served in the field of academic librarianship as a science librarian. Here she discusses her career path and is questioned about barriers faced by Asian Americans in the field of library science.

20. Anderies, John F. "Ethel Louise Lyman and the Beginnings of the Indiana University Music Library." ***Notes*** **59, no. 3 (December 2002): 264–87.**

The author traces the career and life of Ethel Louise Lyman, including her time at Indiana University Music Library. Ms. Lyman witnessed and perhaps created some of today's standards of music librarianship and helped shape the collections of several important music libraries, most particularly the Indiana University Music Library.

21. Anderson, Dorothy. "Mildred Batchelder: 1901–1998." ***Journal of Youth Services in Libraries*** **12 (Spring 1999): 7–8.**

An excerpt from a forthcoming biography of Mildred Batchelder, chief of ALA's first divisions for school and children's libraries and the first executive secretary of its divisions for children's and young adult services. Batchelder developed a worldwide network of relationships between professional people and organizations that benefit children and libraries. She drew talented people into the professional services of ALA, and through constant promotion of better library services and materials, she sought to enhance understanding among different cultures, races, and nations.

22. Anderson, Dorothy, and Carolynne Myall. "Dorothy Anderson: A Welcoming Climate for International Work." ***Cataloging & Classification Quarterly*** **25, no. 2/3 (1998): 11–21.**

Includes a summary of the career and contributions of Dorothy Anderson, a pioneering contributor to the development of universal bibliographic control (UBC) and international standard bibliographic description, along with Anderson's written responses to interview questions. Born in New Zealand, Anderson earned degrees in history and began work in libraries as an alternative to teaching. She accompanied her husband to England, where she completed a diploma in librarianship, then worked in libraries in England and New Zealand. In 1958 she became a research assistant and historical writer, then served as organizing secretary of the International Conference on Cataloguing Principles (Paris, 1961) held by the International Federation of Library Associations. For economic reasons, Anderson was unable to continue her career as a historical writer and became more deeply involved in IFLA activities, including organizing the conference that set development of International Standard Bibliographic Descriptions (ISBDs) in motion. As director of IFLA's International Office for UBC, 1974–1983, Anderson worked to develop and promote ISBDs, to promote creation and international exchange of bibliographic records, and to promote compromise through awareness of differing national approaches due to different language requirements and publishing traditions. She edited *International Cataloguing* from 1972–1983 and contributed extensively to library literature. Anderson replies in answer to a question regarding barriers to accomplishment: "I was not aware of barriers related to race or gender. I was, however, always working against barriers in relation to funding." Includes "Selected Publications of Dorothy Anderson." Also published in: *Portraits in Cataloging & Classification: Theorists, Educators, and Practitioners of the Late Twentieth Century*, 11–21.

23. Ashcraft, Carolyn. "Arkansas Lives: An Interview with Jacqueline S. Wright, Supreme Court Librarian." ***Arkansas Libraries*** **55, no. 3 (1998): 19–21.**

An interview with Jacqueline S. Wright, librarian of the Supreme Court of Arkansas. Wright obtained her J.D. (University of Oklahoma, 1973) before getting her MLIS at University of Arkansas at Little Rock (1985).

In addition to teaching law and clerking at the Arkansas Supreme Court and U.S. District Court, Wright has worked in the library of the Arkansas Supreme Court, the oldest library in the state since 1979. During her tenure, in addition to cataloging the entire collection, Wright established and developed a budget, created a preservation program, and developed one of the leading websites in the state.

24. Bankhead, Detrice. "Augusta Baker." In *Women of Color in Librarianship: An Oral History,* ed. Kathleen de la Peña McCook. Chicago: American Library Association, 1998.

Augusta Baker, a pioneer in children's librarianship and storytelling, talks about her early life and how she became involved in her profession. She was the first black person to be selected coordinator of children's services at New York Public Library.

25. Bankhead, Detrice. "Lourdes Collantes." In *Women of Color in Librarianship: An Oral History,* ed. Kathleen de la Peña McCook. Chicago: American Library Association, 1998.

Born and educated in the Philippines, Dr. Collantes received her graduate degrees at Rutgers University. She is an academic librarian and has held various administrative positions at the State University of New York at Old Westbury. Here she discusses her early years and how she became involved in the profession.

26. Beaudin, Janice. "Lotsee Patterson." In *Women of Color in Librarianship: An Oral History,* ed. Kathleen de la Peña McCook. Chicago: American Library Association, 1998.

Dr. Patterson was born in Okalahoma on her mother's Indian allotment. She began her career as a teacher/librarian at a rural school for Native American children. Dr. Patterson discusses her involvement in establishing libraries on reservations and providing library services for Native Americans.

27. Beaudin, Janice. "Virginia Mathews." In *Women of Color in Librarianship: An Oral History,* ed. Kathleen de la Peña McCook. Chicago: American Library Association, 1998.

Although Ms. Mathews was born in New York City, her father was a Native American of the Osage tribe. In this interview she describes visits with her father in rural Okalahoma. Though not a librarian, Ms. Mathews devoted her life to promoting services to children and youth through her work as a bookseller, reviewer, editor, and teacher.

28. Blake, Noreen B. "Editorial Note." ***Education Libraries*** **23, no. 2/3 (1999): 3.**

Brief tribute to Anne Galler, editor of *Education Libraries* and inductee into the Hall of Fame of the Special Libraries Association.

29. Boucher, Virginia. "So What Did You Do with Your Life, VB? The Autobiography of a Librarian." ***Journal of Interlibrary Loan, Document Delivery & Information Supply*** **11, no. 3 (2001): 45–64.**

Autobiography of the career of a distinguished pioneer in interlibrary loan.

30. Bowden, Russell. "Clodagh L. M. Nethsinghe." ***Library Association Record*** **102, no. 8 (August 2000): 465.**

Clodagh L. M. Nethsinghe (1932–2000) is remembered for her role in establishing the Ceylon (later Sri Lanka) Library Association in 1960. She worked her entire career at the Ceylon Institute of Scientific and Industrial Research, rising from a trainee assistant librarian position (prior to obtaining her master of information studies in London) to head of Information Services. She compiled the first directory of scientific research projects in Ceylon. Having helped to found the Sri Lanka Library Association, she served two terms as its president and was chair of many committees. She was also a Fellow and officer of the Ceylon Institute of Chemistry.

31. Breland, June. "Peggy Jane May, A Remembrance." ***Mississippi Libraries*** **62, no. 4 (1998): 75–76.**

An essay about Peggy Jane May, a driving force for development of library services and recruitment of people into the profession in the 1960s and 1970s. May was a pioneer and early female leader in the field of librarianship in the state of Mississippi.

32. Brisson, Roger. "Interview with Monika Münnich: December 2001." ***Cataloging & Classification Quarterly*** **33, no. 2 (2001): 3–15.**

In an interview with Roger Brisson, Monika Münnich (subject authorities librarian at the national Schlagwordatei [SWD] in the Universitätsbibliothek Heidelberg, Heidelberg, Germany) describes her professional background, her work toward harmonization of *Anglo-American Cataloguing Rules*, second edition (AACR2), and *Regeln für die alphabetische Katalogisierung* (RAK), and her contributions to the International Federation of Library Associations (IFLA), including the development of a multilingual dictionary of cataloging terms and concepts. The interview focuses on the implications of internationalization for librarianship, particularly cataloging practice, and considers such topics as harmonization of practice versus creation of "technology bridges," the introduction of AACR2 into German library practice, and the benefits of internationally accepted rules for easy exchange of data. Münnich compares RAK and AACR2. She posits that AACR2 is a more casuistic rule set, while RAK is a more systematically logical rule set; a particular point of difference concerns treatment of finite multi-parts. She also compares the machine-readable cataloging formats MARC (developed in the United States) and MAB (developed as a specifically German format). Münnich does not discuss gender as a factor in her career. Includes a list of Münnich's "Selected Publications and Recent Lectures." One of a series of interviews with prominent individuals in the specialty of cataloging and bibliographic control.

33. Broward, Marjorie. "Velma King (Memorial Tribute)." *Summary of Proceedings. Fifty-fifth Annual Conference—American Theological Library Association* (2001): 317.

Velma King was a valued member of the library staff of the United Theological College of the West Indies in Kingston, Jamaica. Through her many years of service she was responsible for undergraduate and graduate programs, the Institute of Continuing Studies, OPAC conversion, and helping the library recover from Hurricane Gilbert in 1988. Ms. King was also known as an active member of the American Theological Library Association and was instrumental in the United Theological College's Affiliate Membership designation.

34. Carlyle, Allyson. "An Interview with Martha M. Yee." *Cataloging & Classification Quarterly* 29, no. 3 (2000): 5–19.

In an interview with Allyson Carlyle, Martha M. Yee (cataloging supervisor, UCLA Film and Television Archive, University of California, Los Angeles) surveys her career and summarizes her contributions to cataloging theory and practice. Yee identifies Betty Baughman, former cataloging professor at UCLA Graduate School of Library and Information Science, as a significant influence on her work and career and as "the only master of the Socratic method of teaching . . . and the best teacher from whom I have ever had the honor to learn . . ." (6). Among the topics Yee considers are the concepts *work*, *edition*, and *near-equivalent* in library cataloging; the implications of *Functional Requirements for Bibliographic Records* (FRBR); proposed revisions of *Anglo-American Cataloging Rules*, second edition (AACR2); development of standards for online catalog displays; the influence of her position as a film cataloger on her professional writing;

catalog access to form and genre of works; and the most critical changes that Yee believes need to be made in cataloging, including consistency in work headings and movement in the direction of expression-based bibliographic records. She identifies her greatest disappointments in librarianship, which concern misunderstanding of the role and value of cataloging and a perceived abandonment of concern for education of public service professionals in the U.S. university system. As the cataloger of a film archive, Yee also provides a list of her favorite movies. Yee does not discuss gender as a factor in her career. Includes "Bibliography of Works by Martha M. Yee." One of a series of interviews with prominent individuals in the specialty of cataloging and bibliographic control.

35. Carter, Betty. "Margaret Alexander Edwards: Reaching Out to Young Adult Librarians." ***Journal of Youth Services in Libraries*** **11 (Winter 1998): 175–80.**

A tribute to Margaret Alexander Edwards and her work for young adults and young adult librarianship. The article highlights some of the projects made possible through a trust enacted at her death. The trust, established before her death in 1988, most recently underwrote a series of ALA programs on adult books for young adults, something Edwards championed.

36. Carter, Ruth C. "The Editors of CCQ." ***Cataloging & Classification Quarterly*** **25, no. 2/3 (1998): 5–9.**

Describes the careers of the three editors of *Cataloging & Classification Quarterly*, a peer-reviewed international journal in the specialty of bibliographic and information organization. The third editor is the first woman to hold the position, article author Ruth C. Carter herself. Carter explains that she started her work life as a teacher, next obtained a master's degree in history and worked as a curator of manuscripts, then spent two years in the 1960s as a systems analyst for the U.S. Army. After assisting her husband with a bibliography and index in his discipline, she decided to apply to library school, where Kathryn Luther Henderson became her cataloging teacher. In various positions at the University of Pittsburgh libraries, including assistant director for technical services, Carter was an active participant in CONSER and other cooperative cataloging ventures. Carter does not discuss gender as a factor in her career.

37. Chan, Karen. "From AACR Revision to CONSER's SCCTP: An Interview with Jeans Hirons." ***Cataloging & Classification Quarterly*** **32, no. 4 (2001): 3–13.**

In an interview with Karen Chan, Jean Hirons (CONSER Coordinator,

Library of Congress) surveys her career and summarizes her contributions to serials cataloging theory and practice, training in serials control, and cooperative ventures in serials librarianship. Hirons identifies key conceptual changes that she and her colleagues proposed for *Anglo-American Cataloguing Rules*, second edition (AACR2), particularly the introduction of the concepts *continuing resources* (an umbrella concept that includes serial publications) and *integrating resources*. She describes the evolution of Cooperative Online Serials (CONSER); the development of its successful training program, Serials Cataloging Cooperative Training Program (SCCTP); and other CONSER activities such as the development of a publication pattern database and creation of cataloging manuals and other documentation for use by CONSER participants and library staff generally. She celebrates the pleasures of working with members of the "serials community" (specialists in the treatment of serial publications). Hirons does not discuss gender as a factor in her career. One of a series of interviews with prominent individuals in the specialty of cataloging and bibliographic control.

38. Cherry, Thomas Kevin. "Interview with Elinor Swaim." ***North Carolina Libraries*** **56, no. 2 (Summer 1998): 71–74.**

Interview with Elinor Swaim, politician and advocate of libraries. Swaim's career as a library advocate began after World War II when she was asked to write a radio program for the tenth anniversary of the Asheboro (North Carolina) Public Library. She continued as a campaign worker for the Rowan Public Library bond referendum, focusing on the fact that a new library would cost each taxpayer $3.20 a year (the referendum passed). She eventually served as chairman of the North Carolina Library Commission and served on the National Library Commission under Presidents Reagan and Bush (senior).

39. Clark, Kellie D., and John V. Richardson, Jr. "Edith Guerrier: 'A Little [Warrior] Woman of New England' on Behalf of U.S. Public Documents, 1870–1958." ***Journal of Government Information*** **28, no. 3 (May/June 2001): 267–83.**

A biographical article on Edith Guerrier who served at the Boston Public Library, in the U.S. Food Administration, and on the Public Documents Committee of the American Library Association. Guerrier was a champion for the public's use of government documents and created a precursor to the *U.S. Government Manual*. Guerrier and Edith Brown had a Boston marriage and served as role models for gay and lesbian couples.

40. Clemmons, Nancy W. "Lucretia's View: An Interview with Lucretia W. McClure about Medical Reference through the Years, February 25, 2000." ***Medical Reference Services Quarterly*** **20, no. 1 (Spring 2001): 1–10.**

According to interviewer Nancy Clemmons, medical librarians consider Lucretia McClure "a founding mother, doyen, or matriarch of medical librarianship." McClure, who retired in 1993 as director of the Edward G. Miner Library at the University of Rochester (New York) Medical Center, was president of the Medical Library Association from 1990 to 1991 and has an MLA award named after her. The interview deals with the evolution of medical reference services and the impact of technology on them.

41. Crawford, Holly. "Freedom through Books: Helen Haines and Her Role in the Library Press, Library Education, and the Intellectual Freedom Movement." 1997.

Doctoral dissertation examining the life of Helen E. Haines (1872–1961), author of *Living With Books* (1935, 1950) and *What's In a Novel* (1942), both of which advocated books as a means to opportunity, equality, and freedom. Haines taught at four library schools during her career. A staunch advocate of intellectual freedom, she was vilified during the McCarthy era.

42. Cummins, Julie. "Moore Than Meets the Eye: How a Librarian with Little Experience with Kids Became One of the Most Powerful People in Children's Publishing." ***School Library Journal*** **45, no. 7 (July 1999): 27–29.**

Traces the career of Anne Carroll Moore, the first head of children's services at the New York Public Library. Hired by NYPL in 1906, Moore began Children's Book Week in 1912, wrote a regular column on criticism of children's books for the *Bookman*, and started the "Holiday Books for Boys and Girls" lists that became the NYPL's list of the one hundred best children's books for each year.

43. Cummins, Julie. "A View from the '90s: A Chat with Frances Lander Spain." ***Journal of Youth Services in Libraries*** **13, no. 1 (Fall 1999): 28.**

A tribute to Frances Lander Spain, who died in January 1999. In 1953 Spain was recruited for the position of head of children's work at NYPL. Prior to assuming this position she had earned a Ph.D. from the University of Chicago. She served as assistant director of the library school at the University of Southern California. While there she received a Fulbright Scholarship to go to Thailand in 1952 to establish a library training program, which led to the creation of the Thailand Library Association.

44. Dahlberg, Ingetraut. "Ingetraut Dahlberg: A Brief Self Report." *Cataloging & Classification Quarterly* 25, no. 2/3 (1998): 151–55.

Includes a summary of the career of Ingetraut Dahlberg and her contributions to classification and knowledge organization, along with her brief written responses to interview questions. Having studied philosophy and other subjects, Dahlberg entered the field of classification through documentation (a predecessor of information science), rather than through librarianship. After compiling bibliographies of the literature of inorganic chemistry, she became head of the library and documentation center of the Deutsche Gesellschaft für Dokumentation (German Documentation Society) and wrote a thesaurus for the field of documentation. Dahlberg proposed a revision of the Universal Decimal Classification, edited the journal *International Classification* (later, *Knowledge Organization*) from 1974 to 1996, and authored an influential monograph that examined existing classification systems and proposed a structure for a possible universal classification system; her particular interest is the identification of the relationships between concepts and between concepts and terms. Dahlberg replies in answer to a question regarding barriers to accomplishment: "There were no barriers in my career related to race, gender, or to the level of funding and support" (154). Also published in: *Portraits in Cataloging & Classification: Theorists, Educators, and Practitioners of the Late Twentieth Century*, 151–55.

45. Dawson, Alma. "Celebrating African-American Librarians and Librarianship." *Library Trends* 49 (Summer 2000): 49–87.

This detailed article describes prominent African American librarians and significant achievements by African American librarians. It addresses demographics of the profession, library school education, historical events, and writings by African American librarians. In particular it provides information about significant leaders in librarianship in the twentieth century as identified by *American Libraries* in 1999. These include Augusta Baker, Sadie Peterson Delaney, Virginia Proctor Powell Florence, Virginia Lacy Jones, Joseph Henry Reason, and Charlemae Rollins.

46. De Loach, Marva. "Clara Stanton Jones." *Women of Color in Librarianship: An Oral History*, ed. Kathleen de la Peña McCook. Chicago: American Library Association, 1998.

Jones was the first woman and the first African American to be appointed director of the Detroit Public Library, and she was the first African American to be elected president of the American Library Association. In this interview she talks about her upbringing, how she became a librarian, and her involvement with the American Library Association and the NAACP.

47. Dockter, Sally. "Librarian of thè Year—Betty Gard." ***The Good Stuff*** **32, no. 4 (December 2002): 8.**

Outlines the accomplishments of Betty Gard, North Dakota Library Association's 2002 Librarian of the Year. She is a leader in professional organizations at both state and national levels and is described as a mentor to many librarians.

48. Field, Judith J. "The Crest of Opportunity: A Conversation with Nettie Seabrooks, Chief Operating Officer for the City of Detroit." ***Information Outlook*** **2, no. 6 (1998): 33.**

In an interview with past SLA president Judith Field, Ms. Seabrooks shares how her experience as a librarian with General Motors has helped her meet the challenges of shaping public policy for the city of Detroit.

49. Flatley, Robert. "Characterizing the Role of the Public Librarian: A Survey." ***Rural Libraries*** **22, no. 2 (2000): 8–28.**

The author discusses the results of a survey of rural librarians serving populations of 2,500 or less. The goal of the survey was to learn how rural librarians view librarianship, libraries, and the futures of both. The majority of the 232 surveys analyzed were from women between the ages of forty to fifty-nine. Results of the survey showed that rural librarians have a positive attitude toward the profession, its future, and their work.

50. Ford, Bob. "Arkansas Lives: Louise Schaper." ***Arkansas Libraries*** **57, no. 3 (2000): 8–11.**

A profile of Louise Schaper, director of the Fayetteville Public Library, Fayetteville, Arkansas. After years as a corporate librarian, Schaper revitalized the struggling Fayetteville Public Library. She developed the library's vision, mission, values, and goals; streamlined work processes; filled vacant positions; and revamped the library's financial management practices. Schaper is also credited with creating a computer lab, an active website, and a plan for construction of a new library building.

51. Fry, Linda L. "Elizabeth Balz (Memorial Tribute)." ***Summary of Proceedings. Fifty-fifth Annual Conference—American Theological Library Association*** **(2001): 311.**

Elizabeth Balz received her BS in Library Science from Columbia University in 1939 and went on to succeed in several reference and cataloging positions before becoming the first librarian for the Evangelical Lutheran Theological Seminary Library of Capital University in Columbus, Ohio. Not only was she the first librarian at the seminary, she was the only woman on the staff for many years. She retired as associate librarian for technical processing in 1982 but continued to work in the library, cataloging a backlog of rare books, some of which had been uncataloged for over a century. Elizabeth Balz was also a founding member of the Ohio Theological Library Association and was active in her church and community.

52. Gallimore, Howard. "Elaine Bryant (Memorial Tribute)." ***Summary of Proceedings. Fifty-fifth Annual Conference—American Theological Library Association*** **(2001): 313.**

Elaine Bryant graduated with an MLS from Vanderbilt University in 1987 and went on to become supervisor of the E.C. Dargan-Carver Library, serving both the Baptist Sunday School and the Historical Commission of the Southern Baptist Convention. During her tenure as supervisor, she brought the library up to technological standards by automating circulation, acquisitions, and cataloging as well as helping the library weather difficult economic times. Bryant was also an active member of the Tennessee Theological Library Association, the American Theological Library Association, and the Baptist Agency Library Association.

53. Glick, Andrea. "Storyteller Leaves Lasting Legacy." ***School Library Journal*** **44, no. 4 (April 1998): 13.**

Long-time children's librarian and acclaimed storyteller Augusta Baker died on February 23, 1998. Baker worked at NYPL for thirty-seven years, including serving as coordinator of children's services. At NYPL she began producing lists of books that accurately portrayed the life and culture of African Americans. In the 1950s, she served as the library's storytelling specialist. In 1980 she became storyteller-in-residence at the University of South Carolina's College of Library and Information Science. An annual storytelling festival was begun there in her honor in 1986.

54. Göranson, Ulf. "Birgitta Bergdahl (1937–2001): A Tribute." ***IFLA Journal*** **27, no. 4 (2001): 280–81.**

Birgitta Bergdahl was the first director of IFLA's Core Programme ALP (Advancement of Librarianship Programme). Because of Sweden's neutral position in world politics, she made Uppsala University Library the focal point for ALP. Before assuming the leadership of ALP, Bergdahl held positions at Linköping University Library, where she was director, and at the

Stockholm School of Economics, Stockholm University, and the Royal Library. She traveled the world to work with librarians in developing countries and is remembered as "a powerful, inspiring, and result-oriented force in international library cooperation."

55. Hansen, Debra G. "A Lion in the Hennery: Charles Fletcher Lummis and the Los Angeles Public Library, 1905–1910." ***Vitae Scholasticae*** **19 (Spring 2000): 5–33.**

In this biographical essay, Hansen discusses the work and life of Charles Fletcher Lummis, writer, anthropologist, magazine editor, and librarian for the Los Angeles Public Library (LAPL) from 1905–1910. Lummis was a controversial figure for the LAPL to hire as he was the first male to hold the position of librarian, replacing Mary L. Jones, and had no library administrative or management experience or training. Lummis was also controversial for his plans for the library, some of which were before their time (casual reading areas) and others that failed. One failed plan was to masculinize the library, and though Lummis did hire the LAPL's first male librarian, the plan went no further than that one hire. Ironically, given his views on female librarians and female readers, Lummis did advocate for higher salaries, merit raises, improved training, giving librarians the choice of what department to permanently work in, and the establishment of the Library Senate, allowing the female librarians a voice in the administrative and bureaucratic matters of the library. Lummis resigned in 1910 after a confluence of negative reactions to his approach to the Library Senate as a "rubber-stamping" body, his failure to raise funds for a new, modern library building, and the librarians' dislike of his closing of branch libraries, cutting funds for children's and fiction collections, and general administrative mediocrity.

56. Harrison, K. C. "Elsa Granheim." ***Library Association Record*** **101, no. 6 (June 1999): 362.**

In this follow-up to the official obituary of Elsa Granheim (*Library Association Record* 101, no. 5 [May 1999]: 303), past Library Association president K. C. Harrison shares personal memories of her. Granheim was "one of the great international librarians of the world" who rose from a position in the public library of her native town, Trondheim, to become president of IFLA. She was actively involved in the Anglo-Scandinavian public library conferences in the 1950s and 1960s.

57. Henderson, Kathryn Luther, and Mary Piggott. "Mary Piggott: A Long Long-Distance Friendship." ***Cataloging & Classification Quarterly*** **25, no. 4 (1998): 243–52.**

This two-part article surveys the career and summarizes the contributions of Mary Piggott (retired from the faculty of the School of Library, Archive and Information Studies, University College London, London, England) to bibliographic control and library education. The first part of the article, by Henderson (Graduate School of Library and Information Science, University of Illinois at Urbana-Champaign), who is Piggott's longtime friend and colleague, presents reminiscences of their participation in catalog code revision and the development of *Anglo-American Cataloging Rules* (AACR1), and of their professional and personal friendship. The second part, by Piggott, describes her decision while she was an undergraduate to become a librarian, her professional study, and her career in teaching cataloging, classification, and related topics. She discusses her philosophy of cataloging education and notes that "it was always my aim to show cataloguing as an integral part of the whole library organization and not as an isolated exercise in applying rules" (248). As a participant in the International Conference on Cataloguing Principles (Paris, 1961), the development of AACR1, and the *Guidelines for the Content, Organization and Presentation of Indexes*, and as the author of *A Topography of Cataloguing* (1988), Piggott played an important role in developing and explicating standards in information organization in the twentieth century. Piggott does not discuss gender as a factor in her career. Includes "Bibliography of Works by Mary Piggott." Also published in *Portraits in Cataloging & Classification: Theorists, Educators, and Practitioners of the Late Twentieth Century*, 243–52.

58. Herman, Deirdre A. "ALA's Carol Henderson Moves Beyond the Beltway." ***American Libraries*** **30, no. 8 (September 1999): 14–15.**

Interview with former executive director of the ALA Washington office Carol Henderson. She describes her experiences while working for the ALA and the politics of working in Washington, D.C.

59. Hickey, Damon. "Doralyn Joanne Hickey, 1929–1987: A Brother Librarian's Perspective." ***Cataloging & Classification Quarterly*** **25, no. 2/3 (1998): 157–69.**

Surveys the life, career, and professional contributions of Doralyn J. Hickey, a library school administrator and educator in the area of cataloging and classification; this essay was written by her brother, also a librarian. Hickey came from a family that valued education, for women as well as men. After majoring in mathematics, she entered graduate school in the field of religion; in later life, she wondered whether she would have remained in professional church work had women been eligible for ordination in her denomination at the time. Since she could not be ordained, Hickey enrolled in a Ph.D. program in religion. She began working in a theological library during a break in her education, completed an MLS, and returned to divinity school to complete the Ph.D. in religion before beginning a career in library science education. During twelve years at the School of Library Science, University of North Carolina at Chapel Hill, Hickey received many awards for her work in library organizations, publications such as *Problems in Organizing Library Collections* (Bowker, 1972), and participation in cataloging code revision; she was an unsuccessful candidate for president of the American Library Association. In 1974, she became professor and dean of the School of Library and Information Science at the University of Wisconsin at Milwaukee and guided the school to accreditation. In 1977, she became a professor at the School of Library and Information Science at North Texas State University, where she remained until her death in 1987. She prepared doctoral students to play leading roles as professors and emphasized both rigorous analysis and commitment to service. Hickey believed that the women's movement was "important in bringing to light barriers to the full realization of women's potential and to bringing those barriers down." However, she herself had not felt she experienced impediments to her career and believed that she "had always received encouragement and support from men in positions of authority . . ." (168). Notes that Hickey was skillful and comfortable in the area of technology and that "most of the stronger influences in her life and career were men" (168). Also states that she "benefited . . . from being in a predominantly female profession where women's contributions were generally respected" and from coming from a family in which gender was considered irrelevant to intellectual achievement. Also published in *Portraits in Cataloging & Classification: Theorists, Educators, and Practitioners of the Late Twentieth Century*, 157–69.

60. Hildenbrand, Suzanne. "Library Lives in Multidimensional Reality." In *Women of Color in Librarianship: An Oral History*, ed. Kathleen de la Peña McCook. Chicago: American Library Association, 1998, 3–7.

Hildenbrand's introduction to this important oral history of women of color in the field of librarianship discusses library biography and declares this particular volume as "a major step forward" in terms of bringing out a richer history of the profession. The nature of history and how history can be truly captured by historians and writers is discussed, using examples from the oral histories as evidence that our identities are never one-dimensional and thus neither are our perspectives or choices. Public libraries and serving the public good are core topics in the collection, as six of the eight librarians interviewed in this collection were or are public librarians first and foremost. Hildenbrand recognizes each of the women included in this collection for their personal qualities and strength in times of adversity.

61. Hildenbrandt, Irma. "Blick über Mainhattan und Mainhattan hinaus: Elisabeth Niggemann, 1954, Generaldirektorin der Deutschen Bibliothek." In *Tun wir den nächsten Schritt: 18 Frankfurter Frauenporträt.* Hildenbrandt, IrmaKreuzlingen, München: Hugendubel, 2000.

Elisabeth Niggemann, who holds a doctoral degree in molecular biology, additional education in Anglistics, and a degree in library science, worked in different leading academic library positions before she was appointed general director of the Deutsche Bibliothek in 1999. As a professional woman with an outstanding career, she states that she herself has not experienced any discrimination or prejudices due to her gender. English chapter title: View over Mainhattan and Beyond: Elisabeth Niggemann, born 1954, General Director of the Deutsche Bibliothek.

62. Holthoff, Tim. "Across Kansas, People and Events in Arkansas Libraries: Jacqueline S. Wright: She Takes the Tired out of Retired." *Arkansas Libraries* 56, no. 2 (1999): 31–32.

A profile of Arkansas Supreme Court librarian Jacqueline S. Wright upon her retirement. Includes a description of Wright's many accomplishments during her twenty-year tenure.

63. Hybki Kerr, Sharon. "Arkansas Lives: An Interview with Kathy Sanders, UALR Library Director." *Arkansas Libraries* 55, no. 5 (1998): 22–26.

An interview with Kathy Sanders by Sharon Hybki Kerr, head of reference/documents services, University of Arkansas, Little Rock. Sanders was appointed director of the Ottenheimer Library at UALR after twenty-nine years in various positions in UALR libraries. She was the first student in the library program at the University of Missouri, Columbia. Sanders was also the first reference librarian at UALR and the first head of public services.

64. IFLA Headquarters Staff. "Else Granheim." *Library Association Record* 101, no. 5 (May 1999): 303.

Else Granheim, president of the International Federation of Library Associations and Institutions (IFLA) from 1979 to 1985, died in March

1999. Prior to her retirement in 1991, she was the director of the Norwegian Directorate for Public and School Libraries and a member of the Norwegian UNESCO Commission as well as various committees within IFLA. Her legacy includes strengthened ties between IFLA and its sister organizations IFID (International Federation for Information and Documentation) and ICA (International Council on Archives).

65. Ingle, Leanne. "Southwest Washington Loses Pioneer, First Director of Timberland." ***Alki: The Washington Library Association Journal*** **18, no. 2 (July 2002): 18.**

Summarizes the career of Louise "Becky" Morrison, a prominent librarian in Washington State who was the founding director of the Timberland Regional Library system. Briefly describes Morrison's role in developing a unified regional library district in a large multicounty area that had previously had small city and county libraries, as well as extensive scattered areas with no public library service. In 1999, TRL dedicated the Louise E. "Becky" Morrison Conference & Learning Center, housed in the library's service center in Olympia. Includes portrait.

66. Jacobs, Mark A. "Cataloging and Classification Standards and Practices, Library and Information Science Education, and a Student Legacy: An Interview with Kathryn Luther Henderson." ***Cataloging & Classification Quarterly*** **33, no. 1 (2001): 3–16.**

In an interview with Mark A. Jacobs, Kathryn Luther Henderson (professor, Graduate School of Library and Information Science, University of Illinois at Urbana-Champaign) surveys her career and summarizes her contributions to library education and cataloging. Henderson describes her philosophy of education for librarianship, her approach to teaching library technical services and particularly cataloging (a combination of history, theory and principles, standards, codes, and practice), the impact of colleagues on her career, and her successful mentoring project, in which former students now working in library technical services mentor current GSLIS students through e-mailed "conversations." Several questions touch on the impact of technological changes on librarianship and library education. Henderson notes that "the materials, tools, and technology change, but the goals [of librarianship] are the same" (8), and observes that "technology has always been a part of librarianship . . . However, it sometimes seems overemphasized today to the detriment of consideration of the history and development of the profession, the values and ethics of the procession and our basic tenets, principles, and theory" (11–12). She describes her collaboration with her husband, William T. Henderson, in library practice and in teaching. Henderson does not discuss gender as a factor in her career. One of a series of interviews with prominent individuals in the specialty of cataloging and bibliographic control.

67. Johnson, Carole. "Library Employees without the ALA-Accredited Master's Degree." *Public Libraries* 37, no. 1 (January 1998–28 February 1998): 40–46.

Highlights the results of a 1995 survey done in Iowa, Minnesota, and Wisconsin public libraries in order to understand jobs held by non-MLS workers, gauge impact on positions and salary, and predict the potential impacts of library science education. The survey results are compared to a 1952 public librarians study. Survey participants were largely female, and the majority were over forty years of age. The article includes summary tables of data to accompany the narrative. The authors offer several conclusions based on their data, including that traditional hierarchical structures in libraries can be a source of frustration, an MLS degree should not be the only advanced degree represented in libraries in the future, and that further assessment of jobs is necessary beyond the current models.

68. Jolly, L. "Meet the President: Liz Jolly." *Impact, the Journal of the Career Development Group* 3, no. 1 (January 2000): 2–4.

Interview with Liz Jolly, the 2000 president of the Career Development Group in the United Kingdom. Jolly describes her career as a professional librarian and her involvement in the Career Development Group. She also elaborates on service goals for the group, forthcoming changes with the unification of the Library Association and Institute of Information Scientists, and her interest in promoting equality of opportunity and lifelong learning.

69. Kerslake, Evelyn. "My Famous Kate Pierce: Biographies of and in the Archive." *Vitae Scholasticae* 19 (Spring 2000): 35–58.

Kerslake explores Kate Pierce within the context of biography. She begins by analyzing the conventional approach to biography as outlined by M. H. Abrams, critiquing this approach by presenting another view that biographies should include facts as well as the creation of new narratives for women. Kerslake proposes a new model for biographical writing using elements of both approaches using the work of Monika Bernold and Johanna Geumacher. Lastly, Kerslake experiments with this approach by applying it to the study of Kate Pierce.

70. Kniffel, Leonard. "First Lady, First Librarian." *American Libraries* 32, no. 2 (February 2001): 50–51.

Gives an overview of the life and library career of Laura Welch Bush, the only spouse of an American president to be a librarian. She is predicted to champion literacy while first lady.

71. Kniffel, Leonard. "The Way She Made Children Believe." ***American Libraries*** **32, no. 8 (September 2001): 40.**

Discusses the career of the late Betty J. Morrison who was the head of the public library in Armada, Michigan. She was instrumental in promoting the library as a place of community. She is saluted by the author, who knew her personally, for her warmth, wit, and exemplary service to patrons.

72. Koot, Geert-Jan. "Obituary [Jacqueline Viaux]." ***IFLA Journal*** **25, no. 1 (1999): 67.**

Jacqueline Viaux, who died at the age of eighty-five in October 1998, was a leader in art librarianship. She directed the Bibliothèque Forney in Paris from 1948 to 1980. She also taught courses on the history of the book at the Ecole de Bibliothécaire-documentaliste from 1958 to 1985. Active in the art section of the Association des Bibliothécaires Français, she went on to organize an art libraries round table within the International Federation of Library Associations. When this group became the official IFLA Section of Art Libraries, Mme. Viaux was its first chair. She wrote many books on art and art librarianship and received several awards, including the 1991 Distinguished Service Award from the Art Libraries Society of North America.

73. Kurth, Martin. "An Interview with Barbara B. Tillett." ***Cataloging & Classification Quarterly*** **32, no. 3 (2001): 3–24.**

In an interview with Martin Kurth, Barbara B. Tillett (director, Integrated Library System Program Office, and chief, Cataloging Policy and Support Office, U.S. Library of Congress) surveys her career and summarizes her contributions to cataloging theory, particularly with regard to the concept of bibliographic relationships. Tillett describes her initial work concerning the taxonomy of bibliographic relationships as a conceptual foundation for online catalogs (under dissertation director Elaine Svenonius) and her subsequent work with Svenonius, Tom Delsey, and others toward the development of *Functional Requirements for Bibliographic Records* (FRBR). Tillett considers FRBR a new and helpful conceptualization of the bibliographic universe and speculates about the impact FRBR will ultimately have on cataloging. Several questions consider the emerging internationalization of bibliographic control and the benefits of internationalization. Tillett presents her vision of linking authority records for a single entity internationally, rather than adopting a combined single international authority record for that entity; the linking approach preserves the syndetic structure of individual library catalogs created using different cataloging codes and would enable users to see forms of names, etc., in the language they are using to search. Tillett identifies many international projects that are underway. Other topics covered in the interview include revision of *Anglo-American Cataloging Rules*, second edition (AACR2) and Tillett's role in this endeavor, implementation of an integrated library system at the Library of Congress, functionality and lack of standardization of current integrated library systems, and LC's engagement in digital futures planning. Tillett does not discuss gender as a factor in her career. One of a series of interviews with prominent individuals in the specialty of cataloging and bibliographic control.

74. Laird, Judy. "The Power of Persistence . . . Life is Beautiful." *CSLA Journal* 24, no. 1 (Fall 2000): 33–34.

A profile of CSLA member Doris Dillon, a library media teacher with Lou Gehrig's disease (ALS), who continued to manage two media centers in the San Jose Unified School District after her diagnosis. Dillon, who is no longer able to speak due to the disease, is "shadowed" by a library clerk funded by the Americans with Disabilities Act. She continues her research and communication via e-mail, and throughout her career has been named Site Teacher of the Year four times, has been featured in a *Time* magazine article, and has been awarded the California Reading Association's Marcus Foster Memorial Award, the California State Department of Education Shining Star Award, and the Voice of Courage Award from the ALS Association.

75. Lapides, Linda F. "Margaret Alexander Edwards, 1902–1998." *Journal of Youth Services in Libraries* 15, no. 4 (Summer 2002): 44–49.

A biographical portrait of Margaret Alexander Edwards to commemorate the one hundredth anniversary of her birth. The article also describes the work of the Margaret Alexander Edwards Trust, which was established in 1989 through the bequest of the bulk of her estate. The trust has awarded grants to librarians from New York to California to perpetuate Edwards's philosophy of bringing books and youth together. The Alex Awards, given by the trust, are also described.

76. Layne, Sara Shatford. "Miss Elizabeth (Betty) Baughman." *Cataloging & Classification Quarterly* 25, no. 2/3 (1998): 83–92.

Surveys the life, career, and teaching methods of Betty Baughman, cataloging professor at the Graduate School of Library and Information Science, University of California, Los Angeles, and discusses her influence on students. Born to a working-class family, at age three Baughman contracted tuberculosis spondylitis; she recovered from the disease by age ten but was left with crippling effects that left her hospitalized until she was fourteen. After earning degrees in history, Baughman planned to teach; she was unable to find a teaching position, due to her disability, and became a reference librarian at a historical society. Here she discovered an interest in the library catalog. Following graduation from library school, she became an assistant and then a faculty member at the Graduate School of Library Science of the University of California, Los Angeles, and taught cataloging there for more than twenty years. Her approach to teaching cataloging was to design "encounters with bibliographic hazards in such a way that the students naturally absorbed the limitations of rules and the importance of principles in negotiating these hazards and preparing catalogs" (83), to encourage creative analysis, and to discourage overly pragmatic approaches that ignore the complexity of bibliographic problems. While Baughman's "contribution to cataloging was the creation of librarians, public service and technical service alike, who can think creatively about cataloging . . . Betty's life may be seen as an example of how one can break rules and get a better result than one would have by following those same rules" (91). Does not discuss gender as a factor in Baughman's career. Also published in *Portraits in Cataloging & Classification: Theorists, Educators, and Practitioners of the Late Twentieth Century*, 83–92.

77. Long, Sarah. "Now, Then, and Next: A Year in the Life of the ALA President." ***Illinois Library Association Reporter*** **18, no. 3 (June 2000): 1–2.**

Sarah Ann Long discusses her experience as president of the American Library Association including the challenge of being the profession's chief spokesperson for the ALA policy on filtering of the Internet.

78. Long, Tracy. "Meet the President: Tracy Long." ***Impact, the Journal of the Career Development Group*** **5, no. 3/4 (Summer 2002).**

Interview of Tracy Long, the 2002 president of the Career Development Group in the United Kingdom. Long describes her career as a professional librarian and her prior experience in the Career Development Group, the benefits of involvement in a national organization, and changes in the organization's publication, *Impact*.

79. Margolis, Rick. "A Measure of Respect." ***School Library Journal*** **48, no. 9 (September 2002): 56–58.**

In this interview Katherine Bassett, a New Jersey school media specialist who helped the Educational Testing Service create an evaluation process for media specialists, talks about the significance of including media specialists in the certification process of the National Board for Professional Teaching Standards. She offers advice to those who would like to become nationally certified.

80. Maxwell, Margaret F. "Margaret F. Maxwell: Bequest of Joy: A Life with Books." ***Cataloging & Classification Quarterly*** **25, no. 2/3 (1998): 191–97.**

An autobiographical essay by Maxwell, a library science educator in the field of cataloging and classification, and a writer and researcher in U.S. women's history. Maxwell came from a family that valued education; she entered college with the ambition of earning a Ph.D. in English and becoming a professor. She initially decided to attend library school and enter librarianship in order to support herself during further graduate education, but found that she enjoyed cataloging and classification. She worked for a time at the Library of Congress and other institutions. Following completion of a Ph.D. in library science in 1971, Maxwell taught at the School of Library and Information Studies at the University of Arizona for many years. Observing students' difficulties with the complexities of cataloging practice, she wrote *Handbook for AACR2, Explaining and Illustrating the Anglo-American Cataloguing Rules, Second Edition* (American Library Association, 1980), which became a library classic and appeared in many subsequent editions (as of 1998, it was edited by her son, Robert L. Maxwell, also a librarian). In addition to her work in library education and cataloging, Maxwell wrote in the area of U.S. Western women's history. Among her many works in this field is an award-winning essay about Mary Jones, a prominent early female library administrator. Also published in *Portraits in Cataloging & Classification: Theorists, Educators, and Practitioners of the Late Twentieth Century*, 191–97.

81. McAllister-Harper, Desretta V., Virgina Purefoy Jones, and Mary Beth Schell. "Annette Lewis Phinazee: Visionary, Cataloger, Educator." ***Cataloging & Classification Quarterly*** **25, no. 2/3 (1998): 227–41.**

Surveys the life, career, and contributions of Annette Lewis Phinazee to library education, classification study, and preservation and promotion of library materials concerning African Americans. Phinazee came from a family of educators; in 1961, she became the first woman to receive the DLS from Columbia University. Following work in a wide variety of libraries, including many years of teaching cataloging at the Atlanta University

School of Library Service, Phinazee became dean of the School of Library Science at North Carolina Central University. Under her leadership, the school expanded its enrollment, sought and achieved accreditation from the American Library Association, and added innovative new programs. One of Phinazee's major research interests was the Library of Congress Classification System, about which she wrote her dissertation and conducted institutes for librarians; she also was instrumental in organizing the Cooperative College Library Center, a centralized processing service for a group of historically African American colleges. Phinazee developed two major collections of materials by African American artists and librarians while she was at NCCU and was a guiding force behind the African-American Materials Project that established its headquarters there. Widely recognized as an advocate for African American librarianship, Phinazee was active in library professional organizations and addressed the 1961 Annual Conference of the American Library Association on the subject of racism in the profession; she also edited the proceedings of the Institute on Materials By and About American Negroes and of the Conference on the Georgia Child's Access to Materials Pertaining to American Negroes. Also published in *Portraits in Cataloging & Classification: Theorists, Educators, and Practitioners of the Late Twentieth Century*, 227–41.

82. McCarty, Laura. "Cindy Cunningham: Part of the R/Evolution." *Alki: The Washington Library Association Journal* 16, no. 2 (July 2000): 9–11.

In an interview with Laura McCarty, Cindy Cunningham (head of Catalog/Browse at Amazon.com) discusses her career in libraries and the commercial sector and as president of the Washington Library Association. Cunningham describes the "library skill set" that made her attractive to Amazon.com, including an understanding of the importance of information organization, subject retrieval, and classification; also attractive to a private-sector corporation was her ability to adjust to a "fast-paced, unsafe kind of environment" (10), which she advises other librarians to consider. Other topics covered in the interview include WLA's work toward adoption of a revised intellectual freedom statement, the benefits of maintaining relationships with vendors for the purpose of influencing development of products and services for libraries, the role of mentoring, and the impact of librarians' modeling "someone who is not afraid to speak out or to be extremely direct . . . to be bold and take risks" (11). Cunningham stresses the critical importance of librarians' marketing their values and making them more widely known, since she perceives that librarians' passionate belief in the values of intellectual freedom and service to all members of the community will not be enough, by itself, to protect their institutions and principles. Cunningham does not discuss gender as a factor in her career. Includes photos.

83. McCawley, Christina Wolcott. "An Interview with Lucia Rather." ***Cataloging & Classification Quarterly*** **25, no. 4 (1998): 253–62.**

This article, based on a 1997 interview by McCawley of Lucia Rather (retired as director for cataloging, U.S. Library of Congress), surveys Rather's career and summarizes her contributions to cataloging. Rather explains that her father influenced her to enter librarianship; after library school, she began work as a cataloger at LC. When she married John Rather, a cataloging administrator, LC's nepotism rules prohibited her continuing work in cataloging. Subsequently, in 1966, she joined the staff of LC's Information Systems Office, which was then creating the original MARC format for the exchange of machine-readable cataloging data. Rather worked closely with Henriette Avram on the continuing development of MARC, which became the most influential twentieth-century standard in library automation. Rather discusses her work in implementing *Anglo-American Cataloguing Rules*, second edition, at LC, her role in organizing CONSER (Cooperative Online Serials) and the cooperative authority file project, NACO, the conversion of cataloging at LC from a manual to an automated operation, and the reorganization of LC's cataloging workflows. Rather comments on cataloging code changes ("Lucia personally feels that successive entry in the cataloging of serials was a mistake," 255), the rewards of working at the international level of librarianship, and the future of cataloging and librarianship. Rather states that having to leave her position as serials cataloging when she was married was "the only thing [she] experienced in the way of discrimination because of gender" (260–61). Also published in *Portraits in Cataloging & Classification: Theorists, Educators, and Practitioners of the Late Twentieth Century*, 253–62.

84. McCook, Kathleen de la Peña. ***Women of Color in Librarianship: An Oral History.*** **Chicago, Ill.: American Library Association, 1998.**

Includes interviews with eight ethnically diverse female librarians, all leaders in the profession. Each interview begins with family history. Personal and professional experiences are recounted, including how they first became interested in library and information science. Challenges they faced in their careers including encounters with racial discrimination are also discussed.

85. McElderry, Margaret K. "Remarkable Women: Anne Carroll Moore & Company." In *School Library Journal's Best: A Reader for Children's, Young Adult & School Librarians,* ed. Thomas W. Downen, Lillian N. Gerhardt, and Marilyn L. Miller, 160–64. New York: Neal-Schuman Publishers, 1997.

McElderry's stories provide a glimpse of what it was like working in the Children's Services department at the New York Public Library during the reign of its founder and head, Anne Carroll Moore. Moore not only was an innovator in developing library services for children but was also an advocate for children's literature. She encouraged its development as its own separate literature and influenced publishers, authors, illustrators, and critics of children's books.

86. McGarry, Dorothy. "An Interview with Elaine Svenonius." *Cataloging & Classification Quarterly* 29, no. 4 (2000): 5–17.

In an interview with Dorothy McGarry, Elaine Svenonius (professor emerita, Graduate School of Education and Information Studies, University of California, Los Angeles) surveys her career in library education and her research in cataloging, classification, and indexing. Svenonius presents her views concerning the relevance of philosophy to the organization of information and the need for both basic research and practical research in librarianship; she explains how she progressed from an interest in the subject approach to information to an interest in the problems of descriptive cataloging as well. Svenonius describes teaching experiences at the University of Western Ontario, the Documentation Research Training Centre (Bangalore, India), and UCLA during the 1980s, when students often took "four or five courses devoted to the organization of information" (15). Other topics include discussion of her recent work, including *The Intellectual Foundation of Information Organization*, a monograph that attempts to synthesize subject and descriptive cataloging within a common conceptual framework, and a collection of the writings of Seymour Lubetzky. Svenonius describes as a major disappointment of her career "a fallen idealism" regarding the nature of information science. Initially, Svenonius believed "it was truly a science of information," but by the 1970s, "it was clear that information science was segueing into information technology and management. [She] couldn't believe it: At some schools men taught online reference and were called 'information scientists' while women taught book-based reference and were called 'librarians'" (14). One of a series of interviews with prominent individuals in the specialty of cataloging and bibliographic control.

87. McIlwaine, John. "Maria Skepastianu." *IFLA Journal* 27, no. 4 (2001): 281.

Maria Skepastianu, secretary of IFLA's Section on Preservation, died at the age of thirty-nine in April 2001. Skepastianu dedicated her career to promoting conservation of library materials, particularly in Greece. She earned an MA and Ph.D. from University College London. She taught preservation management courses at library schools in Thessaloniki and Corfu and published important reference works on this and other subjects in Greek.

88. McKechnie, Lynne E. F. "Patricia Spereman and the Beginning of Canadian Public Library Work with Children." *Libraries & Culture* 34, no. 2 (Spring 1999): 134–50.

Surveys the career and accomplishments of Patricia Spereman, possibly the first children's librarian in Canada, and illustrates the emergence of children's library services in Ontario. Spereman was the daughter of the Sarnia (Ontario) Public Library Board's secretary-treasurer, an individual known for his commitment to library development; she served as assistant librarian there from 1904 to 1908. Reports of the inspector of public libraries of the Ontario Department of Education indicate that under Spereman, Sarnia Public Library instituted the first story hours for children in the province, assembled model children's collections, and worked cooperatively with schools. By 1906, Sarnia Public Library demonstrated all critical elements of children's library services. In 1908, Spereman was appointed to the library division staff of the Ontario Department of Education, where she initially served as a consultant who traveled through the province setting up children's departments. In 1908, she gave a major paper on "Library Work with Children" at the conference of the Ontario Library Association. Spereman remained at the department until her death in 1946, but gradually moved into other areas of librarianship. Includes photographs.

89. Mediavilla, Cindy. "A Look Back: We Need More Edna Yellands." *California Libraries* 9, no. 5 (May 1999): 5, 8.

Profile of past California Library Association executive secretary and librarian Edna Yellands, who served in the position for seventeen years. Educated at the California State Library, Yellands began her career as a reference librarian at the State Library and soon moved to a small county library in Monterey. CLA's most prestigious scholarship, named after Yellands, is given to a library school student each year.

90. Meyer, Jennifer. "R/Evolution in YA Services: An Interview with Susan Madden." ***Alki: The Washington Library Association Journal*** **16, no. 2 (July 2002): 15–17.**

In an interview with Jennifer Meyer, Susan B. Madden (retired as coordinator of young adult and literacy services, King County Library System, Washington) surveys her career and contributions as a youth services/teen librarian. Among the career "highs" that Madden recounts are coauthoring the American Library Association/American Correctional Association standards for libraries in juvenile correctional facilities; writing, advising, and team-teaching a grant program, "Courtly Love in the Shopping Mall"; receiving the Allie Beth Martin Award; and "finally getting a frequent Youth Service Center kid to trust me to help him." (This teen, who knew only Spanish, had been tested in English and misdiagnosed by his school [16].) Her advice to librarians about getting teens into the library is "be honest and consistent and really, really happy they're there" (17). Madden does not discuss gender as a factor in her career. This interview was conducted on the occasion of Madden's winning two major awards bestowed annually by the Washington Library Association: the President's Award and the Visionary Library Services to Youth Award of the Children's and Young Adult Services Interest Group (CAYAS). Includes photos of the award presentations. Includes "Susan Madden: CAYAS Visionary Award Citation: A Tribute by Angelina Benedetti" (one column).

91. Mitchell, Carol R. "In Memoriam: Farewell to Anne, a Personal Perception." ***Education Libraries*** **23, no. 2/3 (1999): 5–6.**

Mitchell remembers Anne Galler, mentor, former director at the Concordia Library Studies Program, and active member of IFLA, for her many achievements and personal attributes.

92. Moran, Robert F. "Intellectual Freedom: An Interview with Judith F. Krug." ***Library Administration and Management*** **15, no. 4 (Fall 2001): 200–203.**

This is an interview with Judith Krug, director of the American Library Association's Office for Intellectual Freedom and executive director of the Freedom to Read Foundation. Krug says that children must learn to evaluate information found on the World Wide Web so that they can make wise choices.

93. Morton, Elizabeth. "Marianne Scott Fêted on Her Retirement as National Librarian." ***Feliciter*** **45, no. 6 (1999): 330.**

Reports on a gala held September 30, 1999, to honor Marianne Scott, national librarian of Canada, on her retirement and summarizes her career. Scott was appointed national librarian of Canada in 1984; previously she was law librarian at McGill University, then lecturer in the faculty of law, and finally director of libraries. Scott has served as president of the Canadian Library Association, the Canadian Association of Law Libraries, the Canadian Association of Research Libraries, and the Quebec Library Association, and has been active in the International Federation of Library Associations. Scott noted that the public good has been a constant throughout her career.

94. Myall, Carolynne, and Ruth C. Carter. *Portraits in Cataloging & Classification: Theorists, Educators, and Practitioners of the Late Twentieth Century*. New York: Haworth Press, 1998.

A collection of biographical and autobiographical essays, personal reminiscences, and interviews of major contributors to the specialties of cataloging, classification, and bibliographic organization during the last half of the twentieth century. Subjects include library and information science faculty members, cataloging theorists, classificationists, cataloging code and machine-readable format developers, and cataloging administrators. The majority of the subjects are from the United States, though Australia, Canada, England, and Germany are also represented. Slightly more than half the subjects are women; these include Dorothy Anderson, Henriette Davidson Avram, Betty Baughman, Ruth C. Carter, Doris Hargrett Clack, Ingetraut Dahlberg, Doralyn Joanne Hickey, Margaret F. Maxwell, Jeanne Osborn, Annette Lewis Phinazee, Mary Piggott, Lucia Rather, and Paule Rolland-Thomas. All authors and interviewees were sent a set of suggested questions, though not all responded to all questions. One question concerned barriers to achievement, including barriers related to gender; some contributors explicitly responded to this question. Also published as three numbers of *Cataloging & Classification Quarterly* 25 (2/3–4) (1998), in celebration of the publication of the journal's twenty-fifth volume.

95. Olson, Renee. "Ending a 32-Year Run: *SLJ's* Renowned Editor-in-Chief Lillian N. Gerhardt Lowers the Curtain on an Influential Career." *School Library Journal* 44, no. 9 (September 1998): 96, 98.

This article traces the career and contributions of retiring *SLJ* editor, Lillian Gerhardt. After several public library positions, Gerhardt went into publishing, joining *School Library Journal* in 1966. In 1971 she became editor-in-chief. Gerhardt has also been active in ALA, serving as president of the Association for Library Services for Children and as an ALA councilor. The article includes short tributes from other library notables.

96. Osborn, Jeanne. "Jeanne Osborn: Gladly Lerning and Teching (sic): With Apologies to Chaucer." ***Cataloging & Classification Quarterly*** **25, no. 2/3 (1998): 217–26.**

An autobiographical essay by Osborn, a library science educator in the field of cataloging and classification. In the 1930s, Osborn entered college as a music major, but a vision problem made a career in teaching music problematic; encountering an article about the American Library Association and schools offering training in librarianship, she decided to become a librarian instead. After many years of work in libraries, particularly in the area of cataloging, Osborn earned a Ph.D. in philosophy from the University of Illinois and became a professor of library science. She taught for four years at Northern Illinois University, then she joined the faculty of the University of Iowa. Osborn discusses the impact of automation on cataloging. She does not discuss gender as a factor in her career. Includes a selected bibliographic of works by and about Osborn. Also published in *Portraits in Cataloging & Classification: Theorists, Educators, and Practitioners of the Late Twentieth Century*, 217–26.

97. Partridge, A. "Meet the President: Anne Partridge." ***Impact, the Journal of the Career Development Group*** **4, no. 1 (January 2001–28 February 2001): 2–4.**

Interview with Anne Partridge, the 2001 president of the Career Development Group. Partridge describes her career as a professional librarian and her prior experience in the Career Development Group. She also discusses the unification of the Library Association and Institute of Information Scientists.

98. Pattie, Lin-yuh W. "Henriette Davidson Avram: The Great Legacy." ***Cataloging & Classification Quarterly*** **25, no. 2/3 (1998): 67–81.**

Includes an interview with Henriette D. Avram, along with a summary of her life and career. Avram explains that she was not a librarian by training but rather a "brainwashed computer systems analyst" (71) who stumbled into librarianship when she was assigned in 1965 to work with librarians at the Library of Congress on the design of a machine format for bibliographic data. This project resulted in the first version of MARC (Machine-Readable Cataloging), which became an international standard enabling libraries to create and exchange bibliographic data. Widely admired for her development of MARC and her pursuit of national standards, Avram subsequently became director of the Network Development Office at LC, director for processing systems, networks, and automation planning, assistant librarian for processing services, and finally associate librarian of Congress for collections services, a position in which she directed a staff of over 1,700 individuals working in acquisitions, cataloging, network and automation planning, preservation, collection development, and other functions. In answer to a question about possible barriers to her success, Avram states, "Regarding barriers to my career related to race or gender, there were none. Yes, I noted that there were hardly any or no women in certain high-level positions [of LC]. But as time passed, I, along with others, did attain, and with pride for managing to do so, a series of positions on the ladder" (75–76). Includes a selected bibliography of her publications and major conference presentations. Also published in *Portraits in Cataloging & Classification: Theorists, Educators, and Practitioners of the Late Twentieth Century*, 67–81.

99. Raseroka, H. Kay. "Birgitta Bergdahl, 13011-1937–20-3-2001: A Tribute." *IFLA Journal* 27, no. 4 (2001): 279–80.

IFLA president-elect Kay Raseroka recalls Birgitta Bergdahl as the "wind under the wings" of IFLA's ALP Core Programme, which aimed to strengthen library services in less developed countries. Bergdahl, formerly the chief librarian of Linkõping University, was appointed project manager of ALP in 1989 while it was still a pilot project and a year later became its official director. Described as sensitive, outcome-focused, and a tireless traveler, Bergdahl convinced donor agencies to support ALP projects, developed publications, facilitated interregional communication, and helped to build the capacities and confidence of librarians in the Third World.

100. Rasmussen, Anne F. "An Interview with Tina Feick." *Serials Review* 26, no. 2 (2000): 55–57.

Tina Feick has had an enormous impact on the serials industry through her involvement in the creation of the North American Serials Interest Group (NASIG). The article consists of an interview with Feick about her career.

101. Robin, Joshua. "Dr. Margaret Chisholm, a Leading Librarian." *Seattle Times* (23 November 1999): B6.

Obituary for Margaret Chisholm, former director of the University of Washington's Graduate School of Library and Information Science. The author of seven books and more than thirty articles, Chisholm played a key role in promoting the idea that librarians should become proficient in information technology, utilizing their expertise not only in academia but also in the business world. Online. Available from Lexis-Nexis Universe. Accessed 10 November 2000.

102. Rolland-Thomas, Paule, and Carolynne Myall. "An Interview with Paule Rolland-Thomas." ***Cataloging & Classification Quarterly*** **25, no. 4 (1998): 263–75.**

In an interview with Carolynne Myall, Paule Rolland-Thomas (professor emerita, École de bibliothéconomie et des sciences de l'information, Université de Montréal, Montréal, Quebec) surveys her career and her contributions to cataloging, classification, and library education. Rolland-Thomas explains that she entered librarianship based on the suggestion of a friend of her grandmother, since Rolland-Thomas loved reading and the friend "thought [librarianship] was a suitable profession for a woman." Rolland-Thomas was stimulated by the intellectual problems of cataloging and found that her "undergraduate degree in philosophy prepared [her] wonderfully for classification and subject analysis"; she was, however, disappointed to find that "fine, articulate, scholarly minds in the profession [of librarianship] were relatively rare" (265). Following work at the Catholic School Commission and at the University of Montreal, Rolland-Thomas became one of the founding faculty members at the University's library school. Believing strongly in international standards and consistency in practice, she became involved in cataloging code development as the editor and translator of the French-language versions of *Anglo-American Cataloging Rules*, first edition (AACR1), and *Anglo-American Cataloguing Rules*, second edition (AACR2), published as *Règles de catalogage anglo-américaines* (RCAA), 1973 and 1980 editions. Rolland-Thomas discusses her views about the value of cataloging, problems in the education of catalogers and librarians generally, new developments in library and information science curricula, the importance of international cataloging standards, and issues with regard to development of a subject cataloging code. She identifies her role in developing the library school at the University of Montreal as the most rewarding activity of her career. Rolland-Thomas notes that the first fifteen years she was on the faculty at Montreal, "the female members of the faculty were paid less—not very much less, but less" and notes that this discrepancy in salaries was not unusual during the 1960s and 1970s (268). Includes "Selected Publications of Paule Rolland-Thomas." Also published in *Portraits in Cataloging & Classification: Theorists, Educators, and Practitioners of the Late Twentieth Century*, 263–75.

103. Salvadore, Maria. "An Interview with Virginia A. Walter, Author of Children and Libraries: Getting It Right." ***Journal of Youth Services in Libraries*** **14, no. 3 (Spring 2001): 42–44.**

An interview with children's librarian and author of *Children and Libraries: Getting It Right*, Virginia A. Walter, wherein she outlines strategies that will improve library services for children.

104. Simon, Rose. "Interview with Florence Blakely." ***North Carolina Libraries*** **56, no. 2 (Summer 1998): 60–64.**

Interview with Florence Blakely, head of the reference department at Duke University from 1956 until the mid-seventies, which recounts her career as a reference librarian and collection development librarian in North Carolina and South Carolina. Blakely's achievements include building an alternative press collection, lobbying for professional status at Duke University, founding a discussion group for heads of reference in ALA's Reference and Adult Services Section, founding a chapter of the Reference and Adult Services in the North Carolina Libraries Association, and being awarded a Council on Library Resources Fellowship in 1970.

105. Smith, Jessie Carney. "Black Women, Civil Rights, and Libraries." In ***Untold Stories: Civil Rights, Libraries and Black Librarianship*****, ed. John Mark Tucker, 141–50. Urbana-Champaign, IL: Graduate School of Library and Information Science, 1998.**

Smith profiles seven black librarians to highlight their contributions to the field of librarianship: Anne Spencer, Effie Lee Newsome, Charlemae Hill Rollins, Augusta Braxton Baker, Virginia Lacy Jones, Annette L. Phinazee, and Hannah Diggs Atkins. Each librarian also had other professions that added to their experiences and value as librarians: Anne Spencer was a poet during the Harlem Renaissance and her home became "the equivalent of Gertrude Stein's famous salon in Paris in the 1920s." Hannah Diggs Atkins was a state legislator, becoming the highest-ranking woman in Oklahoma state government. Each woman is profiled not only as a librarian but also as a civil rights activist who used her knowledge and experience as a librarian to further the cause and advocacy of libraries and their users.

106. Spaulding, Amy. "A Good-bye." ***Journal of Youth Services in Libraries*** **11 (Spring 1998): 211–13.**

A memorial tribute to Augusta Baker (1911–1998), which recounts memories of Ms. Baker as a storyteller, a lady commanding respect, and a friend of Maurice Sendak and Eleanor Roosevelt. Born in Baltimore, Augusta Baker went to work at the Countee Cullen branch of the New York Public Library in 1934; in 1961 she became the coordinator of children's services at the New York Public Library. Upon retiring in 1974, she became storyteller-in-residence at the University of South Carolina College of Library and Information Science.

107. Steinhagen, Elizabeth N. "Leaders of Bibliographic Control—The Chilean Experience: María Teresa Sanz Briso-Montiano and Soledad Fernández-Corugedo." ***Cataloging & Classification Quarterly*** **31, no. 1 (2000): 3–13.**

Based on interviews with the subjects by Elizabeth N. Steinhagen, this article summarizes the careers and accomplishments of María Teresa Sanz Briso-Montiano (former coordinator at the Biblioteca Nacional de Chile) and Soledad Fernández-Corugedo (coordinator of Red Nacional de Información Bibliográfíca), particularly with regard to standardization, automation, and cooperative ventures in library cataloging in Chile. Following studies in librarianship in the late 1940s, Sanz developed the library of Pontificia Universidad Católico (PUC) into one of the best and most modern academic libraries in Chile, represented Chile at the 1961 International Conference on Cataloguing Principles (Paris), introduced these principles and other internationally accepted cataloging codes into Chilean practice, coordinated a seminar on centralized cataloging and library automation sponsored by the Organization of American States, and established ground rules for cooperative cataloging by Chilean academic libraries. As Coordinator at the Biblioteca Nacional de Chile (BNC), Sanz obtained a donation of NOTIS software for an online library system and laid the groundwork for the development of a shared network. Following her retirement from BNC in the mid-1980s, this system became the basis of the shared network, Red Nacional de Información Bibliográfíca (RENIB). Fernández-Corugedo, who worked under the leadership of Sanz at both PUC and BNC, joined RENIB in the late 1980s and became its coordinator as the network began to grow. She promoted acceptance of international standards in bibliographic description and information retrieval; established cooperative methods to reach consensus among members about standards, training, and other issues; and lobbied for support and legislation that would encourage membership to cooperate more actively. Both individuals speculate on the future of RENIB. The article does not discuss gender as a factor in the careers of Sanz and Fernández-Corugedo, except to note that Fernández-Corugedo, who had previously studied law, entered librarianship after her children started school. One of a series of interviews with prominent individuals in the specialty of cataloging and bibliographic control but not presented in interview format.

108. Stough, Mary L. "Louise "Becky" Morrison, 1923–2002: Her Legacy." ***Alki: The Washington Library Association Journal*** **18, no. 2 (July 2002): 19, 18.**

Summarizes the career of Louise "Becky" Morrison, a prominent librarian in Washington State who was the founding director of the Timberland Regional Library system. Morrison was known for her dedication to public service and intellectual freedom, her legislative knowledge, her skill in lobbying, and her understanding of the timber tax and its ramifications for library funding. Includes personal reminiscences that demonstrate Morrison's values as an individual and a librarian.

109. Turock, Betty J., and James Anderson. "A Tribute to Pam Richards." *The International Information & Library Review* 33, no. 1 (2001): 1–2.

Celebrates the professional life of Pam Richards, professor at Rutgers University School of Communication, Information and Library Studies since 1977. Professor Richards, who passed away in 1999, was renowned for her teaching career and service to the profession. Her research interests included the exchange of information under stress, such as during wartime.

110. Valentine, Patrick M. "Mollie Huston Lee: Founder of Raleigh's Public Black Library." *North Carolina Libraries* 56, no. 1 (Spring 1998): 23–26.

Profile of Mollie Huston Lee, first African American graduate of the Columbia University Library School, founding member of what became the Negro Library Association of North Carolina, and founder of the Richard B. Harrison Library, Raleigh, North Carolina's first public black library. Under her leadership, the Harrison Library held 3,310 volumes, was open forty-two hours a week, and had an annual circulation of 15,000 within two years of opening its doors. Lee was honored for her achievements by her selection as a UNESCO library delegate and by her appointment to the Board of Trustees of the State Library of North Carolina.

111. Vazquez, Lilia. "Elizabeth Martinez." In *Women of Color in Librarianship: An Oral History*, ed. Kathleen de la Peña McCook. Chicago: American Library Association, 1998.

A native Californian, Ms. Martinez received her library degree from the University of Southern California. She served four years as the city librarian for the Los Angeles Public Library, overseeing sixty-three branch libraries and twenty-eight branch construction projects, including the rehabilitation and expansion of the Los Angeles Central Library. She discusses in this interview her early years, her entrance into the profession, and what she sees as her greatest accomplishments.

112. Vazquez, Lilia. "Lillian Lopez." In *Women of Color in Librarianship: An Oral History*, ed. Kathleen de la Peña McCook. Chicago: American Library Association, 1998.

Ms. Lopez was born in Puerto Rico but came to New York as a child. She received her library degree from Columbia University and began her career at the New York Public Library. She has received many awards for her outreach work with the Hispanic community, which she discusses in this interview.

113. Wartluft, David J. "Catherine Stirewalt (Memorial Tribute)." *Summary of Proceedings. Fifty-fifth Annual Conference—American Theological Library Association* (2001): 319.

Sister Stirewalt graduated with an MLS from Rutgers University in 1961 after a long and varied career as teacher, missionary, and deaconess for the United Lutheran Church, including a period of internment in China from 1941 to 1943. As cataloger for the Krauth Memorial Library at the Lutheran Theological Seminary in Philadelphia, she converted the library's holdings from the Reed classification system to the Library of Congress classification system, simultaneously converting the subject headings from Pettee List of Theological Subject Headings to the Library of Congress Subject Headings, all before the advent of computers. After her retirement, she became the librarian for the Deaconess Center in Gladwyne, Pennsylvania.

114. Wijnstroom, Margreet. "Else Granheim (1926–1999), In Memoriam." *IFLA Journal* 25, no. 2 (1999): 78.

This memorial to Else Granheim, Norwegian librarian and president of ILFA from 1979 to 1985, is in the form of a letter to the deceased. Granheim is described as a hard worker who valued action over talk. She is credited with "breaking down the barriers which prevented the Chinese world from joining IFLA" and with designing IFLA's Core Activity for the Advancement of Librarianship (ALP), which furthers the library profession, library institutions, and library and information services in developing countries.

115. Wilkes, Adeline W. "Doris Hargrett Clack, 1928–1995: Called to Teach." *Cataloging & Classification Quarterly* 25, no. 2/3 (1998): 111–25.

Surveys the life, career, and contributions of Doris Hargrett Clack to library science education, cataloging theory and practice, and bibliographic control of African American library resources. Born into a Florida family and community that valued education highly, Clack taught in public high schools before entering graduate library school and becoming a cataloging and technical services librarian. With the active support of her husband, Clack ultimately earned a Ph.D. in librarianship from the University of Pittsburgh in 1973; she then taught cataloging and other subjects in librarianship at Florida State University for twenty-three years. Among her publications were *Black Literature Resources: Analysis and Organization* (M. Dekker, 1975), widely regarded as a major contribution to bibliographic control of African American library materials, and *Authority Control: Principles, Applications, and Instructions* (ALA, 1990). Discusses Clack's success as a professor and mentor, her devotion to equal opportunity and high standards, her service to the profession through the organization of workshops and conferences, and her work in African libraries and library schools. Notes that she chaired her university's Equal Opportunity Committee, which investigated charges of violations of policies concerning discrimination on account of race or gender. Includes brief reminiscences by several of her students on whose careers she was a major influence. Also published in *Portraits in Cataloging & Classification: Theorists, Educators, and Practitioners of the Late Twentieth Century*, 111–25.

HONORS AND AWARDS

116. "1999 CAYAS Award for Visionary Library Service to Youth Presented to Evie Wilson-Lingbloom." ***Alki: The Washington Library Association Journal*** **15, no. 2 (July 1999): 11.**

Reports that the Children's and Young Adult Services Interest Group (CAYAS), Washington Library Association, presented its 1999 Visionary Award to Evie Wilson-Lingbloom, author of *Hangin' Out at Rocky Creek*, manager of the Edmonds Library of the Sno-Isle Regional Library System, and a leader and mentor among youth services librarians. Briefly reviews Wilson-Lingbloom's career.

117. "And the Winners Are . . . : The Official Results of the 1999 ACRL Elections." ***College and Research Libraries*** **60, no. 6 (June 1999): 467–69, 471.**

Reports the results of the 1999 elections of the Association for College and Research Libraries: Lizabeth (Betsy) Wilson, associate director of Libraries for Research and Instructional Services, University of Washington, was elected vice president/president-elect. Summarizes Wilson's education, previous library positions at the University of Washington and the University of Illinois at Urbana-Champaign, participation in library and educational organizations, and awards (including the Miriam Dudley Instruction Librarian Award).

118. "AzLA Award Winners." ***AzLA`Newsletter*** **32, no. 10 (November 1999–31 December 1999): 1.**

Highlights winners of the Arizona Library Association awards for 1999, including Donna Larson-Bennett, awarded for Distinguished Service, and Judy Register, named Librarian of the Year. Larson-Bennett retired in 1999 from the Ross-Blakley Law Library after a distinguished career in government documents librarianship. Register, director at the Scottsdale Public Library System, was recognized for her promotion of literacy on a large scale.

119. "AzLA to Present Awards at Annual Conference." ***AzLA Newsletter*** **33, no. 10 (November 2000–31 December 2000): 1.**

Profiles winners of several awards, including Carla J. Stoffle, named Librarian of the Year. Stoffle is dean of the University of Arizona Libraries and acting director of the School of Information Resources and Library Science. She is active in several associations and has published extensively.

120. "Elizabeth Moys Awarded MBE." ***Catalogue and Index*** **135 (Spring 2000): 3.**

Law librarian and indexer Elizabeth Moys was awarded the MBE (Member of the British Empire, awarded for outstanding service to Great Britain) for "services to classification and indexing." Moys, a founding member of the British and Irish Association of Law Librarians, created the Moys classification and thesaurus for legal materials, now used in legal and academic libraries in the United Kingdom, United States, and Europe. Previously, Moys earned the Wheatley Medal, the top prize for indexing, for her work on the 8,000-page British Tax Encyclopedia.

121. "Elizabeth Wallis MBE." ***Catalogue and Index*** **129 (Autumn 1998): 7.**

Wallis was awarded an MBE for her work for the Society of Indexers, for which she serves as registrar. She was also the recipient of the Carey Award for her dedication to the Society and her high professional standards.

122. "IFLA President Honoured." ***IFLA Journal*** **27, no. 1 (2001): 42.**

In early 2001, Christine Deschamps, president of the International Federation of Library Associations and Institutions, received the "Chevalier de la Légion d'Honneur," the highest decoration awarded in France.

123. "Jean Arnot Memorial Fellowship Winner 1999." ***LASIE*** **30, no. 3 (September 1999): 71.**

Judith Hurst was awarded the Jean Arnot Fellowship for 1999 for her paper titled "A Journey as a Teacher-Librarian through the Nineteen Nineties." Another entry that was highly commended by the judges, titled "Evidence-Based Practice and its Relevance to Library and Information Services" by Julie Hooke, is published in the same issue.

124. "Judith Krug Wins Lippincott Award." ***Newsletter on Intellectual Freedom*** **47, no. 4 (July 1998): 103.**

Reports that Judith Krug, editor of the *Newsletter on Intellectual Freedom* and director of the Office for Intellectual Freedom of the American Library Association, is the 1998 recipient of the ALA Joseph W. Lippincott Award, the highest honor in U.S. librarianship. Briefly summarizes Krug's career in which she has vigorously defended the First Amendment and promoted librarianship's commitment to intellectual freedom.

125. "Marianne Scott Named Winner of the CLA Outstanding Service to Librarianship Award." ***IFLA Journal*** **26, no. 4 (2000): 325–26.**

Marianne Scott received the Canadian Library Association's Outstanding Service to Librarianship award in 2000, the year she retired. Dr. Scott began her career at the Bank of Montreal. From 1955 to 1984, she worked at McGill University as the first law librarian and later as director of libraries. From 1985 until 2000, she served as national librarian of Canada. She was president of CLA from 1981 to 1982.

126. "Mary E. Krutulis wins 2002 Beta Phi Mu Service Award." ***Focus on Indiana Libraries*** **56, no. 3 (March 2002): 5.**

Describes the professional accomplishments of Mary E. Krutulis, director of admissions for the Indiana University School of Library and Information Science. She also served for eight years as assistant dean of the Indiana University SLIS.

127. "Meralyn Meadows: Winner of the 1999 Outstanding Support Staff award." ***Library Personnel News*** **13, no. 1/2 (Spring 2000–Summer 2000): 5.**

Meralyn Meadows, administrative assistant at the Stanly County Public Library in Albemarle, North Carolina, is the winner of the annual *Library Mosaics* and the Council on Library/Media Technicians 1999 Outstanding

Support Staff award. Meadows has served on the board of the ALA Support Staff Interests Round Table since the group's founding, serves as the editor of the group's National Directory, and served as chair of the North Carolina Library Paraprofessional Association.

128. "Osborn Wins Cheyenne ATHENA Award." ***Outrider (Wyoming Library Association)*** **(November 1999).**

An announcement and description of an award for "advancing women in professional excellence and librarianship." The ATHENA award is made by more than three hundred cities nationwide including Cheyenne, Wyoming, and is designed to recognize an individual who "demonstrates excellence, creativity and initiative in business and professions" among other endeavors. The winner announced in this piece is a librarian who was recognized for her leadership and direction of the Laramie County Library System.

129. "The Professor G. Rao Award to Dr. K. Sarada." ***Herald of Library Science*** **37, no. 2–3 (July 1998–31 October 1998): 260.**

Dr. Sarada received the award for her outstanding services to rural libraries. She is the former head of the Department of Library and Information Science, Andhra University.

130. "Resolution on the Retirement of Alexandra Mason." ***RBMS Newsletter*****, no. 31 (Fall 1999).**

Honors Alexandra Mason, who retired after thirty-one years as librarian of the Kenneth Spencer Research Library at the University of Kansas, Lawrence.

131. "Roll of Honor Award Presented to Dorothy M. Broderick." ***Freedom to Read Foundation News*** **23, no. 3 (1998).**

Announces Broderick as the annual recipient of the Freedom to Read Foundation award at the 1998 American Library Association annual conference in New Orleans. The award citation is printed in full, including praise for Broderick's work as a library educator in the field of intellectual freedom.

132. "Shirley Fitzgibbons Receives Beta Phi Mu Award." ***IFLA Journal*** **26, no. 4 (2000): 326.**

Shirley Fitzgibbons, an expert in children's and youth services on the faculty of the Graduate School of Library and Information Science at Indiana University, Bloomington, received the ALA Beta Phi Mu award in July 2000 for her distinguished service to education in librarianship. Fitzgibbons implemented a minority recruitment plan for the school, has mentored hundreds of children's librarians, and has been active in ALA's youth divisions.

133. "Sue Mahmoodi Winner of the 2001 Outstanding Supporter of Support Staff Award." ***Minnesota Libraries News*** **32, no. 4 (April 2001): 1.**

Sue Mahmoodi, recently retired continuing education and library research specialist for the Minnesota State Library, is the winner of the *Library Mosaics* and the Council on Library/Media Technicians 2001 award for Outstanding Supporter of Support Staff. She has been instrumental in developing and providing successful continuing education efforts such as Branch Out, Soaring to Excellence, and Minnesota Voluntary Certification. She was also successful in getting two other statewide programs off the ground: Minnesota Opportunities for Reference Excellence (MORE) and Minnesota Opportunities for Technical Services Excellence (MOTSE). During her thirty-year career Ms. Mahmoodi has also provided education for public library trustees around the state and has worked with other continuing education specialists at the state agency level from other states as well.

134. "Susan Fuller Is *Library Journal* Librarian of the Year." ***California Libraries*** **9, no. 3 (March 1999): 1.**

Brief profile of Santa Clara County Library director Susan Fuller, who was named Librarian of the Year in 1998. She is known for her political savvy and kept the Santa Clara library system afloat in the post–Proposition 13 era of fiscal hardship.

135. "Washington Library Association 1999 Awards." ***Alki: The Washington Library Association Journal*** **15, no. 2 (July 1999): 25–26.**

Presents excerpts of the citations for Washington Library Association Awards for 1999, including summaries of the recipients' careers. Award winners for 1999 included the following female library employees and librarians: Ruth Poynter, Evie Wilson-Lingboom, Janice Hammock, Sharon Hammer, and Gail Willis.

136. "Winner of the Jean Arnot Memorial Fellowship 1998." ***LASIE*** **29, no. 3 (September 1998): 20.**

Sue Scott, senior project officer of the Education and Client Liaison Division at the State Library of New South Wales in Sydney, Australia, was awarded the Jean Arnot Fellowship. The Fellowship is in honor of Jean Fleming Arnot, former head cataloger of the State Library of New South

Wales, who retired in 1968 after nearly fifty years of service. The annual award goes to a woman who is a librarian or student of librarianship for an outstanding original paper on librarianship. Arnot was active in women's organizations and active in the campaign for equal pay. An article by Sue Scott titled "Mapping the Internet: Applying Reference Skills to Tame the Web," which is based on her winning entry, is published in volume 29, number 3 of *LASIE*.

137. Ariel, Joan. "Congratulations to our Second Annual WSS Award Winners." ***Women's Studies Section Newsletter*** **16, no. 1 (Spring 2001): 3.**

Announces the ALA Association of College and Research Libraries/ Women's Studies Section award winners for 2001. Career highlights for both Sarah Pritchard, winner of the WSS Career Achievement award, and Marilyn Dunn, winner of the WSS Significant Achievement award, are included in this brief overview.

138. Berry, John N. III. "Susan Kent, Los Angeles Public Library. (Librarian of the Year 2002)." ***Library Journal*** **127, no. 1 (January 2002): 42–45.**

Susan Kent, awarded the *Library Journal* Librarian of the Year award 2002, is profiled. Kent is director of an expanding system currently consisting of sixty-seven branch libraries serving a population of 3.8 million people. As city librarian, Kent also serves the mayor, city council, and numerous foundations and donors. She was chosen for the Librarian of the Year award based on a strong commitment to public service, political acumen, strong vision for public libraries, and ability to realize that vision. Her management and fundraising efforts are highlighted, particularly concerning branch expansion and renovation efforts, along with professional service and career history.

139. Burch, Sue. "Spotlight: Evelyn Richardson—A Lifetime of Achievement." ***Kentucky Libraries*** **66, no. 1 (Winter 2002): 4–5.**

Evelyn Richardson received the Kentucky Library Association's "Lifetime Achievement Award" in 2001 at the association's fall conference. Richardson worked for twenty-five years as a regional librarian with the Kentucky Department of Libraries and Archives, where she developed adult literacy programs. She was influential in the formation of the Kentucky Literacy Commission and its funding by the state General Assembly in 1986. The Barren River Region established an annual award bearing her name for a person or persons who contribute extraordinary efforts to promote literacy. After her retirement in 1992, she volunteered to serve as the unpaid interim director of the Logan County Public Library. After two years, a paid director was hired, but Richardson continued nearly full-time as a volunteer for special projects. This article includes a photograph of Richardson and the text of a radio talk she gave after September 11, 2001, in which she stressed the importance of libraries in difficult times.

140. George, Lee Anne. "Carol Henderson Honored by ARL." ***ARL Newsletter*****, no. 204 (June 1999).**

Carol Henderson, executive director of the American Library Association's (ALA) Washington Office and an associate executive director of ALA, received a standing ovation and certificate for "her significant contributions and unwavering commitment to libraries throughout the United States." She retired on August 13 after nearly twenty-four years of service.

141. Glick, Andrea. "Leaders in Waiting: Are These Eight Librarians Headed for the Top?" ***School Library Journal*** **44, no. 1 (January 1998): 24–29.**

Presents brief profiles of eight youth services librarians, six of them women, who were selected for the 1997 Emerging Leaders Institute. Sarah Knetzer is the first professional librarian for Idyllwild Arts Academy in California. Jayashree Chatterjee, head of children's services at the Library of the Chathams in New Jersey, first worked in a library in Saudi Arabia as a volunteer library aide. Katie O'Dell Madison, a youth services librarian in Oregon, has begun writing for *SLJ.* Denise Sisco, a Bloomington, Indiana, media specialist, moved from being a classroom teacher to librarianship. Susan Hill does outreach to local schools for the Broward County Library in Florida. Susan Moore became a children's librarian after working more than ten years in business.

142. Grim, Jessica. "First Annual WSS Award Winners." ***Women's Studies Section Newsletter*** **15, no. 1 (Spring 2000): 3.**

Announces the first Women's Studies Section award winners. Biographical details are included for Susan E. Searing, winner of the Career Achievement award, and Lynn Westbrook, winner of the Significant Achievement award.

143. Hovendick, Kelly. "WSS Awards Ceremony a Memorable Event!" ***Women's Studies Section Newsletter*** **17, no. 2 (Fall 2002): 1.**

Announces the section's annual awards sponsored by Greenwood Publishing Group and Routledge. The career achievement award went to Joan Ariel, women's studies and history librarian at the University of California,

Irvine, and founding member of the section. The significant achievement award went to Beth Stafford for her work on the Women's Studies Preservation Project, 1997 to 2001, to identify, preserve, and make available on OCLC over a thousand women's studies titles.

144. Jay, M. Ellen. "Wild about Reading: Grolier Award Winner Mary Lankford's Enthusiasm for Reading Made a World of Difference." ***School Library Journal*** **48, no. 8 (August 2002): 54–55.**

In this interview with the 2002 Grolier award winner, Mary Lankford talks about her early career in a school library and the importance of school libraries.

145. Kenney, Brian. "Sue Davidsen Named Director of Internet Public Library." ***School Library Journal*** **48, no. 8 supplement (Summer 2002): 7.**

Announces the appointment of Sue Davidsen as managing director of the Internet Public Library at the University of Michigan School of Information. Her previous position was with the interface design team at Proquest.

146. Kimmel, Margaret Mary. "Building the 'Community of the Book': A Conversation with Amy Kellman, Winner of the 1998 Grolier Award." ***School Library Journal*** **44, no. 9 (September 1998): 106–9.**

In this interview with the 1998 Grolier award winner, Amy Kellman talks about her career (beginning with a series of part-time jobs), the various activities sponsored at her current library, the Carnegie Library of Pittsburgh, and how children's librarianship has changed. Kellman has been at CLP for more than twenty years and has served as president of ALA's Association for Library Services for Children.

147. Ward, Caroline. "A Passion for Her Profession." ***School Library Journal*** **47, no. 9 (September 2001): 52–55.**

In this interview with the 2001 Grolier award winner, Julie Cummins talks about the books she has written and edited, about her decision to become a children's librarian, and about her contributions during the thirteen years she served as coordinator of children's services at the New York Public Library. Cummins has also served as president of the New York Library Association and as an ALA Councilor.

148. Williamson, Nancy. "FID/CR News 46." ***Knowledge Organization*** **25, no. 1/2 (1998): 39–45.**

The section titled "Awards" (40) reports that Emilia Currás was presented the Kaula Gold Medal. Currás is director of the scientific information and documentation unit, Universidad Automata de Madrid, and is well known in international information science research and education circles. The section titled "In Memoriam" (40–41) reports the death of Phyllis Allen Richmond, internationally recognized scholar in classification research, in October 1997. Notes that Richard had "a highly creative mind" (40) and that she tried to instill an interest in classification theory in her students through one of the few advanced courses in the subject in the United States during the 1970s and 1980s. Richmond wrote more than seventy articles on topics ranging from the history of science and medicine to technical articles on aspects of library and information science, particularly classification. Summarizes Richmond's career, including her winning the 1977 Margaret Mann citation.

149. Williamson, Nancy. "FID/CR News 47." ***Knowledge Organization*** **25, no. 3 (1998): 113–17.**

The section titled "Ranganathan Award" (113) reports that Elaine Svenonius was named the eighth recipient of this award, presented every two years by the International Federation for Documentation and Information, Committee on Classification Research, to honor distinguished contributions in classification research. Quotes from the citation for the award, which recognizes "her extensive and impressive range of fundamental papers exploring the theory of the field and for her promotion of the application of that theory in practice." Notes that Svenonius is a distinguished library and information science educator, and briefly summarizes her career.

150. Young, Ann-Christie. "ACRL Honors the 1999 Award Winners: Recognizing Professional Contributions and Scholarly Research." ***College & Research Libraries News*** **60, no. 4 (April 1999): 278–84.**

Announces presentation of honors awarded by the Association for College & Research Libraries, and summarizes the careers and achievements of the winners. Susan K. Nutter, vice provost and director of libraries at North Carolina State University, was the 1999 recipient of the Hugh C. Atkinson Memorial Award. Nutter's action-oriented leadership with regard to employing technological solutions and her important roles in organizations were among the factors in the Atkinson Award Committee's selection. Hannelore B. Rader, university librarian at the University of Louisville, was named ACRL Academic/Research Librarian of the Year. Her work in the field of instructional services and her creation of three model library instruction programs were cited. Bonnie Gratch Lindauer, reference/

instructional services librarian at City College of San Francisco, was named winner of the K. G. Saur award for best article in *College & Research Libraries*; Lindauer's article, "Defining and Measuring the Library's Impact on Campus-Wide Outcomes," appeared in the November 1998 issue. Mary Reichel, university librarian at Appalachian State University, won the Miriam Dudley Instruction Librarian award. Jo Ann Carr, director of the Center for Instructional Materials and Computing, School of Education, University of Wisconsin, Madison, won the Distinguished Education and Behavioral Sciences Librarian award. Christine S. Bruce, lecturer in the Queensland University of Technology's School of Information Systems (Brisbane, Australia) won the Instruction Section's Publication award for her book, *The Seven Faces of Information Literacy* (Auslib Press, 1997). Jolande E. Goldberg, senior cataloging policy specialist (law classification) at the Library of Congress, was the recipient of the Marta Lange/CQ award. Alenka Sauperl won the Doctoral Dissertation Fellowship for her work, "Subject Determination during the Cataloging Process." Wanda Johnston Bahde, a consultant and trainer for libraries, educational institutions, and businesses, was chosen to receive the EBSCO Community College Learning Resources Leadership award.

151. Zimon, Kathy E. "Melva J. Dwyer Award." ***Art Libraries Journal*** **24, no. 3 (1999): 9–12.**

This article provides an explanation of the Melva J. Dwyer award, which was established in honor of Melva Dwyer, a founding member of CARLIS (Canadian Art Libraries Section of the Canadian Association of Special Libraries), upon her retirement. It tells the whole story of the award, explains why it was given, and for whom it is named. Contains a brief biography of Melva Dwyer and her lifelong commitment to art librarianship as well as a chronology of the award.

SIGNIFICANT APPOINTMENTS

152. "Alice Yelen Sworn In to Federal Advisory Board." ***ALA Washington News*** **51, no. 6 (July 1999): 7.**

This excerpt from a July 8 press release from the Institute of Museums and Library Services (IMLS) announces the appointment of Alice Rae Yelen to its National Museum Services Board. As a member of the Board she will be providing policy advice to the IMLS, an independent grant-making agency.

153. "Barbara Golden Has Been Appointed by the Minnesota Supreme Court as the New State Law Librarian." ***Minnesota Libraries News*** **33, no. 7 (November 2002): 3.**

Golden has held various positions at the State Law Library since 1983, most recently Electronic Services Librarian. Prior positions include County Law Library project coordinator for the Minnesota State Library and head of outreach services for the Law Library Service to Prisoners program. She replaces Marvin Anderson, who retired.

154. "BL Picks Access Specialist." ***Library Association Record*** **101, no. 3 (March 2000): 123.**

Lynne Brindley is the new chief executive of the British Library as of July 2000. Brindley, pro-vice-chancellor and university librarian at Leeds University, was the only librarian short-listed for the job and is the first professional librarian to hold the post.

155. "Brandau Takes Helm at Library of Michigan." ***Footnotes: The Official Newsletter of the State Library of Iowa*** **24, no. 2 (February 2000): 1, 3.**

A brief interview with Christie Brandau, assistant state librarian of Iowa, as she prepared to become state librarian of Michigan.

156. "British Library Breakthrough: Female, Professional Head." ***Library Hotline*** **29, no. 6 (14 February 2000): 1.**

Reports appointment of Lynne Brindley as the first female chief executive of the British Library.

157. "DCPS Selects Molly Raphael, First Woman Chief in 50 Years." ***Library Hotline*** **27, no. 7 (23 February 1998): 1.**

News item announcing the unanimous vote to appoint Molly Raphael as director of the District of Columbia Public Library, the first woman director there in fifty years. Briefly chronicles her career.

158. "Evans Above." ***Library Association Record*** **101, no. 6 (June 2000): 316.**

Janet Evans is the new head of the Libraries Division in Britain's Department for Culture, Media & Sport (DCMS). A career civil servant, Evans worked in the DCMS since it was established in 1992 and previously headed the Tourism Division and the Media Division. In the following issue of the *Record* (101, no. 7, July 2000, 384), a letter writer takes the Library Association to task for not protesting the appointment of a nonlibrarian to the post. The association's Principal Policy Advisor responds, noting that senior civil servants have historically been viewed as generalists and that the department has a chief library advisor who is properly qualified.

159. "First Lady Hillary Rodham Clinton to Serve as Honorary Chair for Sister Libraries: A White House Millennium Project." ***ALA Washington News*** **51, no. 3 (March 1999): 7.**

A March 23, 1999, press release from the United States National Commission on Libraries and Information Science (NCLIS) announcing an initiative called Sister Libraries: A White House Millennium Council Project. The NCLIS and Sister Cities International (SCI) are partnering in the initiative, designed to promote the pairing of public and school libraries in the United States with libraries worldwide to focus on programs for children and teenagers. First Lady Hillary Rodham Clinton agreed to chair the Sister Libraries project. Libraries that are selected will receive recognition and designation as official White House Millennium Council Sister Libraries but will not receive funds for staff, equipment, or materials.

160. "From the British Library to Yale." ***IFLA Journal*** **27, no. 3 (2001): 195.**

Alice Prochaska assumed the post of university librarian at Yale University in August 2001. Dr. Prochaska was previously the director of special collections at the British Library. At the time of this announcement, she was chair of the Rare Books and Manuscripts Standing Committee of IFLA.

161. "President Clinton Names Rebecca T. Bingham and Martha B. Gould as Members of the National Commission on Libraries and Information Science." ***ALAWON*** **7, no. 13 (4 February 1998).**

A press release that announces the nomination of Rebecca T. Bingham and Martha B. Gould to serve as members of the National Commission on Libraries and Information Science.

162. "Renée Olson is New *SLJ* Editor." ***American Libraries*** **29, no. 7 (August 1998): 22.**

Announces the naming of Renée Olson as the new editor-in-chief of *School Library Journal*. She replaced Lillian Gerhardt, who retired after thirty-two years of service.

163. "Sheppard Named Acting IMLS Director." ***ALA Washington News*** **51, no. 3 (March 1999): 1.**

A March 25, 1999, press release announcing Beverly Black Sheppard's appointment as acting director of the Institute of Museum and Library Services (IMLS). She will continue as acting director until the president nominates and the senate confirms a new director and will administer the day-to-day operations of the agency.

164. "Wilkins Appointed as Director of Illinois State Library." ***Illinois Library Association Reporter*** **17, no. 2 (April 1999): 21.**

Announces the appointment of Jean Wilkins as director of the Illinois State Library and summarizes her career. Wilkins replaced former director Bridget Lamont, who was appointed director of policy development for the governor of Illinois.

165. Baumann, Sabine. "Interview: Johanna Rachinger." ***Zeitschrift für Bibliothekswesen und Bibliographie*** **49, no. 2 (2002): 251–54.**

Rachinger (born in 1960, doctoral degree in 1986), so far working in a publishing house, was appointed general director of the Österreichische Nationalbibliothek in Vienna in June 2001. In this interview she speaks about her management practices and values, new administrative structures of the National Library, corporate identity, and the funding of a new building and reconstruction, respectively.

166. Herman, Deirdre A. "New Day, New Leadership at ALA Washington Office." ***American Libraries*** **30, no. 11 (December 1999): 14.**

Announces the appointment of Emily Sheketoff as an ALA associate executive director and executive director of the ALA Washington office. Sheketoff's lack of library background and experience is discussed.

167. Long, Sarah. "Reflections on My ALA Presidency." ***New Library World*** **102, no. 1160/1161 (2001): 10–12.**

Long recounts some highlights of her year as ALA president and reflects on what the office meant to her.

168. Rogers, Michael. "D. C. Public Names Raphael Director." ***Library Journal*** **123, no. 5 (15 March 1998): 15, 17.**

Brief news article announcing the permanent appointment of Molly Raphael, formerly acting director, to director of the District of Columbia Public Library. She is the first woman to hold the office in more than fifty years. She succeeds former director Hardy Franklin, who retired in 1997 amid charges of sexual harassment.

169. Wegner, Mary. "State Librarian's Message." ***Footnotes*** **25, no. 12 (2002): 2–3.**

In one of her first columns as the new state librarian of Iowa, Wegner traces her career in the profession from library school to assuming her current duties. Before becoming assistant state librarian in 2000, she had held a public library reference position, had directed a hospital library, and had served as president of the Iowa Library Association.

170. Young, Bill. "State Library Board Names McVey as New Director." ***Oklahoma Librarian*** **51, no. 2 (March 2001–30 April 2001): 1.**

Announces Susan C. McVey's appointment as director of the Oklahoma Department of Libraries. The position encompasses a variety of responsibilities, summarized in the announcement, including state librarian and state archivist. McVey's education and career in Oklahoma libraries are also highlighted.

2

Career Development and Satisfaction

This chapter lists publications related to career planning, barriers women in the field encounter while developing their careers (including the glass ceiling), mentoring and networking, work reentry, and other factors that hinder or help career development and satisfaction. For related entries, see related terms in the subject index.

171. Attle, S. "Career Development Group: Equal Opportunities Policy and Statements." ***Impact, the Journal of the Career Development Group*** **3, no. 5 (May 2000): 73–74.**

Presents the United Kingdom's Career Development Group's policy on equal opportunity and its statements against discrimination based on race, color, religion, ethnic or national origin, disability, age, sex, sexual orientation, or marital status. This statement acknowledges the different manifestations of sex discrimination, such as unequal access to services, impediments to career advancement, sexual harassment, and sexual violence in the workplace.

172. Briscoe, G. "Climb High: High Altitude Mountaineering Lessons for Librarians." ***Law Library Journal*** **92, no. 2 (Spring 2000): 217–24.**

Briscoe is the associate director and head of technical services at the University of Colorado Law Library, Boulder. She uses lessons from high-altitude mountain climbing to describe how to manage one's career in librarianship effectively. She recommends these basic tenets: Follow the leader, prepare properly, pace yourself, prove yourself to your leader, support your teammates, accept adverse conditions, be motivated for the goal, and accept risk.

173. Burton, S., and M. Huckle. "Try Mentoring: Candidates on Route B to Associateship Need Your Support." ***Impact, the Journal of the Career Development Group*** **2, no. 2 (February 1999): 21–22.**

The focus of the article is to encourage chartered librarians in the United Kingdom to participate in mentoring new librarians. New librarians taking Route B to qualify for associateship need guidance and support from an experienced librarian. The article discusses how a chartered member can become involved in the mentoring program.

174. Carson, Kerry D., Paula Phillips Carson, William C. Roe, Betty J. Birkenheimer, and Joyce S. Phillips. "Four Commitment Profiles and Their Relationships to Empowerment, Service Recovery, and Work Attitudes." ***Public Personnel Management*** **28, no. 1 (Spring 1999): 1–13.**

Reports the results of a survey of medical librarians on the "influence of career and organizational commitments on work-related outcomes" (1). Those individuals who were committed both to their organizations and to their careers were found to have the highest job and career satisfaction and the lowest career-withdrawal intentions. While the survey did not use gender as a variable, it was stated that the "majority of the respondents were female with an average age of 46 years" (5).

175. Clark, Donia. "Mentoring: Making the Grass Greener on This Side." ***ILA Reporter*** **20, no. 6 (December 2002): 11–13.**

Veronda Pitchford (Chicago Library System coordinator for membership services and special projects) and Kathryn Deiss (director of the Chicago Library System's Strategic Learning Center) share their thoughts on the importance of mentoring within librarianship and what makes mentor-protégé relationships work. While working as a library assistant in college, Pitchford was given challenging assignments by her first mentor, who then convinced her to go to library school. Now she seeks out mentors at work and in professional associations and has become a mentor herself. Deiss defines mentorship as "simply taking an interest in someone else's interests." Mentor relationships are important not just to encourage people to enter the profession but also to support them through graduate study and in the early years of their careers. Mid-career librarians need mentors, too, as they pursue career tracks into management or explore new aspects of the profession. Since mentoring is about "fostering relationships," Pitchford and Deiss are leery of formal mentoring programs, although such programs can succeed if everyone is trained to have similar expectations and to understand the responsibilities of mentor and protégé roles. There is a difference between "coaching," which aims at improving specific tasks within the organization, and mentoring, which focuses on the protégé's aspirations. Deiss cautions against a paternalistic approach, where the mentor "dump[s] everything in their brains into an inferior." The mentor should learn as much as the protégé. The mentor and the protégé share responsibility for making the relationship work. Research shows that people who are successful librarians have had strong mentoring relationships. To prove this point, nine Illinois library leaders identify their most influential mentor and describe how that person inspired them. Four of the six female leaders name women mentors. One of the three men names a woman.

176. Crane, Hilary. "A Look Inside High-Tech Libraries." ***Feliciter*** **44, no. 6 (June 1998): 36–38.**

Five librarians and library technicians who work in private "high-technology" firms, rather than in more traditional library environments, discuss their careers; all five are women. Librarian Jacquie Halupka is manager of information resources for Clearnet, Inc., a wireless carrier with two digital networks. Barbara Ambrisko, a library technician, was an information specialist with a firm that later became Harris Canada; now she is a sales support coordinator for Harris Canada's wireless access division. Brenda Bryan started work at Semiconductor Insights, Inc., in an administrative position. Finding that she spent her time doing online searches and market research, she became a resource technician and completed library technician courses during evenings. Jessie Marshall is a library technician at Newbridge Networks, a firm that designs, manufactures, markets, and services telecommunications services. Susan Boulette, a library technician with twenty years of experience in special scientific libraries, is the founding library professional for the communications systems division of Computing Devises in Canada. All enjoy their jobs and stress the importance of flexibility for those in working in high-tech businesses.

177. Crane, Hilary. "New Librarians: Recent Graduates on Library Studies and Work." ***Feliciter*** **44, no. 9 (September 1998): 28–31.**

Four recent graduates of Canadian graduate library and information studies programs discuss their school and job experiences; all four are women. Sandy Iverson, a manager at a naturopathic college, credits her M.Ed. rather than her MLIS with securing her new job. Iverson believes that her library program was too strongly oriented around job skills, rather than issues and theory. Laura Robson, who provides fee-based business reference service, has positive feelings about her library school experience but is also working on an MBA, in order to be on a stronger footing in the business environment. Jennifer Gray is in the third year of a four-year MLIS/LLB program, a lonely experience eased by participation in law library organizations. Gray contrasts library school students—generally dedicated to public service and focused on teamwork and developing group skills—with law students, who are more ruthless and competitive. Kim Silk, who works with Web interfaces, sees many links between what she does in her job and what she learned in library school about the organization of information. Silk hopes to participate in pioneering new, better-structured versions of the Internet.

178. Culpepper, Jetta Carol. "Mentoring Academic Librarians: The Ultimate in Career Guidance." ***College & Undergraduate Libraries*** **7, no. 2 (2000): 71–81.**

This lengthy literature review on mentoring refers to several articles in which gender was a factor. Several points are made about the impact of mentoring on women in librarianship as well as female faculty in library and information science programs.

179. Dickson, Katherine Murphy. "A Work Journal." ***Library Trends*** **50, no. 4 (2002): 687–701.**

This essay, which appeared in a special issue on midlife career decisions of librarians in *Library Trends*, explores (among other things) the author's thoughts on librarianship as a female-intensive profession, the status of women in the profession, returning to work after eight years as a full-time mother, and the economic independence that her profession has given her.

180. Farmer, J., and F. Campbell. "Continuing Professional Development and Career Success: Is There a Causal Relationship?" ***British Library Research and Innovation Report*****, no. 112 (1998): 1–132.**

This report describes a qualitative study of fifty-one women and twenty-nine men from the information, human resources, and accounting fields on the relationship between career success and continued professional development (CPD). Participants were interviewed over the phone and asked to rank how specific activities influenced career success. According to the report, networking and training courses were identified as the top two most-effective types of CPD. While 65 percent of women who participated in the initial telephone interviews identified gender as an issue impacting career success, during in-depth interviews gender appeared as one of the lowest scoring influences on career success. The report states further that though gender is not a specific influence on career success, respondents did indicate that gender did have an impact on perceptions of personalities, that is, how men and women deal differently with difficult colleagues. The authors of the report also commented on respondent statements about the difficulty of combining career and family.

181. Farmer, Jane, Grainne Ward, and Lawraine Wood. "Taking Stock: Career Planning for Isolated, Middle-level Professionals." ***Librarian Career Development*** **6, no. 8 (1998): 3–15.**

Noting that the step-by-step approach to career planning may not be appropriate or even possible for the sole information professional in an organization, the authors offer in this article some practical advice on how to make opportunities happen in such isolated work settings. They also discuss problems that female information professionals have in planning career development. The authors caution against thinking of career development only in terms of moving up a management chain and advise us to recognize opportunities for development within current positions and by moving into other positions at the same level. For information professionals working in specialized fields, there are additional problems. It can be difficult to move from one kind of library to another (public, academic, corporate). Specialized libraries often employ only one professional, so there are few opportunities for advancement. Women may find it difficult to advance while raising children, and many may be unable to relocate because of their domestic situation. Identifying the goal of career planning as realizing the professional's full potential, the authors offer advice to those who cannot leave their current position as well as to those who can move within the profession, those who want to work for themselves, and those who elect to leave librarianship for another field.

182. Gannon-Leary, Pat, and Sandra Parker. "The Round Table on Women's Issues Snapshot Project: The Status of Women in Libraries, Internationally." ***IFLA Journal*** **28, no. 1 (2002): 17–23.**

The Round Table on Women's Issues (RTWI) is a subdivision of the International Federation of Library Associations and Institutions (IFLA) dedicated to enhancing the opportunities and images of women in the library profession and the user community. The RTWI undertook a survey of librarians across world regions and library sectors. A questionnaire was distributed at the IFLA conference in Boston in August 2001 and again by e-mail to conference participants after the event. Of the 169 total respondents, 50 came from the United States. Since the conference attendance exceeded 5,000, the results are not statistically significant but are nonetheless of interest. Numerical data and verbatim quotes from respondents are provided. Survey respondents expressed concern that the important societal role of librarians is not recognized in terms of money or status. The problem is not merely the status of women within the profession but the status of the profession itself. Respondents disagreed whether librarianship is "female-dominated," but most reported that although women make up the majority of librarians in their countries, men tend to hold the top positions and are on a "faster track." However, several examples of women in high positions were reported. North American respondents offered varying assessments of the progress made toward gender equity.

183. Goulding, Anne, and Clare Jones. "Is the Female of the Species Less Ambitious than the Male?" ***Journal of Librarianship and Information Science*** **31, no. 1 (March 1999): 7–19.**

Reports on a study that explores the attitudes of women library and information professionals toward their careers. The attitudes of library and information students were examined using a survey questionnaire to determine whether a difference exists between the career attitudes and aspirations of men and women. The data gathered show that there is little difference between males' and females' attitudes toward their careers. They have the same attitudes toward ambition, aspiration, and commitment. However, social and organizational factors, such as attitudes toward families, parents, children, and wider social commitments, have a greater negative effect on female career attitudes than those of males. Changes in the organizational cultures need to take place before women can become equals.

184. Hambleton, J., and Lois Calvert. "Unplanned Career Paths: The Role of Serendipity (part 1)." ***Trends in Law Library Management and Technology*** **10, no. 4 (October 1999): 1–3.**

Hambleton and Calvert discuss the paths their thirty-year careers have taken since graduating from library school to the director positions they currently hold. Both have worked in private law firms, academic libraries, and various teaching positions. The article compares aspects of each environment, such as staffing, budgets, job security, users, administrative structures, advantages, and disadvantages.

185. Hambleton, J., and Lois Calvert. "Unplanned Career Paths: The Role of Serendipity (part 2)." ***Trends in Law Library Management and Technology*** **10, no. 5 (December 1999): 3–5.**

Part two of Hambleton and Calvert's article continues comparing different work environments (court/government libraries and information vendors) and also discusses career planning and what kind of law library is best to work in. The authors also discuss the impact of moving from job to job due to new jobs or layoffs and offer suggestions for transitioning to a new work environment with different standards, rules, and workflows.

186. Holley, Robert P. "An Interview with Karen M. Drabenstott." ***Cataloging & Classification Quarterly*** **32, no. 2 (2001): 5–29.**

In an interview with Robert P. Holley, Karen M. Drabenstott (professor, School of Information, University of Michigan) surveys her career and summarizes her contributions to the research base of librarianship, particularly with regard to subject searching in online catalogs and enhancing bibliographic databases. Drabenstott describes her early work with Pauline Cochrane in the 1970s and her projects as research scientist at OCLC Online Computer Library Center. These included transaction log analysis demonstrating that users employed subject searching far more frequently than previous library researchers had assumed, incorporation of the Dewey decimal classification into the online catalog as a tool for subject access by end-users, and establishment of online authority records for subject subdivisions. Drabenstott explains her advocacy of enhanced catalog records and "recommender" systems; she expresses her disappointment that catalog records still provide minimal information, and suggests reasons why searchers might prefer using the Web to using libraries. She discusses her recent work concerning Web search strategies, access to images studied by art historians, and multimedia communication. While identifying her research as "practical," Drabenstott states that she still finds it "difficult to affect major changes in the ways we do things in libraries . . . because librarians here in North America and abroad are so heavily invested in the online catalog databases they have created using AACR, MARC, and other authorities" (18–19). Drabenstott does not discuss gender as a factor in her career. Includes "Bibliography of Works by Karen M. Drabenstott." One of a series of interviews with prominent individuals in the specialty of cataloging and bibliographic control.

187. Jones, Elizabeth, and Charles Oppenheim. "Glass Ceiling Issues in the UK Library Profession." ***Journal of Librarianship and Information Science*** **34, no. 2 (June 2002): 103–16.**

Reports on a research study investigating whether the UK library profession suffers from so-called "intraoccupational sex segregation," which is when men dominate the senior positions within the profession. Discusses, in particular, the "glass ceiling" barrier to promotion women find as they reach their forties, although they have enjoyed a reasonably successful career up until then. The study implies that the main barrier appears to be domestic responsibilities, particularly taking a career break to bring up children. Other barriers, which are termed "self-imposed," are choices such as taking a career break, moving to a new location for the sake of their husband's or partner's job, and putting the needs of their families before their own careers.

188. Long, Sarah. "Mentoring: A Personal Reflection." ***New Library World*** **103, no. 1174 (2002): 94–97.**

Long recounts some of her own experiences with mentoring during the course of her career. In one case, a director served as mentor after the fact, as Long copied his style and various documents when she became director of a small public library. While in that job, she was "adopted" by the president of the local Friends group and learned much about collaboration and timing your initiatives. She also gives advice on how to be open to what the mentor can teach and giving the mentor a clear picture of who you are and what you need. She also presents nine tips for mentors.

189. McDermott, Elizabeth. "Barriers to Women's Career Progression in LIS." ***Library Management*** **19, no. 7 (1998): 416–20.**

The first of two consecutive articles based on the author's Ph.D. thesis, which reports the perceptions of British female librarians toward their careers. Female librarians in various stages of their careers were interviewed with regard to their life and career choices. Lack of child care and flexible working hours were listed as major barriers to women's career advancement in the profession.

190. McDermott, Elizabeth. "A Niceness of Librarians: Attitudinal Barriers to Career Progression." ***Library Management*** **19, no. 8 (1998): 453–58.**

The second of two articles that report the results of a study done for a doctoral thesis at a university in Great Britain. Respondents reported that hostile or negative attitudes had an adverse effect on their career progression. Women librarians also perceived their own upbringing and deferential attitudes as barriers to career advancement.

191. O'Brien, Leacy. "From Stacks to Storefront: Library Skills Translate to Bookselling Success." ***Feliciter*** **45, no. 3 (1999): 170–72.**

Three booksellers who are former librarians or library technicians discuss their careers; all three are women. Jane Cooney, president of Books for Business, Toronto, attributes much of her prosperity as a book retailer to the expertise she gained as a business information specialist in libraries. Cooney formerly worked in several public and academic libraries and the library of the Canadian Imperial Bank of Commerce, and as executive director of the Canadian Library Association. She observes that financial management of a store is different from her library responsibilities. Mary

Jane Maffini, co-owner of Prime Crime Books in Ottawa, sees proprietorship of a bookstore as a logical extension of her itinerant career as a librarian. She counts local libraries and librarians among her best customers. Brenda Bickram, co-owner of Top Banana Toys and Books in Toronto, was formerly a library technician. Cooney offers advice to others who wish to make the move from stacks to storefront.

192. Olson, Hope A. *Information Sources in Women's Studies and Feminism*. Munich: Saur, 2002.

Proceedings of the third International Know How Conference on the World of Women's Information in Amsterdam, 1998: twelve articles on the experiences of fourteen information specialists from ten countries (America, Africa, Europe) concerning gender issues, women's studies, and feminism. Reviews: *BuB Forum für Bibliothek und Information* 55, no. 1 (2003): 44–45 (reviewed by Karin Aleksander).

193. Onatola, Ayo. "Career Development and Movement of Librarians in a Nigerian University Library." *African Journal of Library, Archives and Information Science* 10, no. 1 (April 2000): 63–68.

This study investigated barriers encountered in improving the career status of librarians at Ogun State University. The mobility of the staff and the relationship between staff career development and mobility was also studied. The methodologies employed included administration of a questionnaire as well as the use of nonstructured interviews and personal observations. It was concluded that staff left the university for other job opportunities that offered more training and enhancement of skills. Marriage and family obligations were not factors contributing to staff leaving the university.

194. Pagell, R. A., and E. J. Lusk. "A Professional Photo of Academic Business Librarians Worldwide: The Present Picture and a Future View." *Journal of Business and Finance Librarianship* 6, no. 1 (2000): 3–21.

This survey compared U.S. and international librarians, managers, and nonmanagers on the basis of age, gender, ethnic diversity, and other demographic characteristics. The survey found that white females are in the majority in academic business librarianship; however, U.S. managers are predominantly male, and minorities are underrepresented in senior management. The authors surmise that business librarians have not been more successful than other librarians in effectively dealing with the barriers faced by women and other minorities to achieving higher administrative positions. The authors also compare their results with two other surveys examining demographic characteristics of business librarians.

195. Pors, Niels Ole, and Carl Gustav Johannsen. "Job Satisfaction and Motivational Strategies among Library Directors." ***New Library World*** **103, no. 1177 (2002): 199–208.**

This article reports the results of a survey of Danish library directors that was conducted in 2001. The focus is on the directors' level of satisfaction with their jobs and working conditions. The authors contend that a director's satisfaction influences the recruitment and motivation of staff. The survey conducted by the authors was completed by 411 library managers. They found a surprisingly high degree of satisfaction among the managers surveyed. Neither gender nor age was a significant determinant of the level of satisfaction. Top managers were somewhat more satisfied than were middle managers, as they felt a greater freedom to influence the content of their jobs. One of the few differences noted between male and female directors was that the female directors indicated a greater average need for professional development and self-assessment of personal knowledge than did the men.

196. Robertson, Guy. "Alternative Librarianship: Voices from the Field." ***Feliciter*** **44, no. 9 (September 1998): 26–27, 31.**

"Alternative" library practitioners discuss their work; three of the six are women, identified by their first names only. Wendy is a fundraiser for charities and nonprofit institutions; 40 percent of her clients are libraries. Paula is a corporate records manager and Internet security specialist; she appreciates her library education but does not rely on library connections in her work. Paula observes that "higher salaries motivate many traditional librarians to pursue alternative careers" (27). Sarah provides storytelling, journal writing, book discussions, and other programs for seniors in hospitals, community centers, seniors' day centers, etc., on a contract basis. The three women believe that "their work could broaden the intellectual base of librarianship and establish new forms of professional activity" (31).

197. Sabatier, Sophie, and Charles Oppenheim. "The ILS Professional in the City of London: Personality and Glass Ceiling Issues." ***Journal of Librarianship and Information Science*** **33, no. 3 (September 2001): 145–56.**

Reports results of a survey of fifty-three librarians and their managers working in financial institutions in the City of London. The Integrated Psychological Type Indicator (IPTI) personality test was used to investigate glass-ceiling issues. Findings indicated that the major glass-ceiling issues are related not to gender but to commitment, since library and information science (LIS) staff do not seem to have a high enough commitment to corporate goals. The study also indicated that LIS staff in the City of London are extroverted and exhibit business qualities, which is different from LIS staff measured in earlier studies. Includes extensive list of references.

198. Sheih, Chen Su-May. "The Effect of Perceived Leadership Behavior on the Job Satisfaction of Subordinates in Taiwan's University Libraries (China)." Ph.D. diss., University of Wisconsin-Madison, 1998.

Studies the effects of library directors' perceived leadership behaviors on subordinate librarians' job satisfaction in Taiwan and whether the level of satisfaction is affected by the subordinate librarians' background characteristics (age, gender, time in current job, education, supervising level, and time spent interacting with the public). Uses the Minnesota Satisfaction Questionnaire with the 672 full-time subordinate librarians from 26 university libraries who were invited to participate in the study. Library directors' perceived leadership behavior was measured using the Leader Behavior Description Questionnaire—Form XII. Concludes that there is a direct, positive correlation between the subordinate librarian's job satisfaction and their perception of consideration-oriented leadership behavior, their level of supervisory responsibilities, and the amount of time spent interacting with the public. Further concludes that male librarians working in Taiwan universities have higher job satisfaction than their female counterparts.

199. Spalding, Helen H., Deborah Abston, and Mark Cain. "Only Change Is Constant: Three Librarians Consider What Their Jobs Will Be Like in Five Years." ***College & Research Libraries News*** **59, no. 8 (September 1998): 601–3.**

Three academic librarians, including two women, discuss the changes they anticipate in their jobs during the next five years. Helen H. Spalding, a library administrator, emphasizes the emerging importance of collaboration with other organizations and expected changes in workplace conditions and personnel needs. Deborah Abston, a reference librarian, anticipates that reference interactions with library users will last longer, due to the increasing numbers and size of databases. Abston expects to do more library instruction, one-to-one and in classes, but also believes that technology may, to some extent, isolate her from face-to-face interactions with peers and patrons.

200. Tolson, S. D. "Mentoring Up the Career Ladder." ***Information Outlook*** **2, no. 6 (June 1998): 37–38.**

Tolson writes of her firm belief that mentoring is a key strategy for career progression and professional development based on her positive experiences with her mentors over the course of her career. A participant in both the Special Libraries Association's Diversity Leadership Development Program and the St. Louis Community College's Leaders Program (sponsored by the National Institute for Leadership Development), Tolson recounts how her mentors helped her with grant proposals, technology decisions, special projects, office politics, and day-to-day work challenges. Strategies for selecting a mentor are suggested, such as searching out a person with different skills, an interest in the protégée's career development, and the ability to relate effectively to and advocate for the protégée.

201. Weihs, Jean. "The Birth of a Librarian." ***Technicalities*** **19, no. 9 (October 1999): 1, 8–10.**

Describes an informal survey of sixty-two librarians in which they were asked what attracted them to librarianship. Some indicated that it was one of very few viable career options available to respectable women at the time they were entering the workforce.

202. Thornton, Joyce K. "African American Female Librarians: A Study of Job Satisfaction." ***Journal of Library Administration*** **33, no. 1/2 (2001): 141–164.**

Article examines the responses of ninety-eight female respondents to a survey on job satisfaction of librarians of African descent in relation to other gender studies on job satisfaction of librarians. Concludes that African American women librarians make up a very small portion of the overall workforce and that these women have the least satisfaction in their jobs.

3

Education

This chapter covers publications that explore current and historic library and information studies programs, academia and higher education, and the impact of education and the academic environment on women in the field. For information about postdegree and/or job-related training, see related entries in the subject index and in "Career Development and Satisfaction."

203. "Linda Wood Goes to Washington." *ALA Washington News* 51, no. 5 (May 1999): 6.

Linda Wood, a school library media specialist from South Kingstown (Rhode Island) High School, testifies on a panel before the United States Senate Committee on Health, Education, Labor, and Pensions in support of legislation to help support school libraries and recruit more school librarians.

204. Alsereihy, Hassan A. "The Status of LIS Education in Saudi Arabia." *Journal of Education for Library and Information Science* 39, no. 4 (Fall 1998): 334–38.

Documents the current status of library and information science education in Saudi Arabia and presents results of a survey questionnaire sent to all six LIS departments or programs in the country (five at the university level and one at a pre-university level). Notes that "the LIS programs are offered for male and female citizens separately in accordance with Islamic and local guidance" (335). Describes each program in terms of availability to men and women (most programs are available to both), level of instruction and degrees offered, number of graduates at different levels, and computer lab contents. Also gives the number of LIS administrative personnel, teaching assistants, and faculty of different rank at each of the six institutions, divided by gender and by Saudi and non-Saudi citizenship. (For example, of a total of seven full professors, one is female [non-Saudi]; of a total of thirty-six lecturers, fifteen are female, twelve of whom are Saudi and three of whom are non-Saudi.) Faculty received their degrees from American, British, Egyptian, and Saudi schools. Students in LIS university-level programs normally receive financial support equivalent to other students at the university level, roughly $250 per month.

205. Bleier, Carol. *Tradition in Transition: A History of the School of Information Sciences, University of Pittsburgh, 100th Anniversary, 1901–2001*. Lanham, MD: University of Pittsburgh, School of Information Sciences (in cooperation with The Scarecrow Press), 2001.

This history of the School of Information Sciences (SIS) at the University of Pittsburgh provides a wealth of biographical information on notable women in the early years of American librarianship. Among them are Frances Jenkins Olcott, founder of the Training School for Children's Librarians (the earliest incarnation of the SIS); other early heads of the school including Elva S. Smith, Sarah Bogle, and Nina Brotherton (during the years when the school was named the Carnegie Library School); Virginia Proctor Powell, the first African American to be professionally trained as a librarian; and distinguished students and alumni such as Margaret K. McElderry and Vivian Davidson Hewitt. It also chronicles the school's transition in 1962, under Harold Lancour, into the Graduate School of Information Science. Notable faculty members during these years were predominantly male, including John Clement Harrison, Clarence Walter Stowe, and Andrew Delbridge Osborn. Interestingly, a 1962 recruitment ad for the school pictures two male librarians. Over the last two decades notable women faculty members profiled include Margaret Hodges, Martha Manheimer, Sara Fine, Toni Carbo, Ellen Detlefsen, and Margaret Kimmel.

206. Gollop, Claudia J. "Library and Information Science Education: Preparing Librarians for a Multicultural Society." *College and Research Libraries* 60, no. 4 (July 1999): 385–95.

Suggests that LIS programs need to prepare to handle the rapidly changing racial, ethnic, and cultural demographics in the United States. States that when formal education in librarianship began, diversity issues would have focused on the lack of women in the profession, as the vast majority of workers entering the field were men.

207. Goulding, Anne, and Marigold Cleeve. "Breaking Down the Barriers: The Place of Gender Equity in the ILS Curriculum." ***Education for Information*** **16, no. 4 (1998): 295–314.**

Reports the findings of a survey of lecturers and students in UK departments of information and library science. The authors found that issues of gender equity are not featured in the ILS curriculum in any coordinated or systematic way. Lecturers vary greatly in the topics they cover and the amount of time they devote to gender concerns. The majority of lecturers feel that gender issues are of some interest to their students. The authors argue that ILS departments should play a major role in giving their female students the awareness of analytical skills needed to challenge their experiences in the workplace.

208. Hildenbrand, Suzanne. "The Information Age versus Gender Equity? Technology and Values in Education for Library and Information Science." ***Library Trends*** **47, no. 4 (Spring 1999): 669–85.**

In this article, one of the most prominent researchers in issues facing women as librarians discusses the ramifications of increased technology in libraries on women's status in the workplace. Hildenbrand maintains that since the beginning, a "gender hierarchy" has been constructed that has limited women in terms of lower salaries and stagnant careers in the field. Furthermore, she suggests that increased technology will perpetuate the gender hierarchy once again and integrate stratification into library and information science curricula. References and appendices included.

209. Hildenbrand, Suzanne. "The Information Age vs. Gender Equity." ***Library Journal*** **124, no. 7 (15 April 1999): 44–47.**

Addresses the growing emphasis on information technology in library science education and warns about the gender implications of this change. The gendered history of library education, the identification of computers with males, the gender divide of LIS faculty with respect to information science and library science courses, and the omission of key library science courses in ALA-accredited programs suggest a potential loss of women's status in the current high-tech environment.

210. Lorenzen, M. "Education Schools and Library Schools: A Comparison of Their Perceptions by Academia." ***Illinois Libraries*** **82, no. 3 (Summer 2000): 154–59.**

Both education schools and library schools are looked down upon by other academic departments. The author argues that the low esteem in which these two disciplines are held leads to diminished status and lower pay for their faculty. Furthermore, low academic prestige contributed to the closing of several graduate programs in library science. Gender bias toward women is one likely reason for the low status of the two fields. Female graduates' lower salaries result in smaller alumnae donations than other campus departments receive. Other factors include social bias, because many library and education faculty come from the working class, and the tendency of both fields to focus on practical rather than theoretical matters. Because libraries and schools are public entities with significant public involvement in their management, and because other faculty generally learn to use libraries and to teach on their own, they do not perceive library science and education as disciplines possessing specialized knowledge or intellectual rigor. In response to academia's scorn, education and library science faculty have defended the importance of their work and argued that the value system in higher education should be realigned. Although some library schools have dropped "library" from their names in favor of "information," this strategy is not likely to improve the field's prestige.

211. McCracken, P. "The Presence of the Doctorate among Small College Library Directors." ***College & Research Libraries*** **61, no. 5 (September 2000): 400–408.**

Gender is considered in this article that assesses the prevalence of a doctorate degree among small college library directors. The author finds that males with Ph.D.s hold their directorships longer than women on average and predicts gender parity in this arena if the trend continues. Twice as many male library directors hold doctorates compared to women, while women hold 40 percent of directorships.

212. Olson, Hope A. "Education for Cataloging Is/As Women's Studies." ***Serials Librarian*** **35, no. 1/2 (1998): 153–66.**

Proposes that critical-thinking skills and flexibility are necessary to catalog effectively interdisciplinary, dynamic, paradigm-shifting information such as materials in women's studies and uses established concepts from women's studies to construct a framework for cataloging education that inculcates critical perspectives and encourages the development of these skills and approaches. Defines the guiding values of education for critical, flexible cataloging: recognizing that the study of women is important, that sexism exists, that our models of the world (including library classification systems and cataloging rules) need to be reconsidered, and that issues of sexual difference must be addressed. Provides specific applications of these principles to cataloging education. Describes the stages of integrating women's studies into cataloging curricula: paying attention to significant women in the field, problematizing the status of women in cataloging and catalogs, making women and other marginalized groups central in the practice of cataloging, and, ultimately, reconstructing the discipline. Identifies feminist pedagogical techniques such as encouraging cooperative inquiry, avoiding the tyranny of the "one right answer," and others appropriate for use in a reconstructed cataloging curriculum. Suggests that using the academic stance and critical perspectives of women's studies in teaching cataloging will help prepare librarians for an increasingly interdisciplinary, dynamic, diverse, and unpredictable information environment. Also published in *Women's Studies Serials: A Quarter-Century of Development*, edited by Kristin H. Gerhard. New York: Haworth Press, 1998: 153–66.

213. Olson, Hope A. "Feminism and Librarianship—In Practice!" *Women's Studies Section Newsletter* 13, no. 1 (Spring 1998): 3.

Describes Professor Olson's efforts to develop an online version of her seminar on feminism and library and information studies at the University of Alberta's School of Library and Information Studies. The course includes sampling feminist theory, feminist professional practice, and feminist perspectives on information policy. The design elements include the course Web pages, a discussion list, and virtual guest speakers.

214. Parker, Sandra, Catherine Hare, and Pat Gannon-Leary. "National Vocational Qualifications (NVQs): One Route to Improve the Status of Women in Libraries?" *IFLA Council and General Conference: Conference Proceedings (66th, Jerusalem, Israel, August 13–18, 2000)* (August 2000): 8.

Addresses National Vocational Qualifications (NVQs) and Scottish Vocational Qualifications (SVQs) in relation to improving the status of women working in Information and Library Services in Great Britain. Provides historical background for NVQs and defines the process involved for qualification, including mandatory and optional units designed for information and library staff. Presents the benefits to women, including the ability to meet qualifications while working, schedule flexibility, exemptions for existing skills, costs, and career progression and development. Disadvantages are also listed, including the standards' extensive use of jargon or complex language, the frequent underestimation of the time required for completion, and the absence of theoretical foundations. ERIC Document Reproduction Service No. ED450760. www.ifla.org/IV/ifla66/papers/115-151e.htm.

215. Small, Ruth V. "A Comparison of the Resident and Distance Learning Experience in Library and Information Science Graduate Education." ***Journal of Education for Library and Information Science*** **40, no. 1 (Winter 1999): 27–47.**

Presents the results of a survey of full-time resident students, part-time resident students, and distant-learning students in the LIS program of Syracuse University. Data was collected from students and faculty using a questionnaire, focus groups, and structured interviews. Data analysis includes identification of respondents by gender as well as by distant/resident status, age group, and relevant work experience; the majority of both resident and distance students were women, with distance students generally older, married with children, and with more LIS experience. Most analysis focuses on part-time resident and distance students; results indicate that part-time resident students often found balancing academic responsibilities with personal and work lives more difficult than did the distance students. Resident students had a more difficult time bonding with peers and getting to know faculty than distance students did. Faculty found that distance courses required more preparation time, heavier student-advising demands, and more technological support; they identified working with highly motivated students and learning about new methods and technologies as advantages in distance teaching. Concludes with recommendations related to the study's six conclusions.

216. Wardrup, Eva, Carol Bishop, and Lee Ann Cline. "Not Your Mother's Library School." ***The Georgia Library Quarterly*** **39, no. 3 (Fall 2002).**

A study that examines the experiences of the first class in the Master of Library and Information Science (MLIS) program at Valdosta State University compared to the experiences of students in the MLIS Program at the University of South Carolina. Gender is one of the factors examined.

217. Winston, Mark D. "Communication and Teaching: Education about Diversity in the LIS Classroom." ***Journal of Library Administration*** **33, no. 3/4 (2001): 199–212.**

Stresses the importance of addressing diversity, including gender diversity, during library science education, especially since literature is beginning to show how diverse organizations are also often successful ones. While discussing diversity can often be difficult, the author encourages an open dialog starting in library science classes.

218. Yakel, Elizabeth. "The Future of the Past: A Survey of Graduates of Master's-Level Graduate Archival Education Programs in the United States." ***American Archivist*** **63, no. 2 (Fall 2000): 301–21.**

This article reports the results of a survey of graduates of archival education programs in the United States. The goal was to profile the next generation of archivists by focusing on a variety of demographic, economic, and professional issues. Findings indicate that the new generation of archivists is younger, predominantly female, and slightly better compensated than previous generations. Furthermore, interesting contrasts and comparisons can be made between graduates of history- and library- and/or information science–based programs as well as between men and women in terms of employment sectors, salaries, and the length of the graduate programs.

4

Employment Issues

This chapter encompasses publications that treat employment and job-related issues affecting women in the field, such as benefits, flexible work schedules, part-time work, and work expectations. For information related to career development generally, see the chapter "Career Development and Satisfaction."

219. "Atlanta-Fulton Library Hit with Bias Suit: Eight Women Librarians File Racial Discrimination Lawsuit." ***American Libraries*** **31, no. 9 (October 2000): 14.**

Announces a racial discrimination lawsuit that was filed in federal district court against thirteen members of the Atlanta-Fulton County Library board and director Mary Kaye Hooker. The plaintiff claims that the library left eight women jobless as a result of targeting white women in management positions.

220. "Atlanta PL Board, Director Named in Discrimination Suit." ***Library Hotline*** **24, no. 34 (28 August 2000): 1.**

Brief news item about a lawsuit against the Atlanta-Fulton Public Library. Internal memos indicate that there were "too many older, white women in management positions at AFPL who should be replaced with African American managers and administrators."

221. "A Group of Female Librarians Proved Victorious in Their Racial Bias Suit." ***Library Hotline*** **31, no. 4 (28 January 2002): 5.**

Brief news piece is about a racial bias suit brought about by eight women librarians. When the suit was filed, they attributed the quote "There are too many older, white women in management positions" to the library board chair. The plaintiffs were awarded $25 million.

222. Abell, Angela. "Information Professionals? Knowledge Professionals? Or Support Staff?" *The Law Librarian* 29, no. 1 (March 1998): 11–14.

Abell describes the increasing importance of "Know-How," "Intranet," and "Knowledge Management" skills and abilities for information professionals in the legal and financial sectors. The article offers examples of how companies are using information professionals to improve services, and how information professionals' skills in structuring, organizing, and evaluating information help them collaborate with other professionals within a company or organization. An addendum to the article lists the annual salary survey results from the British and Irish Association of Law Librarians, respondents to which were 80 percent female. Abell notes that only in commercial law firms do women make more money, and that the difference in men's and women's salaries is 5 percent, down from 13 percent in 1994/1995.

223. Abram, Stephen. "Pushing the Pay Envelope: Y2K Compensation Strategies." *Information Outlook* 3, no. 10 (October 1999): 18–22.

Abrams discusses the Special Libraries Association's efforts to improve the image, compensation, benefits, and manager perceptions of librarians. He offers several avenues of improvement from within the profession aimed at raising confidence of librarians, increasing value to each other as professionals, improving job descriptions by using more active, less clerical language, improving understanding of evaluation models, narrowing the gender gap in salaries by strengthening equity legislation, and most importantly, improving communication and marketing strategies to managers, supervisors, and human resources departments.

224. Adeeb, Y. "The Gender Trap in Library Work." *Assignation* 15, no. 3 (April 1998): 5–7.

Adeeb argues that women face a challenge in reaching upper administrative positions: the perception that they are not as invested in their careers as men due to lower rates of publication and professional activity at conferences and meetings. Citing studies done in the late 1980s by Mary Niles Maack, G. Burrington, Nick Moore and Elaine Kempson, and Colin Steels and Margaret Henty, she offers a number of strategies for women to use to improve their prospects for promotion and increased responsibility. However, she also acknowledges the responsibility of the field of librarianship in general to recognize and reward women's management, communication, and leadership skills.

225. Aleksander, Karin. *Wie Speziell ist eine One-Person Library für Frauen- und Geschlechterforschung?* Berlin, Germany: Humboldt-Universität zu Berlin, Institut für Bibliothekwissenschaft, 1999.

Translation of abstract in book: For the first time a one-person library (OPL) for women and gender studies is examined in regard to its unusual qualities in comparison to other OPLs and traditional libraries. In the first part, the mostly English-language specialist literature that has been produced since the mid-1970s is analyzed in regard to the changing concept "one-person library/one-person librarian." The definitions put forth by Guy St. Clair and others (Martha R. Rhine, Judith Siess) verify the trend that professional activities are developing into consultation, service, and management. In the second part, the unusual qualities of an OPL for women and gender studies are discussed with a look at library science: 1. its special subject area; 2. "interdisciplinarity"; 3. the relationship to users; 4. the unity of library, information/documentation, and archive; and 5. its place in the library system. Since OPLs work primarily as special libraries, it is possible to work on tasks and test possibilities that are just future tasks for other libraries (for example, the reworking of the systems for gender equity, the indexing, and the problem of "interdisciplinarity").

226. Alemna, A. A. "Career Development: Follow-Up Studies of Former Graduate Students of the Department of Library and Archival Studies University of Ghana, 1991/1992 to 1996/1997." *Education for Information* 17, no. 1 (1999): 35–43.

For fifteen years the University of Ghana offered a one-year graduate diploma program in library studies. This article reports the results of the third five-year survey of program graduates. Out of a total of forty-three graduates during the last five-year period, eighteen (42 percent) were female. The earlier percentages had been 31 percent and 34 percent female, and for the first time, in the 1991/1992 academic year, there were more females than males. At the time of the survey, all but four graduates were employed. Tables and references.

227. Calle, E., T. K. Murphy, C. Rodriguez, M. J. Thun, and C. W. Heath, Jr. "Occupation and Breast Cancer Mortality in a Prospective Cohort of U.S. Women." *American Journal of Epidemiology* 148, no. 2 (15 July 1998): 191–97.

This study examined the association between lifetime occupation and breast cancer mortality among a large population of U.S. women. Occupation was divided into fourteen broad groups and sixteen more narrowly defined occupational titles, which included the category "teacher/librarian." In comparison with housewives, women in "administrative support" were at a small increased risk, and "executives" also showed an increased risk. However, no significant increases were shown for teachers and librarians, nurses, managers, or women in sales. As a whole, the results showed little support for an association between occupation and breast cancer mortality in general.

228. Colorado Libraries Volunteer Manager's Council. "Who is Mrs. K. Allen?" *Colorado Libraries* 27, no. 4 (Winter 2001): 47.

This brief contribution to the "Volunteer Line" column addresses the changing status of the fictional "Mrs. K. Allen," who receives prompt and respectful attention from library staff whether she's a model patron, a problem patron, or a library advocate in the community. But "when the same Mrs. K. Allen indicates she wants to be a library volunteer, she often and suddenly is transformed into a 'nobody.'" The authors do not state explicitly that volunteers are more likely to be women, although the choice of the name strongly suggests it. Library volunteers should be viewed as valued members of the library team, the authors conclude, not "just volunteers" who drain staff time.

229. Currie, Leah H., Vicki Coleman, and Jeff Bullington. "Reflections on the Big 12 Plus 'Diversity Now' Conference." *ARL Newsletter*, no. 210 (June 2000).

Report on the Diversity Now conference at the University of Texas, Austin, April 4–6, 2000. Four themes—recruitment and retention of a diverse workforce, communicating across cultures, building diverse collections, and managing a diverse workforce—were expressed through a combination of keynote speakers, panel discussions, contributed papers, and table talks.

230. Davis-Packard, Kent, and Alexandra Marks. "Museum Strike Highlights New Face of Unions." *Christian Science Monitor* 31 (August 2000): 1.

Reports on the changing demographics of union members, focusing on UAW Local 2110, the 240-member bargaining unit of librarians, educators, and curators that went on strike in April 2000 at the Museum of Modern Art in New York. The union, which is 70 percent female, is demanding better pay and healthcare benefits, and although other MoMA unions are not honoring the picket line, they are getting local support from renowned artists such as Steven Spielberg and Susan Sontag. Online. Available through EBSCOhost, Masterfile Elite.

231. DiMattia, Susan. "LAPL, Librarians Reach Contract: Salaries to Top $48K after Six Months, Near $56K at Four Years." ***Library Journal*** **127, no. 20 (December 2002): 17.**

The administration of the Los Angeles Public Library and the Librarians' Guild reached an agreement on a contract that provides a significant improvement in librarian salaries and will help LAPL in recruitment efforts. Starting salaries for Librarian I positions will now start at $45,518, will increase after a six-month probationary period, and after a total of forty-two months will reach nearly $56,000. The rank of Principal Librarian II will start at $74,000 and will reach $78,500 by July 2003. LAPL has thirty-six new buildings being opened between 1999 and 2004, five of which are new service points for previously unserved parts of the city.

232. Duhn, Linda. "Who is the Volunteer of the Future." ***Church and Synagogue Libraries*** **31, no. 5 (January 1998–28 February 1998): 1, 6–7.**

In view of the shrinking pool of women volunteers, strategies for recruiting new volunteers are presented as well as different demographic groups to be targeted. Strategies to draw volunteers are provision of child care facilities and offering opportunities to learn skills for re-entry into the job market.

233. Gedeon, J. A., and R. E. Rubin. "Attribution Theory and Academic Library Performance Evaluation." ***Journal of Academic Librarianship*** **25, no. 1 (January 1999): 18–25.**

Introducing bias into a performance evaluation can happen unintentionally. This article investigates gender bias in evaluations that occur due to a social psychological theory referred to as attribution theory. The author suggests that this bias may influence inequities in the library workplace. Evidence and data are given to suggest the existence of these inequities. After a lengthy explanation of attribution theory, the author concludes that it may cause underrepresentation of women in administrative positions, for example. Ideas to combat this introduction of bias are offered.

234. Gilton, Donna L. "Onward and Upward: Promotion of Public Librarians." ***Public Libraries*** **39, no. 4 (July 2000–31 August 2000): 214–19.**

Discusses a study of opportunities for public librarian promotion within an employee's present institution. The narrative includes a literature review, presentation of the research questions employed, and results in table format. The study revealed a gradual promotion to higher positions, although evidence of stagnation did appear after eleven to twenty years in an institution. Differences in promotion trends for librarians of color were evident, although gender did not appear as statistically significant. The author suggests that while promotion may not be the issue previously indicated, there is a need for examining the plateau experienced by some, especially where race is a factor. Bibliography.

235. Glick, Andrea. "Iowa School Librarians Fight Law That Made Them Optional Staff." ***School Library Journal*** **44, no. 6 (June 1998): 13.**

Reports on efforts to change a 1996 state law that deleted the requirements for school library staff and guidance counselors from the state school code. As school districts struggle with reduced funding, they consider not replacing media specialists when they retire. Efforts at reinstating the library requirement have been stalled by conservative Christian schools that feel they cannot afford library specialists.

236. Goulding, Anne, B. Bromham, S. Hannabuss, and D. Cramer. "Likely to Succeed: Attitudes and Aptitudes for an Effective Information Profession in the 21st Century." In ***British Library Library and Information Commission Research Report*****, 97, vol. 8, 1999.**

This report is based on a study completed in the United Kingdom with the goal of exploring personal qualities desired by employers and actual personal characteristics of library school students. The report contains an extensive literature review on the topic as well as informative appendices containing relevant tables, questionnaires, and figures. The methodology used to gather information from employers included content analysis of job postings for creating a list of personal qualities desired by employers, telephone interviews of three recruitment agencies, and a questionnaire sent to chief librarians in several different types of libraries. Chief librarians were also selected for follow-up interviews. Personality assessments and questionnaires were utilized to gather information from library school students. In both groups of respondents, women were the majority (59 percent for employers, 61 percent for students). Findings of the report include recommendations for library schools to alter curricula to develop desired characteristics in students, for employers to rethink approaches to hiring (for example, focusing too heavily on competencies rather than "transformative attributes"), and for information professionals in general to increase interpersonal skills.

237. Goulding, Anne, Beth Bromham, Stuart Hannabuss, and Duncan Cramer. "Supply and Demand: The Workforce Needs of Library and

Information Services and Personal Qualities of New Professionals." ***Journal of Librarianship and Information Science*** **31, no. 4 (December 1999): 212–24.**

Reports on a survey of 888 British library administrators that attempts to determine the relationship between desired qualities in new professionals and those qualities that applicants seem to lack. Of the respondents to the survey, 59 percent were females and 41 percent males. The gender distribution is most unbalanced among those classified as middle managers, where 73 percent are female and 27 percent are male. However, the relationship between job title and gender was not found to be significant. The article includes a literature review on the changing roles of library professionals. It concludes that because there is significant overlap between desired qualities and lacking qualities there is cause for concern since qualities high in demand are also short in supply.

238. Goulding, Anne, et al. "Professional Characters: The Personality of the Future Information Workforce." ***Education for Information*** **18, no. 1 (March 2000): 7–31.**

Reports findings of a UK study that compared the qualities sought by library managers with the attributes of ILS students. Among the findings were that female students are less emotionally stable and more submissive than male students. Female postgraduate students were found to be more resourceful and self-sufficient than both males and undergraduates, and both undergraduate and postgraduate female students tended to be more socially precise than males.

239. Hannabuss, Stuart. "Flexible Jobs: Changing Patterns in Information and Library Work." ***New Library World*** **99, no. 1141 (1998): 104–11.**

The 1990s saw a considerable increase in flexible work arrangements in Britain, including part-time work and job sharing. A 1996 survey of five hundred libraries showed 85 percent of them employing flexible workers with 30 percent employing professionals in such positions. When more than half of library employees are women, this change to flexible work arrangements is particularly relevant. The author describes flexible work patterns, offers pros and cons for the two main arrangements, and comments on the impact on workers and organizations.

240. Harralson, David M. "Recruitment in Academic Libraries: Library Literature in the '90s." ***College & Undergraduate Libraries*** **8, no. 1 (2001): 37–65.**

This lengthy history and literature review of recruitment in academic libraries highlights the role of gender in the profession. The author refers to several articles that point to gender as a factor in recruitment. Such issues as pay inequity and gender-discrimination may hinder recruitment to academic librarianship.

241. Kartman, Jon. "Librarian Sues City in Family Leave Dispute: Derry Public Children's Librarian Discharged after Seeking Extended Leave." ***American Libraries*** **29 (March 1998): 17–18.**

Announces a federal court suit filed by former public librarian Sharon Curtis Phelan against the Derry (New Hampshire) Public Library when she was discharged from her job after asking for additional unpaid leave to care for her terminally ill husband.

242. Kraus, Karin. ***Frauen Wollen Mehr: Frauen in Bibliotheken Melden Sich zu Wort.*** **Frankfurt a.M.: ÖTV Hessen, 1998.**

Statements of unionists and women librarians working in different types of libraries on women's work in libraries (working conditions, salaries, work environment, library users, potential for discrimination).

243. Küster, Heidrun. "Eine Kleine Schwärmerei vom Lande: Die Bibliothekarin als Ersatzlehrerin, Sozialarbeiterin, Unterhaltungskünstlerin, Bildungsbeauftragte, Kulturinstanz . . ." ***BuB-Forum für Bibliothek und Information*** **53, no. 8 (2001): 501–4.**

English title: "A Little Enthusiasm from the Countryside: The Woman Librarian as Surrogate Teacher, Social Worker, Entertainer, Educational Agent, Cultural Authority. . . ." Southwest Germany has strong, vital women who work at miscellaneous tasks in mostly poorly funded rural libraries, but who earn much appreciation from their patrons. The library is viewed as an attractive meeting place for chatting, sharing ideas, learning, and getting novels that might not be the pick of an urban library user. These female librarians—not a single male was spotted—serve their clientele with joy and respect. What they miss and need is networking in order to discuss professional matters and to obtain support for further education.

244. Lan, Debra. "Got Clout? ***SLJ*****'s Groundbreaking New Survey Shows the Increasing Influence of Librarians."** ***School Library Journal*** **48, no. 5 (May 2002): 40–45.**

Reports the results of a survey mailed to two thousand school librarians in February 2002; 770 responses were received. More than half of the respondents have MLS degrees. The survey found that most principals are supportive of library collaboration with teachers and many teach classes without a teacher present; however, fewer than half felt that the principal was well-informed about what the library could offer. The median salary for school librarians is $43,600, and 91 percent said that their pay was comparable to that of other educators. Ninety percent said that they were satisfied with their jobs. The article also highlights the experiences of individual school librarians and media specialists.

245. Lenzini, Rebecca T. "The Graying of the Library Profession: A Survey of Our Professional Association and Their Responses." ***Searcher*** **10, no. 7 (July 2002–31 August 2002): 88.**

The majority of the article focuses on the aging of employees in the library profession, but it briefly touches on women in the profession and how the trends are similar to shortages in nursing and education. While the size of the profession of librarianship grew 62 percent over a twenty-year period, women under thirty entering the profession dropped 9 percent. In sum, "careers dominated by women see shortages."

246. Lim, Vivian K. G., and Thompson S. H. Teo. "Occupational Stress and IT Personnel in Singapore: Factorial Dimensions and Differential Effects." ***International Journal of Information Management*** **19, no. 4 (August 1999): 277–91.**

Factor analysis of data collected from an IT organization in Singapore, described as "a large organization dealing with technology-related industrial products and services," shows six major sources (dimensions) of occupational stress: work demands, relationships with others, career concerns, systems maintenance, role ambiguity, and administrative tasks. The additional personal characteristics of gender and job tenure are considered as differential effects of the six stress dimensions. For female IT personnel, work demands, systems maintenance, and role ambiguity play a larger role in stress than they do for males. Lower stress due to career concerns is reported in workers having more than five years of tenure with the organization. Most of the factors generating stress originate in the work environment, particularly pressures related to job and organizational characteristics. Major implications are seen for IT management in the areas of training, supervision and support, staffing levels, clarification of responsibilities, relationships, and communication.

247. Margolis, Rick, and Amanda Ferguson. "Seeking Greener Pastures: New York City Librarians are Leaving for Higher Paying Jobs in Schools and Businesses." ***School Library Journal*** **45, no. 2 (February 1999): 18.**

The management of New York City's three public library systems appealed for higher salaries for librarians to combat the lost of one-third of new librarians. Children's services staff in particular leave low-paying public libraries to work for schools where they have shorter hours and regularly scheduled raises.

248. Oder, Norman. "New York City PLs Face Crisis; Low Salaries Drive Staff Away." *Library Journal* 124, no. 18 (1 November 1999): 12–13.

New York Public Library administrators are drawing attention to the lack of a minimal living wage for system librarians, stating that the starting pay of $31,296 and insufficient steps for growth in pay and positions are causing many librarians to leave. Factors such as the unresponsiveness of Mayor Giuliani, a weak union, and better pay from city schools and suburban library systems contribute to the problem of retaining qualified staff. About 1,200 union librarians would benefit from the 15 to 25 percent salary increase that union officials are seeking support for from city council members.

249. Oder, Norman. "New York Public Librarians Finally Negotiate an Increase." *Library Journal* 126, no. 9 (15 May 2001): 14.

Announcement of the 16 percent salary increase granted to librarians at the New York Public Library after more than three years of negotiations with city officials. Union leaders are happy with the improvement, which brings the average salary up to $46,100, but say they still face hiring and retention problems.

250. Peterson, Lorna. "The Definition of Diversity: Two Views. A More Specific Definition." *Journal of Library Administration* 27, no. 1/2 (1999): 17–48.

Discusses affirmative action and diversity in libraries. Briefly notes that there continues to be an imbalance between the number of women in the library field and the percentages of women holding top positions. Also notes that salary equity still has not been realized between men and women.

251. Weaver-Meyers, Patricia L. "Conflict Resolution: A Case Study about Academic Librarians and Faculty Status." *College & Research Libraries* 63, no. 1 (January 2002): 25–34.

While this article focuses on the pursuit of faculty status of librarians, the author mentions a case at the University of Oklahoma in which the lack of tenure options for librarians was attributed to gender discrimination. Library representatives stated that "professions generally defined as 'women's fields' are often subjected to repeated challenges because of unconscious and insidious discrimination against minorities and women."

252. Wilder, Stanley J. "The Changing Profile of Research Library Professional Staff." ***ARL Newsletter*****, no. 208/209 (February 2000–30 April 2000).**

This is an update on the 1995 report *The Age Demographics of Academic Librarians: A Profession Apart* (Washington: Association of Research Libraries, 1995). In 1998 ARL collected comparable demographic data on 8,400 professional staff positions in 110 university member libraries to provide an update of the 1995 study. The additional data allow for a broader perspective from which to assess the significance of apparent changes in the population. One of the changes is the hiring of functional specialists, especially in systems work. Among functional specialists, 44 percent are men compared with 28 percent males in other categories.

5

Gender Issues in Librarianship

While all publications included in the bibliography were selected because they pertain in some way to the status of women in librarianship, this category is reserved for those articles and other writings that focus on issues of gender. This chapter therefore touches upon a wide range of topics, some of the broader ones being sex stratification within the profession, gender issues in communication, feminism and feminist theory, and female value systems, to name but a few.

253. "The Daily Bind." ***Ms.*** **9, no. 6 (October 1999–30 November 1999): 81–82.**

This column solicited reader responses to the question, "Can you combine work and feminism?" One anecdote came from a female librarian who had been in a discussion about how to improve the image of librarians. She was appalled when some suggested inviting more men into the profession and said if librarians want more respect and prestige, "we have to demand it from the world," not get it through men joining the field.

254. "National Dress Code Variances Match Seasons, Circumstances." ***Library Hotline*** **31, no. 32 (12 August 2002): 2–5.**

Following the Queens Borough Public Libraries decision to enforce an employee dress code, *Library Hotline* asked other libraries about similar codes. Several libraries have gender-specific codes such as a stocking requirement for women as well as the ban of tight pants and tube tops. One library did state that their dress policy was gender-neutral.

255. Besant, Michele. "Perceptions of Difference: A Grounded Theory Study with White Lesbian Librarians." Ph.D. diss., University of Wisconsin-Madison, 1999.

Utilizes grounded theory methodology and feminist standpoint theory in interviewing twenty-four white lesbian women holding MLS degrees. The interviewees were selected across a range of library types and were interviewed about how their lesbian identities affect their work as librarians. Discusses interviewees' perception of themselves as both librarians and lesbians and their definitions of what makes each identity unique. Evaluates the participants' view that they are "insider/outsiders," a position that affects their understanding and practice of librarianship. Interviewees felt they were "insiders" as part of an educated, white, female profession, but, as lesbians, they admitted feeling like "outsiders" at the workplace. Interviewees also comment on the meaning of feminization of the library profession, the concept of "neutrality," and the cultural dichotomy of the public and private.

256. Bourdon, Cathleen. "Beyond Status Quo." ***American Libraries*** **31, no. 5 (May 2000): 92–93.**

Announcement of the publication of *On Account of Sex: An Annotated Bibliography on the Status of Women in Librarianship, 1993–1997.* Betsy Kruger and Catherine A. Larson with the assistance of sixteen contributors compile a bibliography describing female librarians and the issues and challenges that they face.

257. Carmichael, James V., Jr. "Homosexuality and United States Libraries: Land of the Free, But Not Home to the Gay." In ***64th IFLA General Conference—Conference Proceedings—August 16–21, 1998*****, 26, IFLA, 1998.**

Presents a brief history of gays and lesbians in librarianship and compares the successes and failures of the Gay, Lesbian, and Bisexual Task Force's (now GLBTRT) efforts to promote change in American libraries in the national struggle for lesbigay equality. Carmichael also states that gender dynamics in librarianship presents peculiar problems to the gay situation; because librarians are overwhelmingly female, this adds pressure for male librarians to conform to a masculine stereotype and to closet gay issues. The author also feels that lesbigay rights are inextricably bound to the feminist agenda and the fight for women's rights. While there has been progress both inside and outside librarianship, Carmichael cautions against the accommodationist solution of letting these important issues resolve themselves.

258. Carmichael, James V., Jr. "'They Sure Got to Prove It on Me': Millennial Thoughts on Gay Archives, Gay Biography, and Gay

Library History." *Libraries and Culture* 35, no. 1 (Winter 2000): 88–102.

Carmichael examines the role of gay librarians and archivists in creating, providing access, and promoting lesbigay archival collections. The article includes an overview of the rise in publication of gay studies, history, biography, and autobiography during the 1990s using WorldCat, as well as references to milestones in gay history and criticism and summaries of major reference works in gay studies. Carmichael also analyzes the application of historical principles to the formation of gay archival collections and how historical evidence is at times slim in ascertaining the sexual orientation of some figures in history. He also discusses the preponderance of ambiguity in historical evidence and identity politics and how both can impact historical studies of any population.

259. Cook, Sarah. "Feminist Promotes New Vision for Hierarchical Libraries." *Women in Higher Education* 8, no. 3 (1999): 17.

This brief profile of librarian and professor of library science Deb Nordgren describes how she applies feminist thought to her work and teaching. Having for years felt that her practices as a manager diverged from what she read in the library management literature, she was gratified to find that her collaborative, flexible style was validated in other literature as women's or feminist management. In her teaching she has adopted practices of feminist pedagogy and has students in her cataloging classes work on materials on women's issues, multiculturalism, and homosexuality.

260. Craig, Barbara L. "A Look at a Bigger Picture: The Demographic Profile of Archivists in Canada Based on a National Survey." *Archivaria*, no. 49 (Spring 2000): 20–52.

Reports on a random and self-administered mail survey done with the membership of the Association of Canadian Archivists in 1998. The author summarizes survey results, including tables showing frequency and cumulative data. Variables studied include gender, age, education, scope of professional functions, and geography. The suggestion is made to collect such data on a regular basis in order to compile an accurate picture of the profession and its development.

261. Crew, Hilary S. "Transforming the Hidden Curriculum: Gender and the Library Media Center." *Knowledge Quest* 26, no. 4 (May 1998–30 June 1998): 30–33.

The question of how library media centers can advance gender equity has been largely ignored by library and education literature. Crew discusses how library media centers can encourage the study of women in different professions by collecting and providing access to gender-balanced works about and by women and exploring models of integrating these resources into curriculum and library programs. Crew's article is well-researched, and she cites several articles of high interest to anyone interested in gender equity in education. She also cites several women scientists who are excellent role models and how these women have redefined scientific inquiry.

262. Darvill, G. "Gender, Library Work and Networking." ***Assignation*** **16, no. 4 (July 1999): 9–11.**

In this brief article, Darvill begins by identifying the ability to network effectively as an information skill and then proceeds to investigate and answer the question of whether men or women have better networking abilities. This question is explored by the author in recounting his experiences with both male and female librarians and information specialists throughout his childhood, adolescence, and professional life. The author concludes that women are indeed the better networkers and therefore have superior information skills.

263. Day, David V., William E. Cross, Erika L. Ringseis, and Tamara L. Williams. "Self-Categorization and Identity Construction Associated with Managing Diversity." ***Journal of Vocational Behavior*** **54, no. 1 (1999): 188–95.**

Reports on a study investigating the self-categorization of 254 library employees from a large university library who responded to the question, "Do you consider yourself to be a member of an underrepresented group?" Approximately 70 percent of the respondents were female; of these, two female employees indicated that they felt underrepresented due to their gender, even though 68 percent of the employees in the library at that time were female. Other factors indicating underrepresentation included race/ethnicity, religion, sexual orientation, physical disability, and age.

264. DeCandido, Grace A. "Words Are All We Have: A Very Brief Disquisition on Librarians, Technology, Access, Feminism, and the Truths of Things." In ***Summary of Proceedings. Fifty-fifth Annual Conference—American Theological Library Association*****, 147. Chicago: American Theological Library Association, 2001.**

DeCandido's plenary session speech to the American Theological Library Association discusses the meaning behind the words that define our daily work and our perspectives on our careers: technology, access, choice, truth, librarianship, and more. While words and their power are the main focus of her speech, feminism is at the foundation of her philosophy and practice of librarianship. She eloquently shares how she practices feminism in small ways in her job and life, such as using "female examples" and quoting women. Although there is a focus on feminism, the overarching theme throughout the essay is the role of the librarian in connecting users with words, ideas, and stories.

265. Dudley, Edward. "Libraryland Demographics." ***Library Association Record*** **101, no. 5 (May 1999): 276.**

This column primarily pokes fun at the large proportion of "Elders," also referred to as "Retired Layabouts," who serve on library association committees in the United Kingdom. The author also notes that "by comparison with the '70s, women are now well ensconced on the other side of the glass ceiling." The proportion of women earning top salaries increased nine times between 1988 and 1991. Women are publishing more in library literature, and five women have been president of the Library Association since 1966. The author attributes these improvements to merit, while noting that women outnumber men in the profession three to one. Women's advances are contrasted to "the faltering onward march of the retired" who now constitute 10 percent of the Library Association's membership.

266. Greer, Bertie, Denise Stephens, and Vicki Coleman. "Cultural Diversity and Gender Role Spillover: A Working Perspective." ***Journal of Library Administration*** **33, no. 1/2 (2001): 125–40.**

This article "explores the effect of gender role spillover in the workplace and examines the relationship of men and women in library administration." Since the profession of librarianship is female-dominated, the article explores to what extent gender-related conflicts arise in this setting. The extension of stereotypical gender roles into the workplace can create bias, discrimination, sexual harassment, and other conflicts. Recommendations are given on how to balance gender spillover in the workplace.

267. Hannigan, Jane A. "Gender Equity and Schooling." ***Knowledge Quest*** **26, no. 4 (May 1998–30 June 1998): 8–54.**

Hannigan, professor emerita of Columbia University in New York, served as guest editor of the May/June issue of *Knowledge Quest* in 1998. The theme of the issue was gender equity in school library media centers. Hannigan's editorial describes the content of the issue, which covers areas relating to the library media center such as literacy programs, bias in scientific thinking, reading lists, and use of the Web to highlight women's history.

268. Hildenbrand, Suzanne. "Library Feminism and Library Women's History: Activism and Scholarship, Equity and Culture." ***Libraries and Culture*** **35, no. 1 (Winter 2000): 51–65.**

This essay reviews seminal and influential publications on library feminist history and library women's history in order to trace the development of library women's history from the post–World War II/Cold War period through the 1990s. The essay examines the place of women within the field of librarianship, the struggle for equity throughout the time periods listed above, and the creation of and work of the ALA's Feminist Task Force, Women Library Workers, and the Committee on the Status of Women in Librarianship; it highlights not only what was present in the literature but also what was absent. Writings on or examinations of women of color in librarianship, lesbians in librarianship, and women in children's services were either invisible or extremely brief. Hildenbrand also discusses the shift in methodologies from studying one person's life and work to studying a group of similar people using a set of variables. One example Hildenbrand describes is Joanne E. Passett's *Cultural Crusaders: Women Librarians in the American West, 1900–1917*, in which Passett used both data and primary source material such as letters and diaries. This essay also traces the shift from writings about equity aspects of the profession to how women contribute to the profession, to their workplaces, and to the service ethic of libraries.

269. Hollis, Deborah R. "Affirmative Action or Increased Competition: A Look at Women and Minority Library Deans." ***Journal of Library Administration*** **27, no. 1/2 (1999): 49–75.**

Reports findings of a study that examines twelve years of gender and race data on deans from eighty-six academic libraries and tries to tie the data to affirmative action initiatives. Also reports findings on this issue from affirmative action or diversity efforts.

270. Iverson, Sandy. "Librarianship and Resistance." ***Progressive Librarian*** **15 (Winter 1999): 14–19.**

Argues that librarians should adopt a model of "situated knowledge" based on Donna Haraway's theory of feminist objectivity, which says that objectivity is limited by one's situation. The author states that librarians need to question their practices and recognize their own situated knowledge in order to serve the public in a more equitable manner.

271. Iwe, Josephine I. "Women Librarians and the Challenges of Information Technology in Nigerian University Libraries." ***Information Development*** **17, no. 1 (March 2001): 35–41.**

This article reviews the status of female librarians in Nigerian academic libraries. Librarians there have accepted the challenge of using information technology to ensure the best services. Augmented title: Edited version of paper presented at the International Conference of the National Association of Women Academics, Abuja, Nigeria, September 2000.

272. Kerslake, Evelyn. "Women and Librarianship: A Review Article." ***Journal of Librarianship and Information Science*** **34, no. 1 (March 2002): 53–56.**

Reviews the findings of a report on women librarians in the United Kingdom published in 1966. Compares this report to a contemporary study of women in the profession. The major difference is that since the passage of the Sex Discrimination Act of 1975 women cannot be prohibited from employment on the basis of their marital status. Concludes that while there are more opportunities for flexible and part-time work for female librarians, part-time work impedes women from advancement in their careers and women are still underrepresented in the senior levels of the profession.

273. Kruger, Betsy, and Catherine Larson. ***On Account of Sex: An Annotated Bibliography on the Status of Women in Librarianship 1993–1997*****. Lanham, Md.: Scarecrow, 2000.**

Previous edition of the current work, covering the years 1993–1997. Compiled under the auspices of the ALA Committee on the Status of Women in Librarianship. Contains introductory chapter by Roma Harris, and author, title, and geographic indices.

274. Leisner, Tony. "Not Fit for Print—Are Libraries Sexist?" ***Against the Grain*** **11, no. 3 (June 1999): 80.**

Leisner, a bookseller, compares Home Depot and Barnes and Noble signage to libraries' signage in an effort to prove that libraries are not only difficult to navigate but also sexist. Examples of a sexist library include collecting more information on breast cancer than prostrate cancer, not recruiting men for staff positions, and in general, not providing clear and adequate signage for male customers who may have trouble exploring their topics in the library.

275. Margolis, Rick. "The Women's Room: A High School Media Specialist Insists on Being Herself." ***School Library Journal*** **45, no. 10 (October 1999): 29.**

Short news item reports that the Minnesota Human Rights Department upheld the right of a transgender media specialist to use the school's women's restroom after a complaint filed by a female teacher. Minnesota is the only state that legally protects the rights of transgendered individuals.

276. Morland, Berit. "Bokenes Menn." *Bok og Bibliotek* 65, no. 7/8 (December 1998): 12–16.

Five male librarians from various libraries in Norway share their observations about gender roles within the profession. For example, while men constitute only 25 percent of library school students at the University of Oslo, the numbers even out when it comes to library managers. Library employees are primarily women, but men are the managers. The large number of female employees has an effect on collections as well as the physical environment. However, the author speculates that as technology becomes more prevalent in libraries the number of male employees will increase, since men embrace technology more readily than women.

277. Ogunrombi, Samuel Adewale, H. C. Pisagih, and V. W. Udoh. "The Recognition of Women Librarians in Nigeria: An Evaluative Study." *African Journal of Library, Archives and Information Science* 12, no. 1 (April 2002): 81–89.

This article examines the contribution of female librarians to the profession of librarianship in Nigeria. The study revealed that fewer females than males obtain a master's degree in library and information science. A search of national biographical sources showed that very few women librarians were listed and a literature search produced a lack of materials on women in the profession in Nigeria.

278. Piper, Paul S., and Barbara E. Collamer. "Male Librarians: Men in a Feminized Profession." *Journal of Academic Librarianship* 27, no. 9 (September 2001): 406–11.

Reports on a study exploring "the areas of comfort and bias among male librarians." It also offers updated information originally reported in James Carmichael's 1992 study entitled "The Male Librarian and the Feminine Image: A Survey of Stereotype, Status and Gender Perceptions" published in *Library & Information Research*. While the article focuses on male librarians, many comparisons are drawn in relation to the status of women in librarianship. Therefore, both quantitative and qualitative data are presented in the areas of bias, stereotype, comfort, work community, and advancement for both men and women.

279. Pritchard, Sarah. "Which Guardians and Whose Culture? Feminist Thinking, Libraries, and Information." 5 May 1999. www.library.uiuc.edu/colloquium/pritchard.html.

After presenting a brief historical overview of women in librarianship, Pritchard offers evidence of how feminist thinking informs librarianship at all levels. Feminist critique affects and helps define employment issues, workplace organization, research methods, collection development, and much more. There are also links to Pritchard's biography, papers, and an interview with her by Cory Stier.

280. Rolph, Avril. "The Life and Times of LiL: Lesbians in the Library." In *Gendering Library History*, ed. Evelyn Kerslake and Nick-ianne Moody, 196–208. Liverpool, England: John Moores University Association for Research in Popular Fictions: Media Critical and Creative Arts, 2000.

Rolph discusses the inception, activities, and publications of two library groups in Great Britain: Women in Libraries (WiL) and Lesbians in Libraries (LiL), which grew out of WiL in the mid-eighties. LiL's efforts to improve work environments, educate library staff and personnel, and influence key legislation are included in this history.

281. Samantaray, Moorttimatee. *Indian Women in Librarianship*. New Delhi: National Book Organisation, 1998.

This study reports and interprets findings from structured interviews with ninety-one female librarians in academic libraries in five eastern Indian states: West Bengal, Orissa, Assam, Meghalaya, and Manipur. The introductory chapter reviews the English-language literature from 1960 through the early 1990s on the status of women in society and in the library profession, with particular attention to job characteristics and attitudes among academic librarians. The second chapter describes the sample, the structured interview method (the complete questionnaire is included as an appendix), and the statistical analyses employed. In the third chapter, the data are reported in the aggregate and also in three groupings that reflect the varying degree of economic development of the states. Respondents were asked to describe the work they do and its physical environment, to rate various aspects of job satisfaction and job attitude, and to provide demographic details of their personal and work lives. The most common duties performed are cataloging and classification. While agreeing that librarianship is a women's field, the majority felt that their jobs could be done by either men or women with a bachelor's degree in LIS. The librarians were satisfied overall with most aspects of their jobs, including independence at work, workplace conditions, pay, recognition by staff and users, and cooperation of colleagues and superiors. However, attitudes were mixed on questions about career achievement, job expectations, and so forth. The strongest negative attitudes were expressed about the possibility of moving to another state for a better job. Samantaray was particularly interested in the issue of faculty versus academic status. Although the respondents felt that their salaries should equal those of teachers, the majority did not wish for faculty status and favored seniority as the criterion for promotion. The book concludes with recommendations for enhancing the status and job satisfaction of female Indian academic librarians.

282. Schneider, Jeff, and Ann O'Bryan Cockerham. "Isn't it Queer? Cataloguing the Closet." In *Gendering Library History*, ed. Evelyn Kerslake and Nickianne Moody, 30–39. Liverpool, England: John Moores University Association for Research in Popular Fictions: Media Critical and Creative Arts, 2000.

Schneider and Cockerham discuss queer theory and the role of a queer theorist, comparing it to the role of a rare book librarian. The authors also question libraries' providing equal access to erotica and pornographic literature in a discussion of cataloging rules and subject headings, highlighting the writings of Sanford Berman and Ellen Greenblatt.

283. Sturges, Paul. "Helpless Girls and Female Depravity: Women In and Out of the Public Libraries of the Past." In *Gendering Library History*, ed. Evelyn Kerslake and Nickianne Moody, 5–14. Liverpool, England: John Moores University Association for Research in Popular Fictions: Media Critical and Creative Arts, 2000.

Sturges reexamines his own publications on public libraries using gender as a focal point. In reflecting on his own work he investigates if the subject of women as library users or as members of a profession is ignored by his own writings. He dissects each of the eight articles and finds that in many ways women are "invisible" in his writings.

284. Williamson, Val. "The Role of the Librarian in the Reconfiguration of Gender and Class in Relation to Professional Authorship." In *Gendering Library History*, ed. Evelyn Kerslake and Nickianne Moody, 163–78. Liverpool, England: John Moores University Association for Research in Popular Fictions: Media Critical and Creative Arts, 2000.

The author discusses the initial perceptions of women's writings as unimportant, focusing on regional sagas and romances. While examining the place of these works and their authors within the field of literature, Williamson also discusses the reading, research, and library use habits of contemporary women writers to prove the connection between the increased commercial value of women's writings and the importance of the library.

285. Winter, Michael. "Garlic, Vodka, and the Politics of Gender: Anti-Intellectualism in American Librarianship." ***Progressive Librarian*****, no. 14 (Spring 1998): 5–12.**

Suggests that the new emphasis on information technology in librarianship is more gender influenced than other, older aspects of the profession. Says this is not surprising since computer science is traditionally male-dominated. Author links this to anti-intellectualism in American libraries and the profession's interest in pragmatic management philosophies similar to those used in the corporate sector.

6

Image of Librarians

This chapter includes materials that focus on the stereotypes associated with librarians and on the image of librarians in the media.

286. "Traditional Stereotypes Passé Matarazzo Tells *BW* Readers." *Library Hotline* 31, no. 15 (15 April 2002): 4–5.

In response to a *Business Week* article focusing on the shortages of qualified people to step into the profession, James Matarazzo, dean of Simmons College Graduate School of Library and Information Science, wrote a letter to the editor criticizing the illustration accompanying the piece. The illustration featured a "woman, hair in bun, glasses halfway down her nose, finger to her lips sending a demand for quiet."

287. Adams, Katherine. "Loveless Frump as Hip and Sexy Party Girl." *Library Quarterly*, no. 70 (July 2000): 287–301.

The author uses a theory about the construction of meaning in stereotypes to suggest that librarians appropriate the "old maid" stereotype in order to resist, and even change, the cultural assumptions that helped create the stereotype.

288. Bernier, Catherine. "Bibliothecaires: Editrices sur le Net." *Argus* 30, no. 2 (Autumn 2001): 7–9.

Profiles three women and their websites that challenge the stereotype of the librarian as a woman with her hair in a bun who goes around shushing children. Briefly described are Libraries.net (Jessamyn West), New Breed Librarian (Colleen Bell and Juanita Benedicto), and Ex Libris: an E-Z-Zine for Librarians and Information Junkies (Marylaine Block).

289. Brewerton, A. "Wear Lipstick, Have a Tattoo, Belly-Dance, Then Get Naked: The Making of a Virtual Librarian." *Impact, the Journal*

***of the Career Development Group* 2, no. 10 (November 1999–31 December 1999): 158–64.**

A review of images of librarians on the World Wide Web. Brewerton found that websites fall into one of two categories: "[s]tudies of the image" and "'image busting' sites" (158). In the first category, the websites address representations of librarians, both positive and negative, in comic strips and books, theater and film, newspaper and magazine stories of "real" librarians, and quotations. Image "busting" sites range from the serious (progressive/anarchist) to the fun and risqué (The Lipstick Librarian). Brewerton points out that the profession is still perceived as "book-centered" or "the ideal refuge for the shrinking violet" (163). The profession needs to dispel these misconceptions so that it can draw more people with interpersonal and communication skills, passion, and excitement into librarianship.

290. Burgett, Shelley Wood. "Kentucky Librarians: Do We Fit the Stereotype?" *Kentucky Libraries* 62, no. 3 (Summer 1998): 4–10.

The author conducted a mail survey of members of the Kentucky Library Association "to see if they fit the image [of librarians] prevalent in the popular media." Percentage responses are reported by type of library (academic, public, school, special) and for the total population (n = 100). Some findings fit the stereotype: Ninety-three percent overall were female, and 91 percent were over the age of thirty-six. However, only 17 percent had never married. Reported alcohol and tobacco consumption were low. Nearly half identified themselves as political moderates. Public librarians were less well educated (only 45 percent had master's degrees). Asked "Do you think you fit the public's image of a librarian?" 50 percent said no, 21 percent said yes, and 29 percent were uncertain. A majority of academic and special librarians felt that the media image of librarians is generally negative; the majority of school and public librarians did not. Forty-five percent of the respondents felt that the entry of men into the profession has improved its image. Twenty-four personality traits associated with the librarian stereotype were listed; respondents indicated whether the trait applied to most librarians, whether it applied to themselves, whether it was an asset, and whether it reflected the public's image. Overall, 94 percent said they enjoyed being a librarian, and 84 percent claimed they do not worry about their image.

291. Carle, Daria O., and Susan Anthes. "Gender Images in Library Publications: Is a Picture Worth a Thousand Words?" *Journal of Academic Librarianship* 25, no. 2 (March 1999): 105–10.

Females dominate the library profession as a whole, but the majority of authors and editors of library literature are male. In addition, based on the study reported on in this article, women are also underrepresented pictorially in library journals, especially when compared to the percentages of men and women working in the profession. The authors suggest that their study raises many questions about the role of women in librarianship.

292. Cart, Michael. *In the Stacks: Short Stories about Libraries and Librarians*. New York: Overlook Press, 2002.

These library-oriented short stories come from major authors of the twentieth century, including Ray Bradbury, Alice Munro, and Ursula K. LeGuin. Compiled by Michael Cart, past director of the Beverly Hills Public Library, the collection includes mysteries, ghost stories, and stories about the relationships between librarians and their patrons. Themes include library as sanctuary, the power of books and their characters, and depiction of women librarians at various stages of life and career.

293. Crawford, Jesse. "Image Management: Public and Reference Services." *Arkansas Libraries* 59, no. 2 (April 2002).

A discussion of stereotypes associated with librarians that are demeaning to women and, by extension, women librarians. The author makes suggestions about how to respond to these stereotypes and how to create new positive ones.

294. D'Alessandro, Dario. *Hauptrolle Bibliothek: eine Filmographie*. Innsbruck: Studien-Verlag, 2002.

Examines the depiction of libraries and librarians in film. The different stereotypes are compared to the prosaic reality of the library's everyday life. These movies show an amazing continuity throughout the decades of both the image of the librarian and the library as an institution.

295. Dilevko, Juris. "As the Library Turns: Women, Technology, and Advertisements in the Wired World." Ph.D. diss., University of Western Ontario, 1999.

Examines five library journals and *Wired* between 1991 and 1997 to determine how advertisements depict gender roles in relation to the use of computer information technology. Discusses the traditional, social constructs that have long identified librarianship as a women's profession and suggests that changes in computer technology are shifting gender roles by identifying certain areas of library work, such as computer systems, as an increasingly male-dominated field. Finds that while men account for about 18 percent of librarians in North America, advertisements in the journals studied depict men working with computer information technologies at a rate of about 38 percent. Also finds that women in these ads are overwhelmingly identified with cataloging and circulation functions, but that reference and online searching tasks, bibliographic instruction, and systems work seem to show more equal representation. A thematic study of the advertisements suggests that women are consistently marginalized or identified with the theme of simplicity, particularly in *Wired*, which often invokes traditional physical and domestic stereotypes when it represents women using computers.

296. Duin, Julia. "Libertine Librarians?" *Insight on the News* 15, no. 46 (13 December 1999): 29.

Brief article about the changing image of librarians from the "bespectacled spinster with a pencil stuck in her hair" to the liberal librarian, who according to Will Manley's 1993 survey, most likely has read the *Joy of Sex* and rented an X-rated video. Duin also reports that Manley's survey revealed that 78 percent of female librarians said they had been sexually harassed by a patron, and that 24 percent would pose for *Playboy*. The article reports criticism by Dr. Laura Schlessinger, who thinks librarians have done something evil by opposing Internet filtering, and by Mark Herring, who opposes ALA's support of gay and lesbian issues and organizations. Online. Available from INFOTRAC, Expanded Academic.

297. Fanger, Iris. "Women's Work Informs Back Porch Project." *Dance Magazine* 74, no. 5 (May 2000): 46.

Reports on the Back Porch Dance Company's project, "Celebrating Cambridge Women and Work," which was performed at the Massachusetts Institute of Technology, May 18–19, 2000. The theater-dance piece, as performed by this interracial, intergenerational, all-woman troupe, presents oral histories of eight "ordinary, extraordinary women" who work at diverse jobs such as curtain folder, biologist, welder, and library worker.

298. Feehan, Patricia E., and Jill E. Buie. "Looking Up: The Image of Youth Services Librarians." *North Carolina Libraries* 56, no. 4 (Winter 1998): 141–44.

This article discusses the negative stereotype of librarians and describes two studies (the Heylman Study and the Buie Study), both of which aimed to discover if negative stereotypes of librarians existed in children's literature. The article also discusses the impact of stereotypes on recruitment and training of youth services librarians, focusing on an informal survey sent to 179 faculty whose research and teaching were in the area of young adult services.

299. Garrison, Jessica. "Leaders of the Stacks." ***Los Angeles Times*** **(28 November 1999): B2.**

Interviews with several Los Angeles area librarians who dispel the stereotype of "librarians as cranky old ladies with glasses, orthopedic shoes and a neurotic fixation on silence" by showing today's librarians as young, hip, and cyber-savvy. Online. Available through Lexis-Nexis Universe. 10 November 2000.

300. Hagenström, Juliane. "'Genügt es Nicht, Wenn Sie Welche Abstaubt?' Die Bibliothekarin in der Literatur." ***BuB-Forum für Bibliothek und Information*** **52, no. 1 (January 2000): 62–69.**

Citations of German and international novels and children's books that contain characterizations of women librarians. English title: "'Isn't It Enough If She Dusts Them?': The Woman Librarian in Fiction."

301. Hill, Robert W., and Gregory P. Yousey. "Adaptive and Maladaptive Narcissism among University Faculty, Clergy, Politicians, and Librarians." ***Current Psychology*** **17, no. 2/3 (1998): 163–69.**

Study investigates narcissistic characteristics that may be evident in four sample occupations. Of the four occupations sampled, politicians, clergy, and university faculty were chosen because their work involves frequent appearances before audiences, authority over others, and higher levels of prestige, power, and status. Librarians were selected because of their stereotypical role associated with lower levels of prestige, social attention, and lack of admiration from others. Results were surprising in that while librarians scored lowest in total narcissism, they were not significantly less narcissistic than faculty or clergy. Politicians, however, were significantly more narcissistic than the other three.

302. Kerslake, Evelyn, and Janine Liladhar. "Angry Sentinels and Businesslike Women: Identity and Marital Status in 1950s English Library Career Novels." ***Library History*** **17, no. 2 (July 2001): 83–90.**

The authors examine the image and marital status of female library workers as portrayed in 1950s English career novels. They find that there is a very clear message that women were not expected to remain in their library jobs after marriage, a reflection of the "marriage bar" that existed in a number of professions. However, the image of the unmarried librarian is not strictly that of the unattractive spinster. Some unmarried librarians are described positively, and in one novel the admired head librarian is an unmarried woman.

303. King, Angelynn. "Image Is Everything: So Go Get One Already." ***College & Research Libraries News*** **60, no. 4 (April 1999): 277, 318.**

Humorously dissects the preoccupation of the library profession with its "image problem." Suggests that "when someone remarks that you don't look like a librarian, take a page from Gloria Steinem and say, 'Yes, I do. This is what a librarian looks like.'" Includes a cartoon by Kappa Waugh entitled "Spot the Librarian" (see separate entry). Letters in response to this article appear in *College & Research Libraries News* 60, no. 6 (June 1999): 456.

304. Liladhar, Janine, and Evelyn Kerslake. "No More Library Classes for Catherine: Marital Status, Career Progression and Library Employment in 1950s England." *Women's Studies International Forum* 22, no. 2 (March 1999–30 April 1999): 215–24.

This article explores the constructions of unmarried women through an analysis of three 1950s library career novels. The article explores three novels: *Molly Hilton: Library Assistant* (1954), *Molly Qualifies as a Librarian* (1958), and *A Library Life for Deborah* (1957). The authors argue that while written ostensibly to promote librarianship, the novels may have had the opposite effect due to the marital status of the heroines. Librarians were described as the stereotypical elderly, unattractive, irritable spinster, while "single women" were described as young and heterosexually attractive. While the novels were used as recruitment tools for the library profession, it is argued that they indirectly contributed to the curtailment of single women's library careers. In these books married women did not work in libraries; thus, the young women who entered the field, did not pursue their professional qualifications past the lower levels in anticipation of resignation after marriage. The article includes statistical tables on women in the library field in the 1950s, endnotes, and references.

305. Myers, Marcia J. "Images of Librarians in Science Fiction and Fantasy: Including an Annotated List." (June 1998): 1–44. ERIC Document Reproduction Service No. ED420314.

Examines the image of librarians in science fiction and fantasy novels and videotapes to determine whether the traditional image of the librarian is changing. Reviews sixty-seven authors to form inquiries regarding the librarian characters contained in their work. Analyzes data, such as the importance of the librarian character, their gender, gender of the author, and publication date, and determines the overall image of librarians in science fiction to be positive (44 percent). Male characters predominated the sample (44 percent), but no clear correlation could be found between the librarians' image and author gender. Includes comparisons with results of similar studies on librarians' image in motion pictures, poetry, mysteries, and romance fiction.

306. Park, Daniel S. "Oh Auntie, You Shouldn't Have." ***Library Association Record*** **101, no. 2 (February 2000): 83.**

This letter writer calls attention to the stereotypical portrayal of a librarian in the BBC's broadcast of *The Vicar of Dibley* on December 27, 1999. His first impressions of the character were positive. ("Sporting a sharp suit and some ethnic variation for the first time ever, she seemed a godsend to changing some of the general public's attitudes to information professionals everywhere.") However, she revealed that she had left the library sector ("a wide and varied group of . . . professionals whose combined raison d'être she summed up so succinctly by going 'shhhhh'") for a more exciting job as a daycare inspector. The writer notes that Sean Bean, who made a guest appearance in the episode, has praised libraries.

307. Radford, Marie L. "Approach or Avoidance? The Role of Nonverbal Communication in the Academic Library User's Decision to Initiate a Reference Eounter." ***Library Trends*** **46, no. 4 (Spring 1998): 699–717.**

A qualitative study on the influence of nonverbal communication and reference service was conducted at a university and college library based on Mehrabian's immediacy metaphor. In this study, users identified five major factors that influenced their decision to approach the reference desk. The five factors were: initiation, availability, familiarity, proximity and gender.

308. Swaffield, Laura. "Be Sexy: Draw a Bat on Your Bottom." ***Library Association Record*** **104, no. 3 (March 2002): 192.**

The monthly "Mediawatching" column culls images of librarians from the popular news and entertainment media. The first half of this installment recounts instances where women's fashions were mocked as librarian-like. The sources include commentaries about celebrities Natalie Merchant, Dionne Warwick, and Joan Collins. Swaffield also passes along a story submitted to *Cosmopolitan* by a "library researcher" about a sexual encounter in a stuck elevator. The column is illustrated by a magazine ad, which features a woman's torso, scantily clad, and the legend "Librarian by day, Bacardi by night."

309. Swaffield, Laura. "Change Your Image, Make Money." ***Library Association Record*** **103, no. 5 (May 2001): 316.**

"Mediawatching" columnist Laura Swaffield presents a monthly assemblage of images of librarians gleaned by readers from the popular media, often with a gendered perspective. Following up on her April 2001 column, which quoted from a scathing essay about men (including librarians) with beards, she reports on a stereotype-busting librarian who shaved his beard off as a charity fundraiser, and on two male university librarians/information managers who shaved their heads. "So," she promises, "no more digs about all information scientists having pony-tails." By contrast, recent images of women librarians are nothing to cheer about. When male and female executives were shown two photographs of the same woman—one without makeup, the other with makeup, jewelry, and a dress-for-success suit—they assumed the latter was a high-earning manager, while the former was "either a housewife or a librarian." An ex-stripper, writing in the *Evening Standard*, noted that people don't believe she was a stripper, because she looks "more like a librarian." On the plus side, Swaffield exults because an American TV comedienne was described in the *Guardian Guide* as having "got that chic, sexy librarian look down pat."

310. Swaffield, Laura. "Erica, the Librarian Who Knew Too Much." *Library Association Record* 101, no. 7 (July 1999): 440.

The *Record*'s back-page column, "Mediawatching," offers witty commentary on a wide range of subjects gleaned from various popular media. This month's column leads off by contrasting the image of librarians in *BBC Online*'s career guide ("You get to meet a lot of quirky people in libraries with the widest array of interests and that's what really attracts Marie to the job") to the image on Erica Olsen's website: "Librarians have degrees. Librarians can catalogue anything from an onion to a dog's ear. They could catalogue you. Librarians wield unfathomable power." The rest of the column reports on such diverse press gleanings as rowdy teenagers in a Kent library, Beatrix Potter's pet squirrels, and the latest word derivations discovered by the compilers of the *Oxford English Dictionary*. [NOTE: Erica Olsen's site is now located at www.librarianavengers.com.]

311. Swaffield, Laura. "Fantasy Librarians—Who Needs 'Em?" *Library Association Record* 101, no. 2 (February 2000): 120.

This issue's "Mediawatching" column leads off with the story of Annabel Other, a traveling performance artist who has taken on the identity of the head librarian of the (now closed) Bristol Art Library. She dresses the part—"utility hair-cut, nerdish specs, cardi and all"—and trundles a wooden box filled with miniature books, a card catalog, a book stamp, and other stereotyped tools of the profession. She even says "ssssh." "And what do we make of all this?" asks the perplexed columnist. The cliché head librarian may be an affront to modern librarians or a heartwarming affirmation that "the heart of a library is the librarian." Swaffield moves on to describe other recent images of librarians in the news media, including an article in the *Guardian* on the favorite television programs of public librarians and a survey, also in the *Guardian*, that asked people what they thought various professions earned and what they ought to earn. The column closes with another librarian's long list of her colleagues' eccentric characteristics. Joan Senior, writing a letter to the editor in the following issue (101, no. 3, March 2000, 143) criticizes the column for "pandering to the traditional image and depicting quirky behavior" that only reinforces stereotypes. She calls on the Library Association to promote more accurate and positive images of librarians.

312. Swaffield, Laura. "From Lydia to Whiffles to . . . Fatso?" *Library Association Record* 103, no. 11 (November 2001): 708.

The monthly "Mediawatching" column is a humorous recounting of images of librarians in the popular media, many discovered by readers of the *Record*. This month features a comic strip from a 1960 issue of *Valentine* magazine, in which Lydia the librarian finds a pound note serving as a bookmark in a returned book and uses it as a pretext to meet the handsome borrower. Swaffield contrasts this with a present-day story in *Cosmopolitan* that includes sexual confessions of "Phoebe, 32, librarian, Cardiff." Snippets from other sources use words like "lonely," "disappointing," "genteel," and "mild-mannered" to describe female librarians—even Monika Antonelli, a college librarian in Texas, who moonlights as the voice of a TV cartoon superhero and a shape-shifting cat. Her second career started when she dressed up as Whiffles the white rabbit for the young users of a public library.

313. Swaffield, Laura. "If All Else Fails, Hijack a Helicopter." *Library Association Record* 103, no. 4 (April 2001): 256.

In the *Record*'s back-page column, "Mediawatching," Swaffield presents a potpourri of images of librarians gleaned by readers from the Web, television, newspapers, and other popular media. Her selections this month compare the stereotype of the "sad, lonely woman with her cat" to the caricature of the "lovelorn, frowzy-haired librarian," mock men with beards ("geography teachers, librarians, and folk singers"), and report on an American librarian who swapped jobs with a Las Vegas showgirl. Swaffield also summarizes the story of an Australian librarian who hijacked a helicopter at gunpoint to help her boyfriend, a bank robber, escape from prison. Noting that information scientists do not suffer from an image problem because no one knows what they are, Swaffield declares, "Librarians . . . have an advantage: everyone *thinks* they know what you're like. So you can use that mild-as-milk image to get away with actions that would make even William Hague [a conservative British politician] blush. Or you can fling the image spectacularly to the wind. The media will lap it up."

314. Swaffield, Laura. "It's Better Than Lap-Dancing (Just)." ***Library Association Record*** **103, no. 9 (September 2001): 576.**

"Mediawatching" columnist Laura Swaffield presents a monthly assemblage of images of librarians gleaned by readers from the popular media, often with a gendered perspective. This month ten different instances are described, from an ad for a man's corduroy blazer with the legend "Librarian gear gets butch," to a profile of a powerful female blues singer who "looked like your friendly neighborhood librarian." The media image that emerges from numerous examples is of a sexless, frumpy, stern librarian trapped in a boring life.

315. Swaffield, Laura. "Librarians Are Not the Only Sad People." ***Library Association Record*** **102, no. 10 (October 2000): 600.**

The *Record*'s back-page column, "Mediawatching," gleans mentions of librarians and libraries from the popular news and entertainment media and adds commentary, typically spiced with sarcasm. This month leads off with a profile of Angie McEvoy, a librarian stand-up comic who was a runner-up in a BBC talent search. A sample joke: "When I told my librarian boyfriend I was a month late, he fined me 50p." Other images of librarians reported here are less positive: two allusions to librarians' frumpy clothing, a report that John Lennon's murderer, Mark Chapman, works in the prison law library, and a quote from the *Daily Telegraph*, explaining that the impotence of the protest movement at the Democratic national convention was symbolized by a librarian who was keeping an eye on her protesting son.

316. Swaffield, Laura. "Mad, Sad, Hated—And Overlooked." ***Library Association Record*** **102, no. 4 (April 2000): 300.**

The *Record*'s "Mediawatching" column comments on diverse library-related subjects gleaned from the popular news and entertainment media, often with a gendered twist. Among other tidbits, this month's column recounts an exchange of letters in the *Guardian*, occasioned by a fashion collection said to be inspired by "frustrated librarians." One letter writer urged librarians to fight back "by reviving the old T-shirt slogan 'Librarians are novel lovers.'" Another proposed the more up-to-date slogan, "Librarians do it digitally."

317. Swaffield, Laura. "Mediawatching." ***Library and Information Update*** **1, no. 6 (September 2002): 64.**

Every month, the "Mediawatching" column takes a tongue-in-cheek look at depictions of librarians in the British media and real-life librarians who belie the stereotypes. This month Swaffield mentions *Storm Center*, a 1956 American movie that starred Bette Davis as a censorship-battling public librarian. She also reports a poll on the Barbie doll website, where visitors can vote for Barbie's next career: architect, policewoman, or librarian. The article is illustrated by a magazine ad for earplugs, featuring a lovely swimsuit-clad, earplug-wearing woman and the pronouncement, "She's not your typical librarian." Swaffield muses on the possible links between earplugs and library work: "Something about diving but doing it sensibly? Or a subliminal connection between earplugs and silence?"

318. Swaffield, Laura. "Mediawatching." ***Library and Information Update*** **1, no. 7 (October 2002): 64.**

Every month, the "Mediawatching" column takes a tongue-in-cheek look at depictions of librarians in the British media and real-life librarians who belie the stereotypes. This month spotlights two newspaper accounts of the 2003 IFLA conference in Edinburgh, in which the old stereotype of dull, shushing librarians was repeated. A fashion note in the *Sunday Times Style* magazine described the long, tight pencil skirt as "perfect garb for any librarian with dominatrix tendencies. Or a slutty nurse." While nursing has its own image problems, it's not above taking digs at other female-intensive professions. A humor column in the *Nursing Times* reported on a fictional survey of people who fell asleep at work: Twelve percent woke up to find that "they had been promoted to chief librarian or head of social work." Other media nuggets convey out-of-date images of libraries and misunderstanding of the profession ("technology has made the job easier"). The column is illustrated by a newspaper fashion shot that Swaffield honors with her "Tripe Cliché Award" for depicting a librarian 1. stamping books; 2. saying "sssh"; and 3. wearing a cardigan.

319. Swaffield, Laura. "Mediawatching." ***Library and Information Update*** **1, no. 8 (November 2002): 64.**

Every month, the "Mediawatching" column takes a tongue-in-cheek look at depictions of librarians in the media. This month features websites recommended by readers, ranging from a bizarre spoof (a site for people who sniff books) to the epitome of British humor (a site devoted to the fictional 1901 census for the village of Great Cockup and librarian Edith Tintwhistle's tribulations in putting it online). Of particular interest is the

"You Don't Look Like a Librarian" site (http://atst.nso.edu/library/perception/), which includes links to a paper and bibliography on the image of librarians. Also mentioned is a dystopian description of the library of the future, published in an anarchist magazine, which acknowledges the meek image of librarians but asserts that "these days, however, library workers are having to become a far more radical breed." The column concludes by noting two novels about female librarians: *A Ring in Time*, by Linda Sawley and *La Cucina*, by Lily Prior.

320. Swaffield, Laura. "Mediawatching." ***Library and Information Update*** **1, no. 9 (December 2002): 64.**

Every month, the "Mediawatching" column takes a tongue-in-cheek look at depictions of librarians in the British media and real-life librarians who belie the stereotypes. The illustrations this month include two examples of celebrities dressed in "librarian chic"—in one case, a tight skirt and blouse, in the other case, eyeglasses—that are mocked by fashion critics. Most of the column is devoted to praising *The Library Book Cart Precision Drill Team Manual* (McFarland, 2002), implying that librarians in marching formations are still a novelty in Great Britain. Three films that include librarian characters or references to librarians are pointed out: *Red Dragon*, *Possession*, and *Star Wars 2* (in which a petite gray-haired librarian with a bun assists Obi-Wan Kenobi).

321. Swaffield, Laura. "Mediawatching." ***Library and Information Update*** **1, no. 4 (July 2002): 64.**

The "Mediawatching" column is a humorous recounting of images of librarians and libraries in the popular media. This month Swaffield focuses on library cats but also reprints an ad for a sexual aid from an American lesbian magazine, *On Our Backs.* A woman with a knowing smile clutches a book and the text reads: "After a long day at the library, the last thing Margaret needed to unwind with was a good book." Swaffield asks, "Is this a good image for librarians? Cute-looking and sexually aware—but can't get a woman?"

322. Swaffield, Laura. "Mediawatching." ***Library and Information Update*** **1, no. 5 (August 2002): 64.**

The monthly "Mediawatching" column features images of librarians culled from the popular British media. This installment spotlights several novels that feature libraries or library-related themes. Swaffield also repeats a reference to librarians as "among the scariest people on the planet" and quotes from a novel (*Accidents in the Home*, by Tessa Hadley

[Jonathan Cape, 2002]) that describes a woman who "look[s] like a librarian" when she's tired: "small eyes, neat straight brows, thin lips, a square high forehead." A writer in *Glamour* denounces the bob hairstyle by asking "Who wants to look like a librarian?" Lisa Loeb does, according to Swaffield. The singer was featured in an ad for retro-style eyeglasses that are designed to give the wearer a preppy, "sexy-librarian look."

323. Swaffield, Laura. "Not So Dusty in Leicester or Toronto." ***Library Association Record*** **101, no. 11 (November 1999): 676.**

The *Record*'s back-page column, "Mediawatching," offers witty commentary on a wide range of subjects gleaned from the popular news and entertainment media. This month's column carries over from the September 1999 issue the theme of librarians' image, as Swaffield culls counterexamples to the dull spinster stereotype (some positive, others not). A final anecdote relates how the Toronto Argonauts, a football team, tried to drum up fan excitement through a newspaper ad declaring, "If you want to behave like a librarian, go to a library." Librarians complained, were given free tickets, and were properly raucous during the game.

324. Swaffield, Laura. "Pow! It's the Powerful People!" ***Library Association Record*** **101, no. 3 (March 2000): 180.**

The "Mediawatching" column reports library-related content from the mass media, usually spiked with a large dose of sarcasm. This month, it features a photo of Nadine Cohen, a librarian at the University of Georgia, hoisting a pile of heavy books on her shoulder. "This pleasant-looking person," Swaffield writes, "can dead-lift three times her own weight and is one of only three women in the United States to have official elite status in her weight category of (gulp) just 97 lb." The column also reports how the British news media, when announcing the appointment for the first time of a qualified librarian to head the British Library, headlined the fact "that the new appointee is—gasp!—a woman."

325. Swaffield, Laura. "Strange Ways to Make the Earth Move." ***Library Association Record*** **102, no. 11 (November 2000): 660.**

The *Record*'s back-page column, "Mediawatching," gleans mentions of librarians and libraries from the popular news and entertainment media and adds commentary, typically spiced with sarcasm. This month's collection reproduces an ad for a commercial website, in which an attractive naked woman holds up a sign (strategically positioned) that reads, "British Library claims ancient Greek and Roman texts 'bawdy.'" The ad was featured as the "Ad of the Week" in the *Telegraph* and hailed as a clever parody of tabloid headlines, but Swaffield is not amused. Nor does she enjoy the fashion spread in the *Telegraph Saturday Magazine* that describes an ugly and ill-fitting outfit as "the Librarian's Day Off look." The description of a well-muscled young male librarian in the novel *Inheritance* by Livi Michael, however, is a "treat."

326. Swaffield, Laura. "Where Truth Is Just as Weird as Fiction." *Library Association Record* 102, no. 6 (June 2000): 360.

The *Record*'s back-page column, "Mediawatching," comments on diverse library-related subjects gleaned from the popular news and entertainment media, often with a gendered twist. This month the column presents a photo of a woman behind a pile of books and a sketch of an orangutan and asks "Which is the librarian?" The ape, it turns out, is the librarian in a fantasy series by Terry Pratchett. The attractive woman, on the other hand, is a dental hygienist who dreamed of being a mobile librarian. For her fiftieth birthday, her coworkers arranged for her to spend a day on the local bookmobile, where colleagues reported that she "took to stamping books like a duck to water." Columnist Swaffield reacts with sarcasm: "Good grief, man, it's every librarian's core function, isn't it?"

327. Van Aswegen, Elizabeth S. "Thankless Tasks: Academics and Librarians in the Novels of Barbara Pym." *South African Journal of Library and Information Science (SAILIS)* 66, no. 1 (1998): 34–39.

An analysis of academic and library characters in the novels of Barbara Pym that includes a discussion of the relationship between women librarians and male teaching faculty. Issues of "women's work," a woman's role in the workplace, and the woman librarian's participation in scholarship are explored. These characters are based on academics and librarians Pym encountered during her work at the International African Institute. Van Aswegan demonstrates that women librarians in Pym's work are nurturing and competent while male librarians are malicious and averse to "books and borrowers."

328. Watson-Boone, Rebecca. *How Library and Information Science Research Literature Describes Librarians: A Synthesis of Selected 1985–1995 Journal Articles (CSIP Occasional Papers, No. 1)*. Mequon, WI: Center for the Study of Information Professionals, Inc., 1998.

Watson-Boone sampled studies of "practitioner-librarians" reported in fourteen leading LIS research journals between 1985 and 1995. She thoroughly discusses three themes examined in the research—demographics, employment, and attitudes—each of which includes information relevant to the status of women in the profession. Watson-Boone suggests several topics for future research, including: librarians in specialties other than cataloging and searching, librarians' views of each other across types of libraries, telecommuting, librarians working in academic full-text centers, librarians as library users, librarians' voting behavior, and librarians from non-middle-class backgrounds. A complete bibliography of the sample articles is appended.

329. Watson, Don. "Rocks Are a Girl's Best Friend." ***Library Association Record*** **101, no. 1 (January 1999): 64.**

The *Record*'s back-page column, "Mediawatching," comments wryly on a wide range of subjects gleaned from the popular news and entertainment media. This month's column calls the reader's attention to the Lipstick Librarian website (now found at www.lipsticklibrarian.com). Watson praises its creator, Linda Absher, who "has a mission to celebrate those brave souls who bring a little glamour and pazzaz [sic] to the information profession." Quotes from the site illustrate Absher's tongue-in-cheek views of librarians' fashions.

330. Waugh, Kappa. "Spot the Librarian." ***College & Research Libraries News*** **60, no. 4 (April 1999): 277.**

Cartoon shows a lineup of four women: two fashionably (and skimpily) dressed, one "bag lady," and one conventionally dressed, with her hair in a bun.

331. Weihs, Jean. "Does a Rose by Any Other Name Smell Sweeter?" ***Technicalities*** **20, no. 2 (March 2000–30 April 2000): 1, 8–9.**

Frustrated with the public image of librarians as "boring, dowdy wimps," the author wonders if the fact that the majority of librarians are female contributes to this stereotype. She does not develop this thought, however. Instead, she considers ways in which we might change that perception and questions whether we should alter our titles so that people might be more interested in what we do.

7

Information Technology

This chapter covers issues related to gender and information technology; it includes such topics as the impact of opportunities in IT on women in the field, the relationship of gender and information technology issues, and implications for planning and organizing work and learning opportunities.

332. "Center for Women & Information Technology." 3 July 2002. www.umbc.edu/cwit.

Explores the relationship between gender and information technology, encourages more women and girls to study computer science and information systems and to pursue careers in IT. The site also includes links to bibliographic resources about women and technology, videos of CWIT Speakers Series, and curricular resources to further incorporate IT into gender-related courses.

333. "Women in Information Technology." 9 October 2001. www.womeninit.net/index.shtml.

Provides annotated lists of websites about and for women in information technology, computer science, and library and information science. The sites lean heavily toward women in technology and computer science, but there are useful links to gender-related issues. Formerly McDonough's Web-sters' Net-Work.

334. Bacic, Edita. "Partnership with NGO's as a Great Opportunity for Librarians for Promotions of Women's Information Needs in Croatia." In *67th IFLA Council and General Conference: August 16–25, 2001*. IFLA, 1–4. IFLA, 2001.

Bacic explores the role the women's nongovernmental organizations had in raising awareness of women's information needs within librarianship in

Croatia. She also discusses the history behind women's advocacy for access to education and voting rights and how women's organizations now play a key role in creating democracy in Croatia. Bacic offers three examples of developing and implementing plans to help women with their information needs: creating small libraries or information centers in refugee camps expressly for women, establishing the Women's College in Zagreb and Split, and establishing the Women's Information Center in Split. The Internet is a key element in Bacic's exploration of fulfilling women's information needs, and she also discusses the need to raise awareness among women in librarianship and information science.

335. Booth, H. Austin. "Women, Gender, and Cyberculture." ***Choice*** **37, no. 11/12 (July 2000–31 August 2000): 1917–29.**

This bibliographic essay explores the literature on women and cyberculture in the last few decades. Although advances in science and technology have the potential for transforming women's lives and opening up new opportunities, this has not become the reality for women across the globe. The perpetuation of social hierarchies and devaluing women's skills and approaches to knowledge continue to limit women in the economic and sociopolitical spheres. The literature suggests a lack of progress in some arenas, but technology is being used in exciting ways to create new identities and cultures. In many ways, the interconnectivity of the Internet is more conducive for women's communication styles and creativity. However, the prevalence of sexism and harassment on the Internet undermines notions that women can escape societal ills in the digital world. Advances in reproductive technologies are beginning to fundamentally change the understanding in reproduction and of women's relationship with their bodies and the fetus. In the educational sphere, girls continue to lack role models and the means to access computers and educational software, thus perpetuating the "technological divide" between girls and boys. Women's cyberfiction challenges the male dominance of the science fiction genre and explores issues of gender and subjectivity. References.

336. Cottrell, J. R. "Ethics in an Age of Changing Technology: Familiar Territory or New Frontiers?" ***Library Hi-Tech*** **17, no. 1 (1999): 107–13.**

The author devotes one section of the article to gender bias and technology. As technology becomes more prevalent in the field of librarianship, a historically female profession, more men are entering the profession. Some research suggests that men are overrepresented in high-tech areas of librarianship while women remain in more traditional roles. The author questions whether action needs to be taken to ensure equal representation of both genders in all areas of the library.

337. Duncan, Moira. "From Hairnet to Internet." ***Library Association Record*** **101, no. 10 (October 1999): 578–79.**

Despite the title, this article does not address gender in its analysis of the recent history of workplace libraries (also known as special libraries). Since information has become "hot and glamorous," librarians' profiles have risen within the organizations they serve. Marketing is a key role for librarians in their new work as information managers. Case studies of librarians (all female) in an engineering firm, a law office, and a trade association provide evidence of changing roles and wider responsibilities for core technology-supported services such as knowledge management.

338. Eckhouse, John. "Women Lag in IT Salary Race." ***Information Week*** **(1999): 211–16.**

The article reports that disparities in compensation persist for female IT managers and staffers. The gap is showing signs of narrowing for female IT managers whereas female staffers continue to struggle with pay inequities. Female IT managers received a 7 percent pay increase compared to 6.8 percent for males; however, women in staff roles gained only a median 6.7 percent raise rather than the 7.1 percent that their male counterparts received. Women achieve the highest salaries in enterprise resource planning, security, and application development. The Internet is also a lucrative career path for both women managers and staffers. The article also examines similarities and differences between men and women in work satisfaction and expectations.

339. Fidishun, Dolores. "Listening to Our Side: Computer Training Issues of Middle-Age and Older Women." ***Women's Studies Quarterly*** **XXIX, no. 3/4 (Fall 2001–Winter 2001): 103–25.**

Presents qualitative research on the factors that encourage or block older women's acceptance and retention of computer training. Twelve women, librarians and paraprofessionals, were interviewed to obtain background information on each and to elicit their attitudes toward computers and computer training. Most valued the help of a mentor, trainer, or colleague who would answer questions in language they understood. They recognized the need to feel capable of using technology, but attitudes toward the place of computers differed depending on whether the woman saw library work as people serving or information providing. To a great extent, a woman's success at learning technology on her own related to her previous life experiences: whether she had led a very traditional life or had become more self-reliant following divorce, widowhood, or raising children on her own.

340. Fidishun, Dolores. "People Servers vs. Information Providers: the Impact of Service Orientation on Technology Training." ***Information Technology and Libraries*** **20, no. 1 (March 2001): 29–33.**

Reports on a study that examined female library employees' attitudes and issues regarding technology training and learning. The study also examined whether women's attitudes about technology differed from those of male colleagues. The basis for the study was interviews with twelve library employees (librarians and support staff). Feminist standpoint theory was used to value each woman's view of technology. As a result of these interviews two groups were identified: people servers and information providers. Implications and service issues based on these two types of employees are discussed.

341. Gilley, Jennifer. "2002 WSS Program: Women, Technology & Libraries." ***Women's Studies Section Newsletter*** **17, no. 2 (Fall 2002): 3.**

Reports on the 2002 section program at the American Library Association conference in Atlanta, Georgia. The program, a panel discussion, featured Joan Korenman, director of the Center for Women & Information Technology at the University of Maryland, Baltimore County (www.umbc.edu/cwit/). Korenman stressed the need to encourage women to enter information technology fields and to ensure their involvement in creating information technology. The other panelists, who addressed the topic as librarians, were Kelly Hovendick, Syracuse University; Dolores Fidishun, Penn State Great Valley; and Kristin Gerhard, Iowa State University.

342. Harney, Krista. "A Study of the Attitudes of Library and Information Science Students about Censoring Materials on the Web in a Library Environment." Ph.D. diss., Kent State University, 2001.

Evaluates the opinions of library and information science students toward censoring library patrons' access to controversial materials on the World Wide Web. Uses an anonymous questionnaire consisting of questions about an individual's background and various censoring situations in relation to sexually oriented Internet sites. Suggests personal beliefs influenced students' willingness to support filtering within their library, as did factors such as the type of library, gender, and age. Of the eighty respondents to the questionnaire, 63 were female and 17 were male. Concludes no significant differentiation exists between genders, though female respondents favored censoring slightly less than males overall, except in cases involving explicit sexual materials, which females tended to censor more than males. Suggests a stronger correlation exists between the type of library an individual works in and the level of censorship they are willing to support. ERIC Document Reproduction Service No. ED459858, 37 pages.

343. Harris, Roma. "Gender and Technology Relations in Librarianship." ***Journal of Education for Library and Information Science*** **40, no. 4 (Fall 1999): 232–46.**

Posits that the strong cultural and ideological associations between masculinity and technology in Western society make it impossible to consider the social shaping of technology in librarianship without taking into account the gendered nature of library work, and reports the results of a study of the impact of technological change on library work, as the workers perceive it. Findings are based on interviews with seventy-one employees in six major public and academic library systems in Canada and the United States, including twenty-two men and forty-nine women, with thirty-two respondents from public libraries and thirty-seven from academic libraries. Participants were asked about the nature of their work, the integration of new technologies into work activities, the effects of new technologies on their work, and the extent of control they perceived they had in the introduction and use of new technologies. A sense of inevitability about the change process permeated responses. About 30 percent expressed a sense of lack of control in the technological change process; 41 percent of the men as opposed to 14 percent of the women felt they had a significant impact on the process of integrating new technologies into the workplace. Of the respondents, 48 percent predicted that technological change would have a beneficial impact on their careers or those of others, or else were neutral in their responses; 17 percent (73 percent of whom were men) indicated that adapting to technological change was essential for career survival. Another 18 percent believed that technological change would have a negative impact on their own or others' careers; 11 percent thought that technology would have little impact on their careers or were unsure about its impact, and 6 percent suggested that technological change may cause them to pursue careers outside the library setting. Some respondents commented on a perceived lack of respect for core professional knowledge of librarianship on the part of library managers. Experiences of the respondents are similar to those of workers in other sectors in which technologies have had a significant influence on work processes. The author observes that what remains to be seen is the extent to which work roles once performed by a predominantly female library workforce will migrate from the public to private sector, and whether women will find themselves segregated to the bottom of the occupational hierarchy in the new environment. Presented at the 1999 conference, Association for Library and Information Science Education.

344. Harris, Roma. "Squeezing Librarians Out of the Middle: Gender and Technology in a Threatened Profession." In *Women, Work and Computerization: Charting a Course to the Future*, ed. Ellen Balka and Richard Smith, 250–59. Boston: Kluwer Academic Publishers, 2000.

Technological change has profoundly affected librarianship and radically restructured professional roles in a predominantly female workforce. Other occupational groups have moved into the information sector, which was once librarians' sole domain. As a result, librarians are attempting to reshape their identity in order to survive. By renaming job titles and educational programs, the profession is trying to disguise its female identity. As the information workforce shifts from the public sector to the private sector, lower-end clerical positions are automated and women are displaced at all levels. Women librarians are undervalued, "especially those whose work involves the caring functions of direct service to patrons." Gender stereotypes are evident in ads for library technologies: Women are associated with simplicity, ease of use, and routine functions, while men are associated with complexity, leadership, and future progress. These gender divisions are reproduced in the workplace, where expert status vis-à-vis technology is granted primarily to men. Interviews were conducted with staff (twenty-two men and forty-nine women) at all levels in three public library systems and three university library systems in Ontario, Ohio, and Michigan. The interviewees shared their experiences with the introduction of new technologies and the impact of technological change on their careers. Many respondents reported that library administrators and systems experts were out of touch with the realities of the workplace and did not understand the impact of imposing technological changes on employees. Compared to men, women felt that they had less control over decision making and implementation of new technologies. Even at higher organizational levels, male respondents conveyed confidence in their personal power to influence change, while women respondents qualified and contextualized their power. A "we" and "they" dynamic was often invoked to signify a power struggle around technological change. The findings of this study are similar to other researchers' findings that technological change tends to realign jobs in ways that disadvantage women. Although models exist for involving lower-status workers in technological change processes, these were not used in the library systems studied. Technological changes in libraries appear to squeeze professional librarians out of direct service to patrons and push women's work down the labor hierarchy. This is problematic, not only because women librarians have fewer opportunities for rewarding work and good compensation but also because the public no longer benefits from women's work of care. The replacement of free access to information and information literacy training with self-service and fee-based services compromises the ideals that information technology was supposed to achieve. (IFIP TC9 WG9.1 Seventh International Conference on Women, Work and Computerization, June 8–11, 2000, Vancouver, British Columbia, Canada.)

345. Harris, Roma, and Margaret Ann Wilkinson. "(Re)Positioning Librarians: How Young People View the Information Sector." ***Journal of Education for Library and Information Science*** **42, no. 4 (Fall 2001): 289–307.**

The authors report the results of a survey given to two thousand entering students at a large Canadian university about their perceptions of the work roles, future employment prospects, educational requirements, status, and starting salaries of twelve occupations. The occupations were chosen to include traditional professions, occupations practiced predominantly by men or women, and nonprofessional and emerging occupations in the information sector: lawyer, reporter/news correspondent, Internet researcher, paralegal, animator, systems analyst, librarian, database administrator, announcer/newscaster, physical therapist, computer engineer, and medical records technician. The authors discuss the implications of their findings for library and information science education in the context of gender and identity politics.

346. Heimrath, Rosie, and Anne Goulding. "Internet Perception and Use: A Gender Perspective." ***Program*** **35, no. 2 (April 2001): 119–34.**

This article reports on a late-1999 study in the United Kingdom to investigate gender differences in use of the Internet. Data gathering was accomplished by two methods: questionnaires given to students at the Loughborough University's Department of Information Science and users at public libraries in Loughborough and Slough and interviews with both groups. Results reported in the article include patterns and purpose of Internet use, attitudes toward the Internet, confidence in using the Internet, and opinions on gender prejudice and Internet service providers. The study concluded that though women are using the Internet in increasing numbers, gender stereotyping still plays a role in inhibiting access.

347. Hovendick, Kelly. "*Core Lists in Women's Studies: Information Technology*." January 2001. www.library.wisc.edu/libraries/Womens Studies/core/crtech.htm.

Bibliography of English-language books on the topic of gender issues in relation to information technology.

348. Kingston, Michelle, Elizabeth McDermott, and Christopher M. Baggs. "Design and Implementation of the WOMBL (Women in British Libraries) Database Using Access." *Program* 32, no. 1 (January 1998): 55–65.

The WOMBL database, created at the Department of Information and Library Studies at the University of Wales, Aberystwyth, was conceptualized to improve access to information about women and librarianship in the United Kingdom between the years 1877 and 1914. This article captures the design and implementation processes behind the development of the database. Use of the relational database product Microsoft Access is discussed at length, and the authors conclude that their predesign discussions on the goals of the database and the biographical and bibliographical content of the database greatly facilitated the design of the database itself.

349. Mottin-Sylla, Marie-Helene, Jennifer Radloff, and Rebecca Holmes. "African Women Organize for Action in Cyberspace." *Focus on International and Comparative Librarianship* 30, no. 1 (May 1999): 45–46.

A bulletin on the status of African women and their participation with information and communication technologies (ICTs) from 1994 to 1999. Article includes information on Women'sNet, an electronic information, training, and support project for South African women; the Communication pour les Femmes, a program that aims to promote the utilization of electronic communication tools for women's agendas in francophone Africa; and the Gender in Africa Information Network (GAIN), which facilitates the sharing of information and networking on issues of gender justice in Africa.

350. Nath, Vikas. "Empowerment and Governance through Information and Communication Technologies: Women's Perspective." *International Information & Library Review* 33, no. 4 (2001): 317–39.

Places women worldwide within developing knowledge networks, or information and communication technologies. Discusses building such networks, with spaces for women, in order to enhance communication between women. The article includes brief case studies of the use of information to empower women in different parts of the world and illustrates what successful networks might look like. Additionally, the author discusses possible barriers to success, including access, awareness, and linguistic differences. The author recommends intermediary organizations to facilitate and set up prototypes and asks for further macrolevel research to study the impact of growing knowledge networks.

351. Panteli, A., J. Stack, M. Atkinson, and H. Ramsay. "The Status of Women in the UK IT Industry: An Empirical Study." ***European Journal of Information Systems*** **8, no. 3 (September 1999): 170–82.**

The information technology (IT) industry in the United Kingdom is growing faster than in any other European country; however, the number of women in IT has been declining. Using quantitative and qualitative research methods, the authors attempt to answer why women have been underrepresented in the IT industry in the United Kingdom. The authors analyzed the results of the *Computer Weekly* and Institute of Data Processing Management's surveys. Women were represented in all IT specialties, but a higher proportion of women are in administrative and support functions (e.g., help desk). Women in programming or in other technical tracks tend to be assistants or trainees, and only a few move to the position of principal programmer or to a higher technical position. The number of women in managerial positions is also low, and those who do obtain these posts have lower salaries. The authors also used four IT organizations as case studies and found further evidence of gender segregation. Although these organizations have made efforts to recruit women, the male-dominated culture in the workplace and the lack of part-time and flexible work schedules continue to limit women's advancement. The authors recommend that the IT industry expand its career options, develop comprehensive training and development programs that take into account needs of women returning from maternity leave or working from home, and finally, tackle the issue of gender stereotypes in the workplace.

352. Rehman, Sajjad Ur, and Luluwa Ahmad Al-Obaidali. "Internet Use and Capabilities of Library and Information Professionals at the Kuwait University Libraries: Results of a Survey." ***Program*** **34, no. 2 (April 2000): 177–86.**

The authors conducted a study of Internet usage at the Kuwait University Libraries. A questionnaire was administered to gauge the extent of use of the Web, and all participants participated in interviews to gauge training methods and problems with the Internet. The majority of participants in the study were female, were about thirty years of age, had a degree in library and information science, and had been working in public services for six to seven years. The study found that more than half the respondents did not use the communication applications associated with the Internet (newsgroups, FTP), and that librarians working in the science or engineering libraries typically had better Internet skills. Other findings of the study are also discussed.

353. Sierpe, Eino. "Gender and Technological Practice in Electronic Discussion Lists: An Examination of JESSE, the Library/Information Science Education Forum." ***Library and Information Science Research*** **22, no. 3 (2000): 273–89.**

In a study of communications on the Library/Information Science Education Forum (JESSE), the author reports that gender has important implications in the practice of computer-mediated communication. Males tend to participate more and their contributions exceed their proportional representation.

354. Teo, Thompson S. H. "Demographic and Motivation Variables Associated with Internet Usage Activities." ***Internet Research*** **11, no. 2 (2001): 125–37.**

Discusses Internet user behaviors in Singapore using demographic factors (gender, age, and education) and motivational factors (perception of ease of use, enjoyment, and usefulness). Internet use is defined as messaging, browsing, downloading, and purchasing. The author gathered results through a literature review, interviews with sixteen users, and a Web-based and well-publicized questionnaire. Among other conclusions, the research shows that male users make up the majority of users, and that male users tend to use the Internet for downloading and purchasing more than female users. Female users tended to use messaging tools more frequently, however. The article includes tables, the questionnaire, and a bibliography.

355. Turock, Betty J. "Library Media Specialists with a Different Voice." ***Knowledge Quest*** **26, no. 4 (May 1998–30 June 1998): 26–29.**

Reports that from 1994 to 1997, the author, as an officer of the American Library Association in testimonies before federal agencies, learned there is a wide gap between the public perception and the reality of librarians' technological proficiency. Proposes that a feminist perspective can provide insights about librarians' lack of credibility as information-technology experts and also suggests ways to better integrate responsibility for equitable access into the daily management of school library media centers. States that women, who make up the majority of library media specialists, must develop and strengthen their voices of authority and, in order to be effective advocates of equitable access, must be knowledgeable about information technology and networking. Cites the work of Jane Anne Hannigan and Kay Vandergrift as two authors concerned with incorporating the feminist viewpoint into library media services. Suggests that creating an unbiased and gender-balanced atmosphere in the library media center will help develop the voice of authority in students as well as in ourselves. By combining strong voices of authority, school library media specialists can help lead the campaign for just access for all youth, regardless of age, gender, or circumstances.

356. Zoe, Lucinda R., and Diane DiMartino. "Cultural Diversity and End-user Searching: An Analysis by Gender and Language Background." ***Research Strategies*** **17, no. 4 (2000): 291–305.**

Points to the increasing number of foreign students and students from various ethnic groups in American institutions of higher education. Developing innovative instruction models to serve these diverse students is becoming increasingly important. A study on end-user searching using both gender and language variables in analyzing searching success, techniques, and satisfaction is reported. The results indicate that the need for training that takes cultural differences into consideration will become increasingly necessary for students to maximize the use of the wide variety of new information technologies currently available.

8

Leadership and Management

This chapter contains publications covering gender issues in leadership and management, including leadership styles, gender-based differences, characteristics of women leaders, and the effect of leadership practices on women workers in the field, for example.

357. "100 of the Most Important Leaders We Had in the 20th Century." ***American Libraries*** **30, no. 11 (December 1999): 38–46.**

A compilation of the one hundred most important leaders in the profession of librarianship in the twentieth century, as determined by writers at *American Libraries*. Includes profiles of a number of influential female librarians.

358. "Directors Find Running Two Libraries Challenging, Rewarding." ***Footnotes: The Official Newsletter of the State Library of Iowa*** **22, no. 11 (November 1998): 1–2.**

Briefly discusses the work of Linda Adams and Carol French Johnson, both of whom are directors of Iowa public libraries.

359. Ariel, Joan. "Women Moving Mountains: Women and Organizations." ***Women's Studies Section Newsletter*** **16, no. 2 (Fall 2001): 3–4.**

Reports on the 2001 annual section program at the American Library Association meeting held in San Francisco. Kathryn Deiss, Chicago Public Library, spoke on women and organizations, reviewing research and discussing both successes and barriers for women within organizations and their cultures. The author highlights Deiss's challenge to attendees to return to their workplaces and ask what they would change about their workplace cultures to transform their organizations.

360. Barksdale-Hall, Roland C. "Navigating the New Leadership Frontier: African American Librarians and Service in the 21st Century." ***Urban Library Journal*** **11, no. 1 (Spring 2002): 47–60.**

Subscribers to the African American Studies and Librarianship electronic discussion list (AFAS-L) were surveyed. Although the author did not target women, women constituted 96.6 percent of the respondents (N = 30). The survey gathered data on leadership competencies and volunteer service. Nearly all the respondents were African Americans and represented a variety of types of libraries and positions. Most reported participation in professional associations or community service organizations and cited many benefits from their involvement. The author finds, among other conclusions, that "minority librarians lack a sense of empowerment" and that "minority librarians must continue to develop leadership skills."

361. Dasgupta, Kalpana. "Women as Managers of Libraries: a Developmental Process in India." ***IFLA Journal*** **24, no. 4 (July 1998): 245–249.**

Summarizes the history and current status of women librarians in India. Prior to 1975 there were few women in the profession, and men still outnumber women today. Women enter librarianship because the field is viewed as consistent with stereotypical expectations for women in Indian society. Women are clustered in certain sub-fields (children's, school, and academic libraries) and rarely rise to decision-making positions. Several cultural and psychological factors contribute to gender disparities, including women's lack of mobility, their focus on the family, the stigma of careerism, and a lack of training opportunities. The Indian situation has some redeeming features, e.g., women and men who hold similar posts are paid equally. Trends in library management that will affect women include the growing need for information technology skills; the value of women's "understanding, patience and sincerity" as libraries become less hierarchical; and the difficulty both women and men have accepting women as leaders. Despite the barriers, the number of women library managers has increased in the past two decades. The author (herself an exceptional, high-ranking librarian) recommends several approaches to improve the recruitment, retention, and promotion of women.

362. Evans, G. Edward, Patricia Layzell Ward, and Bendik Rugaas. ***Management Basics for Information Professionals*****. New York: Neal-Schuman, 2000.**

This comprehensive textbook on library management updates the 1983 edition (*Management Techniques for Librarians,* 2nd ed., by G. Edward

Evans) and adds a bit more information related to women's status. In chapter 2, "History of Library and Information Service Management Concepts," several paragraphs address the predominance of women in the "semiprofessions." Salaries are low compared to fields that require similar qualifications but are predominately male. Male librarians historically had higher average salaries than female librarians. An "attitudinal problem" still exists in terms of library management, although in the United States the proportion of women to men directors more closely matches the makeup of the field today. In chapter 13, "Leadership," a short section is titled "Do gender differences matter in leadership?" While studies looking for gender differences in leadership styles have reached contradictory conclusions, a meta-analysis of such studies revealed only minor, insignificant differences. In a box labeled "For Further Thought . . . ," the authors ask: "Do you agree or disagree that gender differences matter in leadership? Make a list of four points to justify your view."

363. Evans, Margaret Kinnell. "Managerialism and Women's Roles: Femaleness in Public Service Organizations from 1945 to the Present." In *Gendering Library History,* eds. Evelyn Kerslake and Nickianne Moody, 82–94. Liverpool, England: John Moores University Association for Research in Popular Fictions: Media Critical and Creative Arts, 2000.

Evans discusses her study of women's roles from post World War II to the present in administration and management in a number of professions, including library and information science. She brings in data and legislative information not only from Britain but also from the United States and the European Union, and also brings in organizational structure and culture as a factor in women's success. She concludes by presenting a list of key cultural changes that must occur to ensure women's continued progress in the the management arena.

364. Golian, Linda Marie. "Thinking Style Differences Among Academic Librarians." Ph.D. diss, Florida Atlantic University, 1998.

Investigates whether differences in thinking styles exist among senior-level library administrators working in libraries with institutional memberships in the Association of Research Libraries (ARL). Nationwide distribution of a survey consisting of an Inquiry Mode Questionnaire and a demographic data form yielded an 80.3 percent (106) return rate, with a total of 97 surveys used for data analysis. Includes five analyses of variance to determine relationships between thinking styles and administrative role (public or technical), gender, and thinking style preference (synthesist, idealist, pragmatist, analyst, or realist). The analysis reveals that female library administrators were more likely to be idealist thinkers than men, who tended to be pragmatist and idealist thinkers. Findings of the study suggest the respondents exhibited a predilection towards the flat thinking style; a relationship exists between gender and thinking style; a relationship exists between the area of administrative responsibility and thinking style; a difference exists among administrative peers in the same institution with regards to preferred thinking styles; and that there exists a strong need for aggressive recruitment and diversity efforts for the library profession. 270 pages.

365. Hernon, Peter, Ronald R. Powell, and Arthur P. Young. "University Library Directors in the Association of Research Libraries: the Next Generation, Part Two." ***College & Research Libraries*** **63, no. 1 (January 2002): 73–90.**

The literature review section of this article touches briefly on gender styles of library directors. Specifically, women directors were perceived to lead with charisma, inspiration, and intellectual stimulation.

366. Holley, Edward G. "Librarianship and Scholarship through Five Decades: A Personal View (Beta Phi Mu's 50th Anniversary Speech delivered June 28, 1998). www.beta-phi-mu.org/paper.html.

Dr. Holley's speech on librarianship includes a section on women in librarianship and specifically emphasizes women as library directors and scholars. He also mentions several books written by women librarians, most of which were published the 1970s and 1980s.

367. Lary, Marilyn. "Mentoring: A Gift for Professional Growth." ***Southeastern Librarian*** **47, no. 4 (1998): 23–25.**

A piece that explores the evolution and meaning of mentoring with discussions of the responsibilities and pitfalls of mentoring as well as the development of a mentor and the role of gender in the mentoring process. The author suggests that women have a tendency to defer to men in positions of authority whether or not that deference has been earned. As a result, the sex of a mentor is particularly significant to the mentee.

368. Maxwell Kalikow, Nancy. "Lunchroom Loneliness." ***American Libraries*** **32, no. 1 (January 2001): 54.**

Briefly describes the change in working relationships that occurred when being promoted to library director. States that some women may be reluctant to be promoted to supervisory positions for fear of changing relationships with co-workers and the stigma attached to being "the Boss." Promotes a less hierarchical and rigid workplace structure.

369. McElrath, Rebecca Eileen. "Perceptions Held by Academic Library Directors and Chief Academic Officers about Challenges Experienced by Current Academic Library Directors as an Indication of Cognitive Dissonance." Ph.D. diss., Florida State University, 1999.

Compares the perceptions of academic library directors and their chief academic officers with regard to current challenges in librarianship. While concerned primarily with whether differing perspectives were indications of the presence of cognitive dissonance, the study also considered the respondents' age, gender, and length of employment. A mail survey was sent to 118 academic library directors and chief academic officers from institutions located in the southern region of the American Association of Public Colleges. The respondents' perceptions about user satisfaction were alike, as was their identification that serials posed a great challenge to library service. Concludes that the study's criteria to establish the presence of cognitive dissonance failed to prove its existence.

370. Murgai, Sarla R. "Motivation to Manage: A Comparative Study of Male and Female Library & Information Science Students in the United States of America, India, Singapore, & Japan." ***IFLA Council and General Conference. Conference Programme and Proceedings (65th, Bangkok, Thailand, August 20–28, 1999)*** **(August 1999): 24.**

Compares the managerial motivations of library and information science (LIS) students in the United States with LIS students in India, Singapore, and Japan. Provides a comprehensive overview of the status of women in each of the countries involved in the study, which includes 665 student respondents from 11 Southeastern universities in the United States; 814 students from 23 universities in India; 73 students from Singapore; and 3 students from Japan. Uses a questionnaire consisting of forty-one statements divided into ten categories: task orientation, fear of success, perseverance, reaction to success/failure, future orientation, competitiveness, independence, rigidity, social needs, and acceptance of women as managers. Draws further comparisons based on educational attainment, age, marital status, and mobility. Determines a majority of the respondents were highly educated, persevering, competitive, and achievement or future oriented. Concludes similarities exist between countries and by sexes in the areas of "task orientation," "perseverance," "future orientation," and "competitiveness," but uncovers differences between the sexes with regard to factors such as "women as managers," "reaction to success or failure," "fear of failure, " and "social acceptance."

371. Neely, Teresa Y., and Mark D. Winston. "Snowbird Leadership Institute: Leadership Development in the Profession." ***College and Research Libraries*** **60, no. 5 (September 1999): 412–425.**

Study addresses impact of participation in the Snowbird Leadership program on career development and leadership. Gender is a minor variable in the data.

372. O'Keeffe, Julie. "Small College Library Directors: Getting in the Door and Surviving on the Job." ***College and Research Libraries*** **59, no. 2 (March 1998): 140–153.**

Reports results of a 1996 survey of library directors at four-year colleges in the Midwestern United States that attempted to assess job preparedness. Gender was a factor in the study, which examined work experience, publication records, and involvement in professional organizations. Per the study, men were more qualified than women, had more years of experience, more administrative experience, published more, and held more officer or committee positions in professional library organizations.

373. Turock, Betty J. "Women and Leadership." ***Journal of Library Administration*** **32, no. 3/4 (2001): 111–131.**

This lengthy article focuses on women librarians and leadership. While statistics show that women increasingly continue to occupy leadership positions and achieve salary parity, discrimination and bias remain prevalent in the profession. A goal of the article is to "develop more inclusive patterns for leadership that will provide new understandings and directions for the future." Section headings of the article are as follows: The feminist perspective; womanless leadership; women as anomalies or problems in leadership; women as leaders; Helgesen and the web of inclusion; and leadership redefined or reconstructed. In the conclusion the author states that qualities often possessed by women (such as caretaking tendencies, intuition, emotional intelligence, and relationship-building skills) offer an important balance to leadership in libraries and create a synergy with the leadership qualities of male counterparts. While great strides have been made on the status women in librarianship, the author stresses that the need for continued advocacy for equity remains.

9

Library Associations

This chapter encompasses publications detailing the current and past activities of library organizations and associations and the impact of these activities on women in the field. For publications focusing on particular individuals within an organization, refer to the "Biography and Autobiography" chapter for information on contemporary women and to the "Library History" chapter for women from the past.

374. "ALA Urges Support for Equal Pay Day." ***Library Hotline*** **29, no. 18 (2000): 4.**

Announces Equal Pay Day, taking place on May 11, 2000. This day encourages actions that would help close the wage gap between men's and women's salaries, especially in professions considered to be "women's professions," such as librarianship.

375. "ALISE Announces 2001 Award Winners." ***Library Journal Academic News Wire*** **(12 December 2000).**

Announces winners from the Awards Committee for ALISE (Association for Library and Information Science Education) for the year 2001. ALISE is an independent nonprofit organization that provides a forum for library educators. ALISE presented the awards at their annual ALISE Conference in January. Shirley Fitzgibbons of Indiana University was awarded the Service Award for Outstanding Contributions to the Association. Jane Robbins at Florida State University won the award for Professional Contribution to Library and Information Science Education. Kay Vandergrift of Rutgers University was designated winner of the award for Teaching Excellence. Norman Horrocks chaired the awards committee.

376. "ARL Welcomes the 2001–02 Leadership and Career Development Program Participants." ***ARL Newsletter*, no. 217 (August 2001).**

Describes the program and lists participants and their projects.

377. "COSWL: Committee on the Status of Women in Librarianship." 9 January 2001. www.ala.org/coswl.

Explains that the mission of COSWL is to represent women's interests in ALA and to ensure that ALA considers the rights of women in the library profession. COSWL also concerns itself with collecting and disseminating information on the status of women in librarianship and on enhancing opportunities for women in the field. There are links to an action list, members, subcommittees/task forces (including the bibliography task force that compiles *On Account of Sex*), minutes, and general Internet sites for professional women.

378. "The Feminist Task Force." 4 December 2000. www.lib.wayne.edu/ftf.

The Feminist Task Force's (FTF) home page describes the history, purpose, and activities of the group. There are also links to feminist research in librarianship, past issues of FTF's *Women in Libraries* newsletter, *The Feminist* discussion list, information on how to get involved in the organization, a form to join the S.H.A.R.E. (Sisters Have Access to Resources Everywhere) directory, and general Internet resources on feminism.

379. "Feminist Task Force Celebrates 30th Year Anniversary, Tackles Issues, and Raises Consciousness within ALA." ***Women in Libraries*** **28, no. 2–3 (Spring 2000–Summer 2000): 14–15.**

Briefly traces the history of the Feminist Task Force, through quotes from *Women in Libraries*, from the 1970 formation of SRRT's Task Force on the Status of Women in Libraries to the first author breakfast in 1992.

380. "*Human Resource Development Liaisoned Committees: Committee on Pay Equity*." 7 August 2001. www.ala.org/hrdr/cpe.html.

Gives a history of the committee's establishment in 1986 and its charge to promote and advocate pay equity for library workers, act as a resource on this issue for ALA, support involvement of the committee in the National Committee on Pay Equity, and maintain a database of resources available to state and local groups. Also lists contact information for all committee members and links to other HRDR sites.

381. "Iowa Library Association Foundation Board—A Mix of Experience." ***Catalyst*** **53, no. 3 (1999): 6.**

Provides brief biographies of board members, including ten women, serving on the Iowa Library Association board and working in libraries statewide.

382. "Johnston Elected Vice President/President-Elect of American Association of Law Libraries." ***ILA Reporter*** **20, no. 3 (June 2002): 22.**

Janis L. Johnston, director of the law library at the University of Illinois, Urbana-Champaign, was elected to lead the American Association of Law Libraries. Johnson served as director of the Marion County Law Library in Indianapolis and as rural development coordinator for the Indian Institute of Cultural Affairs before joining the library faculty at Indiana University in 1982. From 1987 to 1999, she was associate director of the law library at Notre Dame and also served in various administrative posts in the law school. She joined the Illinois faculty in 1999. Johnson has been active in regional and national law library associations.

383. "Kay Raseroka Wins Presidential Election." ***IFLA Journal*** **27, no. 4 (2001): 273.**

Members of the International Federation of Library Associations and Institutions elected Kay Raseroka for a two-year term as president-elect (2001–2003) followed by a two-year term as president (2003–2005). Raseroka was born in Kwazulu-Natal in South Africa and is now a citizen of Botswana, where she directs the University of Botswana library services. She has been an active member of IFLA in many capacities, including serving on its executive board since 1997.

384. "LAMA Women Administrators Discussion Group." 5 December 2001. www.ala.org/lama/committees/div/wadmin.html.

Provides a forum for discussing problems and issues of women in library administration. Also gives contact information for the chair of the group and has links to all other LAMA sites.

385. "Minutes of the Executive Board." ***North Carolina Libraries*** **56, no. 2 (Summer 1998): 87.**

Report on a workshop planned for early spring 1999 titled "Motivation, Satisfaction and Commitment in the Library," to be led by Dr. Richard Rubin. Brief note regarding Ms. Management, a valuable resource for interviews with women leaders, and features on the status of women in librarianship.

386. "Minutes of the Executive Board." ***North Carolina Libraries*** **56, no. 4 (Winter 1998): 166–70.**

Report on the activities of the Executive Board of the North Carolina Library Association (NCLA), including the Round Table on the Status of Women in Librarianship. The Round Table reported that they will contribute $100 to the NCLA Leadership Institute fund and that plans for their program for the 1999 NCLA Conferençe have been developed.

387. "Nancy Kranich Wins ALA Presidency." *American Libraries* 30, no. 6 (June 1999–31 July 1999): 8–9.

In the recent ALA election, Nancy Kranich defeated C. James Schmidt by 64 percent to serve as the 1999–2000 president-elect and to assume the presidency at the close of the ALA Annual Conference in 2000. Kranich, associate dean of the New York Universities Libraries, is chair of the ALA's Committee on Legislation and has served on the ALA Executive Board and Council.

388. "New IFLA President is Prominent ILL Figure." *Interlending and Document Supply* 26, no. 2 (1998): 98.

Christine Deschamps of the Bibliotheque de l'Universite Paris V Rene Descartes in Paris, France, was elected president of IFLA in August 1997. Deschamps was active in IFLA as well as a member of the editorial advisory board of *Interlending and Document Supply*. The French government and Ministry of Higher Education and Research recognized Deschamps for her achievement by releasing her from her work responsibilities in France and creating a special job position that allowed her to focus on her IFLA presidency.

389. "New SLA Executive Director." *IFLA Journal* 27, no. 3 (2001): 195.

Roberta Shaffer became the executive director of the Special Libraries Association in September 2001. Shaffer was the dean of the Graduate School of Library and Information Science at the University of Texas at Austin from 1999 to 2001. Previously she directed research and information services at an international law firm in Washington, D.C., and coordinated the law libraries program at the Catholic University School of Library and Information Science. At the time of this announcement, she was vice president of the International Association of Law Librarians.

390. "Paula T. Kaufman Elected ARL President." *ILA Reporter* 20, no. 1 (February 2002): 14.

Paula T. Kaufman, university librarian and professor of library administration at the University of Illinois, Urbana-Champaign, was elected president of the Association of Research Libraries (ARL) in fall 2001. She chairs ARL's Copyright Working Group and is a former chair of its Information Policy Committee.

391. "Paula T. Kaufman Elected ARL Vice President/President-Elect." ***ILA Reporter*** **19, no. 1 (February 2001): 23.**

Paula T. Kaufman, university librarian and professor of library administration at the University of Illinois, Urbana-Champaign, was elected vice president/president-elect of the Association of Research Libraries. Her term begins in October 2001. Kaufman has directed the library at the University of Illinois, Urbana-Champaign, since 1999. Prior to that, she was dean of libraries at the University of Tennessee, Knoxville, for eleven years. She also held several positions at Columbia University and at an information industry service firm, which she cofounded. Kaufman has served on the boards of the Center for Research Libraries, the Research Libraries Group, and the Southeastern Library Network, Inc. (SOLINET). She chairs the Directors Group of the Committee on Institutional Cooperation, the academic consortium of the Big Ten universities. She has written and spoken on issues such as scholarly communication, privacy, and leadership.

392. "Presidential Candidates Concur at Midwinter Forum: Salaries, Recruitment, and Children's Services Are Crucial Issues." ***American Libraries*** **32, no. 3 (March 2001): 61–64.**

This is an interview with three presidential candidates for the American Library Association. Leonard Kniffel, *AL* editor and publisher, interviewed Ken Haycock, professor and director of the School of Library, Archival and Information Studies at the University of British Columbia in Vancouver; William Sannwald, assistant to the city manager, library design and development manager, for the city of San Diego; and Maurice Freedman, director of the Westchester Library System in Ardsley, New York. The candidates address different issues facing librarians including low salaries as a result of the female predominance of the profession.

393. "Round Table for Women's Issues." 15 October 2001. www.ifla.org/VII/rt14/rtwi.htm.

Home page covers the scope and goals of IFLA's Round Table for Women's Issues, which concerns itself with issues that have particular relevance for women in the library profession and in the user community. RTWI also promotes research, publication, and dissemination of information on the status of women in librarianship and works to identify discrimination and disparities in resources and opportunities for women in the library profession. There are also links to past issues of its newsletter, *Women and Librarianship*, minutes of meetings, medium-term and annual reports, and contact information for officers.

394. "Sarah Ann Long Elected ALA President." ***Illinois Library Association Reporter*** **16, no. 3 (June 1998): 13.**

Announces the election of Sarah Ann Long, director of the North Suburban Library System in Wheeling, Illinois, as president of the American Library Association for the 1999–2000 term and summarizes her career.

395. "South African Library Group Names First Leader." ***Library Journal Academic News Wire*** **(12 December 2000).**

Gwenda Thomas has been named by the Library and Information Association of South Africa (LIASA) to serve as its first executive director, a position funded in part by the Carnegie Corporation of New York. Her term of appointment began January 1, 2001 and ran through December 31, 2003. LIASA was formed in 1997 and unified all previously existing library organizations throughout South Africa. A number of interest groups represent the 1700 members' interests, and a conference is held annually. Thomas began her career at the University of South Africa as a reference librarian, becoming assistant director of reference and then being appointed as head of research and development. She also served as project leader for the library's 1999 reengineering project. Professionally, she had been active in the South African Institute for Librarianship and Information Science (SAILIS) before it became part of LIASA. She has also published and spoken extensively on such subjects as user satisfaction and marketing.

396. "What's In a Name? Association of Assistant Librarians Changes Name to Career Development Group." ***Library Association Record*** **100, no. 1 (January 1998): 36–37.**

The Association of Assistant Librarians, a division of the Library Association of Great Britain, changed its name to the Career Development Group. The new name for the 102-year-old organization reflects the fact that few positions today carry the title "assistant librarian." In addition to an array of activities aimed at librarians in "first- and second-level posts," the Career Development Group will continue "to campaign on a range of key issues, including . . . equal access for women and Black library and information workers."

397. "Wisconsin Women Library Workers Home Page." 10 November 1999. http://danenet.danenet.org/wwlw.

WWLW is a feminist organization that works to improve the status of women in the library field and to eliminate stereotyping and sex bias. The website includes the organization's goals and links to steering committee members with contact information, newsletter contents, calendar of events, e-mail lists, and more.

398. Adams, Megan. "Women's Organizations in ALA." ***Women's Studies Section Newsletter*** **14, no. 2 (Fall 1998): 3.**

Summarizes the scope of women's organizations in the American Library Association. The organizations highlighted include the Feminist Task Force, the Committee on the Status of Women in Librarianship, and the Library Administration and Management Association's Women Administrators Discussion Group.

399. Attle, S. "Equal Opportunities and Being a Christian Librarian: Is There a Conflict?" ***Librarians' Christian Fellowship Newsletter,*** **no. 76 (Winter 2000): 32–35.**

This brief article details the author's position as honorary equal opportunities officer (HEOO) of the Career Development Group, a librarians' association in England, and also her views on being a librarian and a Christian. Attle describes the HEOO's work to encourage and advise on equal opportunity matters on a national level as well as meeting with representatives of groups such as the African Caribbean Library Association, Asian Librarians and Advisers Group, and the Burning Issues Group (a gay/lesbian librarians group) as a member of the Equal Opportunities Sub-Committee. The second part of the article deals specifically with the tension between being a Christian and a librarian, and Attle focuses specifically on Part IV, Section 28 of the United Kingdom's Local Government Act, which prohibits "promoting homosexuality by teaching or by publishing material." Attle discusses how this law is interpreted and how librarians in particular must reconcile themselves with their roles as librarians, Christians, and educators in order to function in a professional manner.

400. Flowers, D., and B. McKee. "Ask Bob McKee." ***Impact, the Journal of the Career Development Group*** **3, no. 10 (November 2000–31 December 2000): 157–59.**

Minutes of the open meeting of the North and South Thames Division of the Career Development Group on September 21, 2000. Liz Jolly, the president of the Career Development Group, raises the issue that the Library Association (LA) is 78 percent female, but male representation on the Council is over 22 percent. As there are more women in the association, a greater number should run in elections and get elected.

401. Fuller, Howard. "SLA Caucuses: Creation, Purpose and the GLIC." *Information Outlook* 5, no. 4 (April 2001): 47.

Howard Fuller interviews Didi Pancake, past SLA president, and Richard Hulser, past division cabinet chair on the SLA Board of Directors, both of whom were instrumental in SLA caucuses. Pancake, as past president, played a major role in creating caucuses within the SLA structure, and Hulser created the Gay and Lesbian Issues Caucus (GLIC). The purpose of the twelve caucuses within SLA is to give members with a common interest an opportunity to network without the requirements of bylaws, officers, or financial support from SLA. The first caucus within the organization was the Women's Issues Caucus. In 1995, the GLIC was formed to give gay and lesbian members of SLA a chance to come together and discuss issues pertinent to their community such as employment and benefits and library-related issues such as catalog headings. GLIC's first conference program in 1999 in Minneapolis was cosponsored by the Insurance and Employee Benefits Caucus and focused on forming employee groups. The other program sponsored by GLIC that year focused on Library of Congress subject headings.

402. Gabel, Gernot U. "Vom Keller zum Waschhaus: Das neue Domizil der Women's Library in London." *BuB-Forum für Bibliothek und Information* 54, no. 10/11 (2002): 609–11.

Describes the history of the Women's Library from its beginning in 1926, founded by the London Society for Women's Service (LSWS), renamed in the fifties (Fawcett Library), and organizationally combined with the City of London Polytechnic (now London Guildhall University) in 1977. Located in the basement of an old building, the Fawcett Library had suffered several floods and therefore had to close its doors again and again. With an impressive and extremely successful fund-raising campaign, led by Betty Boothroyd, speaker of the House of Commons, a modern, state-of-the-art library was opened in early 2001, run by Antonia Byatt. The library contains a collection of more than 60,000 volumes, 2,400 journals, a women's archive, and a café. The aim is to attract a wider public than in the past using an intensified educational program. English title: *From the Basement to the Washhouse: The New Domicile of the Women's Library in London* (www.thewomenslibrary.ac.uk).

403. Galler, Anne M. "Lise Bissonnette and the Grande Bibliothéque du Québec." *Feliciter* 45, no. 1 (1999): 23, 26.

Summarizes the content of remarks by Lise Bissonnette, director of the Grande bibliothéque du Québec, to the 1998 conference of the Quebec

Library Association. Bissonnette, a journalist and writer and not a librarian, said that she believed her experience as publisher of *Le Devoir*, the French-language Montreal daily, would enable her to successfully work with boards, negotiate with banks, and resolve legal tangles. She saw her role as creating a cultural institution rather than just a building—an institution in which technology would be used to the fullest, but reading and the book would remain central. Galler states that Bissonnette's address and responses to questions demonstrated her interest in libraries, her sympathy toward librarians, and her desire to enhance the public's access to books.

404. Greenblatt, Ellen, and Jerilyn Veldof. "LEZBRIAN." 16 July 2001. www.cudenver.edu/public/library/libq/lezbrian.

LEZBRIAN is the Lesbian and Bisexual Library Workers List, a forum for discussing professional issues and concerns. This list also posts announcements about relevant conferences, job listings, and publications. The listowners also state that they would like this list to serve as a "repository for bibliographies, pathfinders, and other items of interest to queer librarianship." Links are provided to FAQs, Who's Who on LEZBRIAN, other related library sites, and general lesbian and bisexual Internet sites.

405. Hildenbrand, Suzanne, and Mary Biblo. "International Library Women: Identifying Problems, Seeking Solutions." In *Libraries: Global Reach—Local Touch*, ed. Katherine de la Peña McCook, Barbara J. Ford, and Kate Lippincott, 187–94. Chicago, IL: American Library Association, 1998.

This article describes the formation and development of the Round Table on Women's Issues (RTWI) in the International Federation of Library Associations and Institutions. The primary objective of the group is to promote research on the status of women in librarianship and to promote the awareness of women's issues in IFLA. It is noted that many countries of the world are not represented in the membership due to such issues as poverty and cultural differences.

406. Hyams, Elspeth. "Raseroka's Radical Evolution." *Library Association Record* 104, no. 2 (February 2002): 94–95.

Kay Raseroka, from the University of Botswana, is the first librarian from a developing nation to serve as president of the International Federation of Library Associations and Institutions (IFLA). She speaks eloquently of bridging the information gaps between the developed and developing worlds. Raseroka, who studied librarianship through distance learning, first attended an IFLA conference in Munich in 1983. She describes that conference as a "watershed experience" that enlarged her professional networks and extended her intellectual reach. Although her ideals and rhetoric appear revolutionary, Raseroka believes in evolutionary change and working through established organizations. Librarians in the developing world, she asserts, need to lobby politicians to appreciate the important role of information and libraries in socioeconomic improvement. The management of intellectual property and copyright are critical in regards to indigenous knowledge systems, and librarians have a responsibility to collect, organize, preserve, and share traditional knowledge. Librarians must also work to promote and reinforce literacy. Asked if librarians in Botswana enjoy more status and respect than their counterparts in Europe, Raseroka replied, "Librarians have a relatively fair status and respect commensurate with the degree of visibility of their professional contributions to their communities." The advent of information and communication technologies (ICT) in Africa is both an opportunity and a threat. Librarians who lack ICT skills feel insecure and dissatisfied with their status, but there are many opportunities for professional growth. In Raseroka's view, librarians must be involved in politics and the shaping of national information policies. Her vision for IFLA includes both a consultative process based on existing structures (sections, divisions, core activities, etc.) and a think-tank approach that will seek partnerships with businesses and other professional organizations.

407. Jay, M. Ellen, and Drucilla Raines. "AASL President-Elect/President Candidate Statements." ***Knowledge Quest*** **26, no. 2 (January 1998–28 February 1998): 73–74.**

M. Ellen Jay and Drucilla Raines, candidates for president-elect/president of the American Association of School Librarians, present their plans and their views about the AASL's role, focus, and activities. Jay believes that individually and as an association, school librarians should balance the needs of technology and literacy, fuse the outcomes identified in AASL revised standards and other curricular standards, actively participate in education reform projects, and transform training opportunities available to school library media professionals. Raines emphasizes making library media and information literacy programs integral parts of the curriculum in each school and district and reaching the grassroots affiliate members, whether or not they are members of AASL. Raines describes her past experience in school library media programs and in the association.

408. Jones, DeEtta. "ARL Initiative to Recruit a Diverse Workforce." ***ARL Newsletter*****, no. 210 (June 2000).**

Highlights the components for this ARL initiative and lists all participating ARL libraries.

409. Jones, DeEtta. "ARL Leadership and Career Development Program." *ARL Newsletter*, no. 202 (February 1999).

The pilot experience of ARL's Leadership and Career Development (LCD) Program was completed in July 1998. The components of the LCD Program consisted of institutes, mentoring relationships, and research projects. The LCD Program has become an ongoing operation of the Diversity Program and will be offered biannually.

410. Jones, DeEtta. "ARL Welcomes the Leadership and Career Development Program Class of 2000." *ARL Newsletter*, no. 205 (August 1999).

Lists the seventeen librarians, along with their research project topics and mentors for 1999–2000. In addition to taking on leadership positions, the librarians are involved in mentoring the ALA Spectrum Scholars, working to design and deliver the Spectrum Leadership Institute, presenting at national and international library and higher education conferences, and publishing their research projects in professional journals and as book chapters.

411. Jones, DeEtta. "Diversity." *ARL Newsletter*, no. 223 (August 2002).

Announces the 2002 stipend recipients for the ARL Initiative to Recruit a Diverse Workforce. Also reports on the successful completion of the ARL Leadership and Career Development (LCD) Program of 2001–2002.

412. Jones, DeEtta. "Millennial Leadership and Career Development Program Comes to a Successful Close." *ARL Newsletter*, no. 211 (August 2000): 15.

With the support of ARL member leaders as mentors, and encouragement from colleagues and administrators at their home institutions, sixteen librarians of color completed the Millennial LCD Program. Article lists participants and mentors.

413. Kelley, H. Neil. "Portrait of the Illinois Trustee Community." *Illinois Libraries* 81, no. 4 (Fall 1999): 222–25.

Reports on a survey of trustees of public libraries in Illinois. Seventy percent are women and 30 percent are men. Most trustees work during the week, making it difficult for the State Library to schedule continuing education programs for trustees. Extrapolating from the sample, the authors report that volunteer trustees donate more than a quarter of a million hours a year to Illinois libraries.

414. Kerslake, Evelyn. "Not Only Suitable, But Specially Attractive." ***Library Association Record*** **101, no. 1 (January 1999): 32–34.**

On the occasion of the hundredth anniversary of the publication of the *Library Association Record*, Kerslake reviews the representation of women in its pages. Women were the majority of Britain's library workforce by 1923 to 1924 and approximately 70 percent by the 1960s. Women in libraries were poorly paid, compared both to male library workers and to women in other professions. In some sectors such as county libraries, however, women held senior posts in similar numbers to men. Throughout the century, the *Record* featured announcements of (and occasional disputes over) women's firsts in libraries. During both World Wars, articles appeared that noted the predominance of women in British librarianship. In 1948, A. G. S. Enser published two incendiary articles in the *Record* in which he alleged that the library workforce was "grossly over-feminized" because women outnumbered men six to one. The predominance of women in the library workforce was assumed to be the cause of the profession's low salaries. In 1940, Rena Cowper urged women librarians to fight against sex discrimination. Yet in 1946 the Library Association's statement to the Royal Commission on Equal Pay reiterated that women were best suited to work with children and men to assume senior posts. The Equal Pay Act of 1970 did not make a noticeable difference, according to a 1978 article by Liz Chapman. Prior to the 1960s, writers often explained that the cause of women's lower pay was their tendency to resign upon marriage. Some unmarried female librarians who stuck with the profession did achieve senior positions. In 1962, W. S. Haugh argued that more men were needed in the profession because librarianship was "facing a society without spinsters." By the late sixties, the letters column featured married former librarians lamenting over the lack of part-time work, under the headline "Library Work for Housewives." Gradually, shifts in the labor market brought more married women into the library workforce. In a special 1985 issue of the *Record* devoted to women, Elaine Kempson showed how the demographics had shifted: No longer were the majority of women librarians under the age of thirty. In the 1990s, articles appeared on topics such as the glass ceiling and the impact on women of taking "career breaks." Kerslake concludes that the *Record*, despite occasional articles and letters, was "determinedly unaware of gender" in the twentieth century. It was not as blatantly sexist as other UK library journals during this period, but it still underplayed issues important to the profession's female members.

415. Kinnaly, Gene. "Pay Equity, Support Staff, and ALA." ***Library Mosaics*** **13, no. 2 (March 2002–30 April 2002): 8–10.**

The fact that library jobs are filled primarily by women has had a negative impact on wages. Since library support staff are generally the lowest paid group among library workers, pay equity issues are of particular concern to them. Author reports on the formation and initial work of the ALA Better Salaries and Pay Equity Task Force.

416. Kranich, Nancy, and C. James Schmidt. "Meet the Candidates for ALA President: Vote in the Election This Spring." ***College & Research Libraries News*** **60, no. 3 (March 1999): 185–88.**

Nancy Kranich and C. James Schmidt, candidates for president of the American Library Association, respond to questions posed by the board of directors of the Association for College and Research Libraries. Nancy Kranich states that, if elected, she will focus on defense of the First Amendment and fair use rights and on reduction of financial, educational, and linguistic barriers to information access. Kranich also comments on the roles of ALA divisions, opportunities offered by technology for distance participation in ALA, representation of library issues to government and press, and the future of libraries and librarianship.

417. Love-Rodgers, C. "Chartership Support Page—Mentoring: What's In It for Me?" ***Impact, the Journal of the Career Development Group*** **3, no. 10 (November 2000–31 December 2000): 160–61.**

The article advocates the mentoring program, Route B Chartership, developed by the Library Association of the United Kingdom, and examines the elements of effective mentoring, both for the mentor (supporter) and the mentee (learner). The article discusses how developing professional networks are also opportunities for mentoring.

418. Lynch, Mary Jo. "Librarians' Salaries: A New Approach." ***American Libraries*** **30, no. 9 (October 1999): 66.**

This article describes recent changes in the formatting of and categorization in the annual 1999 *ALA Annual Survey of Librarian Salaries*. The ALA Committee on the Status of Women in Librarianship requested that the survey collect data on the gender of directors. This information was collected and will be published in a planned separate article on librarian demographics.

419. Pors, Niels Ole. "Perceptions of the Quality of the IFLA Conference in Boston." ***IFLA Journal*** **28, no. 1 (2002): 11–16.**

This article evaluates the 2001 conference of the International Federation of Library Associations and Institutions (IFLA) by analyzing data from questionnaires completed by delegates. Gender is examined as a demographic variable. Female respondents outnumbered male respondents overall. A cross-tabulation of gender with occupation shows that a higher percentage of females identified themselves as "librarians" or "educators," while a higher percentage of males identified themselves as "library directors." There was no meaningful difference in respondents' age by gender. On evaluative factors, there were no differences by gender, age, or occupation, but perceptions of the conference's quality differed markedly by nationality and by how many IFLA conferences the respondents had attended previously. Overall the attendees were highly satisfied with most aspects of the 2001 conference.

420. Pors, Niels Ole. "Perceptions of the Quality of the IFLA Conference in Glasgow." ***IFLA Journal*** **28, no. 5/6 (2002): 328–33.**

Only 10 percent of the participants in the 2002 annual conference of the International Federation of Library Associations and Institutions (IFLA) returned evaluation questionnaires. This report presents demographic factors and composite factors relating to satisfaction with the conference. Women constituted a majority of the sample. Among the men who responded, 27 percent were library directors and 47 percent were librarians. Among the women, 20 percent were directors and 58 percent were librarians. The average age was forty-eight years; there was no difference in age by gender. As in past years, participants from the United Kingdom, United States, Scandinavia, and Western Europe predominated. Perceptions of the quality of the conference did not differ by gender or age, but statistically significant differences by nationality were found.

421. Rabago, Ginny, and Martha Parsons. "Twenty-Five Years of CLEWS/WALE." ***Alki: The Washington Library Association Journal*** **15, no. 1 (March 1999): 18–19.**

Traces the history of the Washington Association of Library Employees (WALE) from its initial organization in 1973 as Classified Library Employees of Washington State (CLEWS), to its silver anniversary at the seventh WALE conference, October 1998. Identifies CLEWS and WALE presidents, all of whom up to 1999 have been women. Includes comments by past WALE chairs and Donna Jones, Pat Kennedy, and Ruth Poynter as well as statements from past and current presidents of the Washington Library Association and others.

422. Thomas, Wendy M. "Women's Conference Affirms Information Access Rights." ***American Libraries*** **29, no. 10 (November 1998): 33–34.**

The International Information Centre and Archives for the Women's Movement hosted this five-day event, which was the largest international conference since the United Nations Fourth World Conference on Women. The "Know How Conference on the World of Women's Information" brought together women from libraries and archival centers from around the world to discuss both community-based and large-scale themes facing librarians around the world.

423. Wand, Patricia Ann, and Lizabeth Wilson. "ACRL Candidates for President Share Plans for ACRL." ***College & Research Libraries News*** **60, no. 2 (February 1999): 98–102.**

Patricia Ann Wand and Lizabeth Wilson, candidates for president of the Association for College & Research Libraries, present their views concerning the role and potential of ACRL and related topics. Wand describes significant aspects of her career from 1973 to 1999. Wilson discusses the role that ACRL mentors played in her professional development.

10

Library History

This chapter covers primarily the general history of librarianship and notable events and individuals from the past who may or may not have been affiliated with formal library organizations and associations.

424. "RTSWL: North Carolina Library Association's Roundtable on the Status of Women in Librarianship." 4 May 2001. www.nclaonline.org/rtswl.

RTSWL's website offers links to a history of the organization, its bylaws, the RTSWL newsletter, listserv instructions, useful news, and membership and contact information. Objectives of the roundtable include uniting NCLA members interested in the status of women in librarianship, providing a forum for discussion of concerns of women in librarianship, giving support and stimulus to NCLA, presenting programs and carrying out other appropriate activities, and fulfilling the objectives of NCLA.

425. "Celebrating Women's Achievements: Women in Canadian Librarianship and Bibliography." 2 April 2002. www.nlc-bnc.ca/2/12/h12–250-e.html.

Presents biographies of ten women who played pivotal roles in the development of library services and bibliographical research in Canada. The women selected represent various regions of Canada as well as all aspects of librarianship.

426. "SLA Timeline: A Glance Back into Our Past." ***Information Outlook*** **3, no. 7 (1999): 10.**

During its ninetieth anniversary year, SLA looked back at significant events in the association's history. One of these events included the election of Carabin Mann as its first female president, a year before the adoption of the Nineteenth Amendment in 1920. Also mentioned was a resolution, approved in the 1970s, not to select conference and meeting sites in states that had not ratified the Equal Rights Amendment.

427. Baggs, Chris. "The Worthing Connection: Marian Frost, Pioneer Woman Librarian, and the Two Committees of Women Librarians, 1913–1915." In *Gendering Library History*, ed. Evelyn Kerslake and Nickianne Moody, 40–56. Liverpool, England: John Moores University Association for Research in Popular Fictions: Media Critical and Creative Arts, 2000.

Surveys British library literature of the early 1900s to determine the representation of women and presents interesting data on the number of women employed as librarians and as assistants in Great Britain and their impact on public libraries. The main focus is on Marian Frost and the activities of two library committees between 1913 and 1915 (the Committee of Women Librarians and Assistants and the Committee of Women Librarians). The committees were both concerned with representation of women within the Library Assistants' Association, membership, and raising the profile of librarianship. Marian Frost worked with both committees and is considered a pioneer in British librarianship for her long and distinguished career.

428. Barth, Robert, and Schneider, Gabi. *Bibliotheken, Bibliothekarinnen und Bibliothekare in der Schweiz: hundert Jahre bibliothekarischer Branchenverband 1897–1997 = Bibliothèques et bibliothècaires en Suisse*. Vevey: Ed. de l'Aire, 1997.

Explores the history of the Swiss library association (which now has more than two thousand members and libraries). It shows the development of the library profession and its professionalization. Also contains short biographies, mainly of women librarians, whose biographical "footprints" were—compared to their professional achievements—hard to track down. In German and French.

429. Bartle, Lisa R. "Women in the History of American Librarianship." 27 February 2001. www.pe.net/~ellerbee/wom_lib.html.

This website provides biographical sketches and photos of ten notable women in the history of American librarianship. These women represent all fields of librarianship and were chosen for their activism and their roles in the development of the profession.

430. Beck, Clare. "Adelaide Hasse: The Historiography of the Difficult Woman." In *Gendering Library History*, ed. Evelyn Kerslake and Nick-

ianne Moody, 16–30. Liverpool, England: John Moores University Association for Research in Popular Fictions: Media Critical and Creative Arts, 2000.

Beck argues that the biographical and historical treatment of Adelaide Hasse trivializes her accomplishments as a leader and role model by instead using her personality as a measure of her achievements. Using what little analysis exists of her work, including histories of the New York Public Library and histories of female librarians, Beck shows that the library literature of the past and present have diminished her contributions to the NYPL and to the library profession. Reasons for this omission are offered, and Beck closes with a discussion of sex discrimination and its impact on library management.

431. Bier, Lois. "Atomic Wives and the Secret Library at Los Alamos." ***American Libraries*** **30, no. 11 (December 1999): 54–56.**

Describes the role of Los Alamos National Laboratory's scientists' wives in the staffing and formation of the affiliated library. Discusses how the government specifically sought out women without backgrounds in librarianship to work in this library.

432. Black, Alistair. "Man and Boy: Modifying Masculinities in Public Librarianship, 1850–1950. With a Case Study of the Inter-War Librarianship Masonic Circle." In ***Gendering Library History*****, ed. Evelyn Kerslake and Nickianne Moody, 209–21. Liverpool, England: John Moores University Association for Research in Popular Fictions: Media Critical and Creative Arts, 2000.**

Black categorizes the types of stereotypes attributed to male librarians and juxtaposes these against the ideals of manliness in the nineteenth century to demonstrate how stereotypes affected male librarians. Black also discusses the strong networking among male librarians and the formation of the Librarianship Masonic Circle in 1927.

433. Bowen, Judith. "Librarians as Guardians of Memory: The Case of France." In ***Gendering Library History*****, ed. Evelyn Kerslake and Nickianne Moody, 232–40. Liverpool, England: John Moores University Association for Research in Popular Fictions: Media Critical and Creative Arts, 2000.**

Bowen focuses on librarianship in France from 1830 to 1850. During this time, historian and politician Guizot convinced the king that the preservation of historic national documents was of great value. At the same time, women were increasingly excluded from intellectual pursuits and were instead encouraged to contribute their time and creativity to family and home life. By limiting women's participation in the pursuit of politics, history, and any field requiring use of the scientific method, librarianship became a male-dominated profession. Bowen does provide examples of exceptions to the rule, discussing George Sand, Madame de Swetchine, and others.

434. Campbell, Patty. *Two Pioneers of Young Adult Library Services*. Lanham, MD: Scarecrow Press, 1998.

Campbell's book provides biographical accounts of two pioneers of library services to children and young adults and, through these accounts, details the development of youth services librarianship in the United States in the early twentieth century. Mabel Williams was the first young adult librarian at the New York Public Library, which she joined in 1914, and Margaret A. Edwards was the author of *The Fair Garden* and *The Swarm of Beasts*, a manual on library services to young adults.

435. Carmichael, James V., Jr. *Daring to Find Our Names: The Search for Lesbigay Library History*. Westport, CT: Greenwood Press, 1998.

This collection grew from papers presented at the summer 1995 conference of the American Library Association in Chicago. The session was titled "The Importance of Lesbigay Library History." The issues covered here include stereotyping within the profession, the strong connections between libraries and sexual minorities, the struggles of the Gay, Lesbian and Bisexual Task Force, and the efforts to collect and make accessible the historical archives and ephemera of lesbian and gay communities. Essays are inclusive, addressing issues in librarianship of importance to women as well as men, and over half of the authors, leading scholars in a variety of disciplines and activists, are women. Reviews: *Lambda Book Report* 7, no. 6 (1999): 18 (reviewed by Victoria Hill), *Harvard Gay and Lesbian Review* 6, no. 2 (Spring 1999): 54–55.

436. Crane, Hilary. "Librarians Honoured at Festival of Words." *Feliciter* 45, no. 3 (1999): 144–45.

Reports that librarians will be recognized by the Festival of Words in Moose Jaw, Saskatchewan. The 1999 Festival, expected to attract over two thousand readers and writers, was dedicated to "the Canadian librarian of yesterday and today." The late Margaret McGregor Young Gzowski Brown, a children's librarian and mother of writer Peter Gzowski, was chosen to embody the spirit of the dedication. The article reproduces the Festival of Words 1999 dedication, which extols the work of children's librarians and includes a photo of Gzowski Brown.

437. Eddy, Jacalyn. "'We Have Become Too Tender-Hearted': The Language of Gender in the Public Library, 1880–1920." ***American Studies*** **42, no. 3 (Fall 2001): 155–72.**

During the period between 1880 and 1920, the public library was "up for grabs," caught among competing visions of its role in American culture. Official rhetoric from the library expressed the broadly accepted belief that women represented the cultural/moral/private domain, while men dominated the intellectual/civic participatory/public domain. However, the admission of substantial numbers of women into librarianship, whatever the motives, increased their visibility and helped "unhinge the connection between public/private and male/female." Accepting the importance of gender as a metaphor helps one recognize that the library, in accomplishing its goal of becoming a leading cultural institution, was also an active shaper of dynamic social change in America.

438. Everitt, Jean. "Co-operative Society Libraries." ***Library History*** **15 (May 1999): 33–40.**

Briefly notes that librarians in British cooperative society libraries were generally men until the First World War when women began to take such positions.

439. Goedeken, Edward A. "The Library Historian's Field of Dreams: A Profile of the First 9 Seminars." ***Libraries and Culture*** **35, no. 1 (Winter 2000): 161–72.**

Goedeken analyzes the first nine seminars of the American Library History Round Table (LHRT), held between 1961 and 1995. His study uses data on the seminars themselves, including presenters, institutional affiliation, geographic locations, regional breakdown, and presentations by subject and time period. The data suggests that even though women represent a majority in librarianship, their activity in LHRT was non-existent until the second meeting in 1965, when they made up 30 percent of participants. In 1995, the percentage increased sharply to 57 percent. Goedeken also uses the rise of women members in American Library and Information Science Education (ALISE) (41 percent in 1976 to 49 percent in 1995) and history degree attainment figures for women, which increased by 30 percent between 1960 and 1994, to indicate women's increasing representation in those fields. In terms of the representation of women in library history at the seminars, women in librarianship was not explored until 1995, when two papers on women in librarianship were presented.

440. Goedeken, Edward A. "The Literature of American Library History, 1995–1996." ***Libraries & Culture*** **33, no. 4 (Fall 1998): 407–45.**

Surveys publications in the area of U.S. library history for the years 1995 to 1996, with discussions organized under various subtopics (e.g., "Sources and Historiography," "Technical Services, Preservation, and Technology"). One of the subtopics is "Women in Librarianship." In this section, essays in Hildenbrand's *Reclaiming the American Library Past: Writing the Women In* and in a theme issue of *Library Trends* devoted to women and children's library services, as well as several individual articles, are briefly considered. Notes that "historical writings on women in librarianship show encouraging promise for the future" (421). One in a regular series of biennial reviews of the literature of U.S. library history in *Libraries & Culture*.

441. Graham, Patterson Toby. "Public Librarians and the Civil Rights Movement: Alabama, 1955–1965." *Library Quarterly* 71 (January 2001): 1–27.

Although most librarians in Alabama during the civil rights era did not actively work against segregation, three female librarians who actively spoke out are profiled in this article. Juliette Hampton Morgan, a reference librarian at the Montgomery Carnegie Library, wrote a letter to the Montgomery newspaper supporting the Montgomery bus boycott. In response to her letter she was harassed by whites over a period of eighteen months. Rocks were thrown at her home, she received threatening phone calls both at work and at home, and she was insulted on the streets. Emily Wheelock Reed became the focus of controversy when, as the director of the Alabama Public Library Service Division, she refused to remove *The Rabbits' Wedding* from circulation. The book portrayed the wedding of a black rabbit and a white rabbit. In 1959 an Alabama legislator attempted to get a bill passed that would remove Reed from her position. The attempt failed; a compromise bill, which left Reed in her position, was passed. However, in 1960 Reed left Alabama for the Washington, D.C., Public Library when she accepted a position as an adult education consultant. Patricia Blalock was one of the few librarians who worked toward desegregation of public libraries before it was mandated by law. She was the director of the Carnegie Library in Selma, Alabama. Working with a board, whose members were opposed to desegregating the public library, Blalock finally gave the board an ultimatum in May 1963: "I think we need very badly to get this library integrated, and I don't believe I can open up Monday until we've made a real decision." The Carnegie Library of Selma opened as an integrated library on May 20, 1963.

442. Graham, Patterson Toby. *A Right to Read: Segregation and Civil Rights in Alabama's Public Libraries, 1900–1965*. Tuscaloosa, AL: University of Alabama Press, 2002.

Graham's book, based on his 1998 dissertation, explores the connections between access to public libraries and issues of racial equality, freedom of expression, and intellectual freedom in Alabama from 1900 through 1965. Profiled are many women who were instrumental in the development of biracial library services and the eventual desegregation of those services. The career of Mattie Herd, the state's first African American public librarian, illustrates the intersection of racism and sexism. She was paid one-third the salary of other branch heads of the Birmingham Public Library, was excluded from staff meetings, and after four months, the board replaced her with an African American man. Dulcina DeBerry was instrumental in establishing the first African American branch of the Huntsville Public Library. Juliette Morgan was a white librarian who was publicly vilified for her support of the Montgomery bus boycott. Emily Wheelock Reed was the director of the Alabama State Library in 1959 when state legislators attempted to oust her from her position because she refused to remove from the library's collections a children's book that featured the marriage of a black rabbit and a white rabbit.

443. Hansen, Debra Gold, Karen E. Gracy, and Sheri D. Irvin. "At the Pleasure of the Board: Women Librarians and the Los Angeles Public Library 1880–1905." *Libraries & Culture* 34, no. 4 (Fall 1999): 311–46.

Notes that during the late nineteenth and early twentieth centuries, the development of U.S. librarianship was marked by both increasing feminization and professionalization, with librarianship consequently offering women both opportunities and limitations. Uses biographical material concerning the careers of three female librarians at the Los Angeles Public Library, 1880–1905, to demonstrate and analyze the impacts of feminization and professionalization on U.S. librarianship during the period and the impacts of gender on librarians' relationship with boards of trustees. Initially founded as the Los Angeles Library Association in 1872, the Los Angeles Public Library became a tax-supported public library in 1878; the city charter indicated that the librarian "served at the pleasure of the board," with the board holding authority to appoint and dismiss librarians at will or whim. While the city's first two librarians were male, from 1880 through 1905, LAPL was headed by female administrators; the initial decision to hire female librarians may have been economic. Mary E. Foy

(1880–1884), the eighteen-year-old daughter of a prominent local merchant, had no previous library training or experience but may have been perceived as needing a job. She established a cataloging system, kept library accounts, answered questions, served as hostess, etc.; a new mayor reorganized the board and did not reappoint her. After her departure from the library, Foy had a full career of teaching and political activity. Under Tessa L. Kelso (1889–1895), LAPL enjoyed a period of remarkable development and accomplishment. A newspaperwoman and prototypical Progressive Era feminist, Kelso introduced the Dewey Decimal System, interlibrary lending, open stacks, and delivery services to neighborhoods; she abolished dues and established one of the first training classes for library staff. An unconventional and independent woman, Kelso and her progressive policies were unacceptable to some powerful constituencies; while she initially had the board's support, Kelso and her assistant Adelaide Hasse were ultimately forced to resign. Kelso was replaced by a woman without library or literary experience who was appointed in an apparent political payoff; Kelso did not work in librarianship again. A graduate of the New York State Library School and an experienced librarian, Mary L. Jones (1900–1905) expanded programs, emphasized children's and readers' services, extended the library's outreach role, and modernized practices and collections. Within four years, the library nearly doubled its collection size and its circulation. Deteriorating physical conditions, low wages, etc., resulted in discontented library employees and personnel problems. A prominent board member engineered Jones' replacement by a "man of letters." Jones took her cause to the American Library Association and the city's women's organizations; she gained support from Susan B. Anthony and had some initial success. In the end, however, the city council determined that the librarian served "at the pleasure of the board." The board male entrepreneurs and lawyers took a "boosterish" rather than a professional approach to library development and did not comprehend Jones's dedication to professional standards; the board also regarded personnel problems as demonstrations of the inherent weaknesses of female employees rather than as the result of poor working conditions and wages. Ultimately, the "men [of the board] were determined to refashion the library in their own image, but to do this the LAPL had to have a man at its head" (341). Includes photographs of the subjects. Originated in a panel presentation at the 1997 conference of the California Library Association.

444. Hearne, Betsy, and Christine Jenkins. "Sacred Texts: What Our Foremothers Left Us in the Way of Psalms, Proverbs, Precepts, and

Practices." ***Horn Book Magazine*** **75, no. 5 (September 1999–31 October 1999): 536–47.**

This article examines the works written by the foremothers of children's librarianship, including *My Roads to Childhood*, written in 1920 by Anne Carroll Moore, who founded children's services at the New York Public Library in 1900. The authors find in the works of these nine women and one man commentary on the importance of reading for children, advice on encouraging children to read, and recommendations of books appropriate for children.

445. Herrada, Julie, and Tom Hyry. "Agnes Inglis: An Anarchist Librarian." ***Progressive Librarian*** **16, Special Supplement (Fall 1999): 7–10.**

Describes the life and work of Agnes Ingles, an early twentieth-century activist in the anarchist and antiwar movements. Working as an unpaid volunteer, she organized and expanded a collection of primary and secondary materials donated to the University of Michigan Library by her friend and fellow activist, Joseph Labadie.

446. Hoadley, Irene B. "Reflections: Management Morphology—How We Got to Be Who We Are." ***Journal of Academic Librarianship*** **25, no. 4 (July 1999): 267–73.**

The author looks at issues in librarianship over the last twenty-five years, including gender and management. In the 1970s, library directors tended to be male. Department heads, especially in cataloging, were female. The late 1970s to early 1990s showed an increase of women directors and upper-level female administrators.

447. Holley, Edward G. "Academic Libraries over Twenty-five Years." ***Journal of Academic Librarianship*** **25, no. 2 (March 1999): 79–81.**

The 1960s and 1970s showed great expansion in academic scholarship and publishing, which in turn had a great impact on libraries and librarianship. During this time, there was also an increase in the number of female librarians. Affirmative action helped boost the salaries of female and minority librarians.

448. Howsam, Leslie. "In My View: Women and Book History." ***SHARP News*** **7, no. 4 (Autumn 1998): 1–2.**

This issue of the newsletter of the Society for the History of Authorship, Reading & Publishing features several articles related to women's history. The lead piece touches on the image and role of librarians. Contemporary popular culture equates bookishness with feminine qualities of respectability and delicate physical features. The book itself is gendered, but "contrary to familiar stereotypes of frail bookworms or of bespectacled spinster librarians," the book has historically been identified as masculine. In the dominant theory of book history espoused by Robert Darnton, books exist in an endless circle of authorship, publication, and reading, and researchers have found women at every node in the cycle. With the exception of bookbinders and librarians, however, the women have been anomalies in a male domain. Howsam asks book historians to "think about how the book has been implicated in those structures of masculine power and authority known to feminist scholarship as patriarchy." She calls not for compensatory efforts to add women to the existing research agenda but rather for a focus on the "gender identity of the book itself both as physical object and as cultural product." Ripe areas for feminist scholarship include the collecting and possession of books by men, the uses and sharing of books by women, and the functions of nonliterary books such as cookbooks. Wondering how bookishness came to be associated with feminine attributes, she speculates that impressionable children who used public libraries and received books from female librarians may have grown up perceiving the books themselves as feminine. Although admittedly this may be a "far-fetched" idea, it illustrates how feminist analysis can be brought to bear on book history.

449. Hubber, Brian. "The Proto-profession of Librarianship: The Richmond Public Library 1884." ***Australian Library Journal*** **47, no. 4 (November 1998): 315–25.**

Includes a brief recounting of RPL's search for a replacement for its retired librarian, a woman. Of the one hundred applicants, only sixteen were women, but five of the women made the fourteen-person shortlist. All five were rejected for lack of experience.

450. Ishizuka, Kathy. "Acclaimed Film Tells Librarian's Heroic Story." ***School Library Journal*** **47, no. 11 (November 2001): 23.**

A film about San Diego librarian Clara Breed won a Special Gold Jury Award at the 2001 Houston Film Festival. When Japanese Americans were put in camps after Pearl Harbor, Breed kept in contact with incarcerated children, answering their letters and sending them care packages.

451. Jackson, Mildred Louise. "'A Delightful Entertainment': Study Groups as Part of the Kalamazoo Ladies' Library Association." ***Annual Meeting of the Popular Culture and American Culture Associa-***

tion (San Diego, CA, March 31–April 3, 1999) **(March 1999–30 April 1999): 18.**

Examines the Kalamazoo Ladies' Library Association during the latter half of the nineteenth century, including the establishment of Social Meetings (1856 and 1861, 1867), a Reading Circle (1861–1868), and Ladies' Library Club (1873–1890s). Focuses on the structure and subject matter of the Reading Circle and the Social Meetings, examines the organizations' various rules and procedures, and discusses their differences in approach. Explores the way gender influenced differences in the interpretation of literature by men and women in the Reading Circle. (ERIC Document Reproduction Service No. ED429296)

452. Jackson, Mildred Louise. "'Do What You Can': Creating an Institution, the Ladies' Library Associations in Michigan, 1852–1900." Ph.D., diss., Michigan State University, 1998.

Presents a history of the Ladies' Library Association in Michigan through the discussion of institution-building activities, reading practices, and community involvement. Local newspaper articles supplement the study, but the core research material is based primarily upon records of the Kalamazoo, Ann Arbor, Ypsilanti, and Galesburg LLAs. Examines minutes of board meetings, annual meetings, and study groups as well as the LLAs' organizational principles as presented in their constitutions, bylaws, and mission statements. Describes how women used state laws to gain status and power for libraries. Explores reading circles and study groups in Kalamazoo, in addition to studying LLA members' public and private reading practices. Topics of study, the format of meetings, and the educational opportunities provided for members are also discussed. Also, investigates thirteen library catalogs in an attempt to determine what women purchased and read, including popular genres and authors, between 1850 and 1902. Studies the minutes of the associations to identify the policies and practices for book purchasing and the many ways that the LLAs functioned to serve reader request trends. Concludes by analyzing LLA fund-raising efforts, their physical meeting spaces, and the way women of the LLA served as visible leaders in their communities.

453. Jenkinson, Penelope. "Travelling Hopefully: Progress and the Nineteenth Century Public Library." ***Library History*** **15 (May 1999): 23–32.**

Notes the absence of female employees in early British public libraries. Smaller libraries employed women in greater numbers than did large libraries, probably because women were cheaper to employ than men.

454. Jones, Plummer Alston. "The Librarian as Advocate: Jane Maud Campbell, 1869–1947." In *Libraries, Immigrants, and the American Experience.* Westport, CT: Greenwood Press, 1999.

Jane Maud Campbell's advocacy and service to immigrants is discussed. Campbell used the library not only as a tool for teaching immigrants but also as a source of trust. Maud developed foreign language bibliographic guides for the ALA Publishing Board and served on the New Jersey Immigration Commission and the Massachusetts Free Public Library Commission. Eventually, Campbell won national recognition for her consulting work with public libraries in the northwest.

455. Jones, Plummer Alston. "The Librarian as Educator: Edna Phillips, 1890–1968." In *Libraries, Immigrants, and the American Experience.* Westport, CT: Greenwood Press, 1999.

This chapter discusses the impact of Edna Phillips in her role as secretary for Library Work with Foreigners in the Division of Public Libraries. Phillips advocated for Americanization through the public library system. The chapter also traces Phillips's involvement and work with the ALA Committee on Work with the Foreign Born.

456. Jones, Plummer Alston. "The Librarian as Social Worker: Eleanor (Edwards) Ledbetter, 1870–1954." In *Libraries, Immigrants, and the American Experience.* Westport, CT: Greenwood Press, 1999.

Describes the approach that Eleanor Ledbetter took while working with immigrants at the Cleveland Public Library's Broadway Branch. Ledbetter used community outreach programs to bring immigrants into the library and transform it into a model community center. Her programs for educating other librarians about effectively serving immigrant populations are examined as well as her contributions to the ALA Committee on Work with the Foreign Born.

457. Joyce, Steven. "A Few Gates: An Examination of the Social Responsibilities Debate in the Early 1970s & 1990s." *Progressive Librarian*, no. 15 (Winter 1999): 27–30.

This article traces the origin of the social responsibility debate and the Social Responsibilities Round Table within the American Library Association. Feminism and services to women are briefly mentioned as an aspect of social responsibilities.

458. Kerslake, Evelyn. "Constructing Women in Library History: Responding to Julia Taylor's 'Left on the Shelf?'" *Libraries & Culture* 34, no. 1 (Winter 1999): 52–63.

Responds to an essay on female library workers in Great Britain titled "Left on the Shelf? The Issues and Challenges Facing Women Employed in Libraries from the Late Nineteenth Century to the 1950s," by Julia Taylor (*Library History* 11 [1995]: 96–107). Stresses the importance of analysis and interpretation in historical writing, with postmodern doubts about the existence of "truth" and "objectivity" giving rise to pluralities rather than absolutes. In this context, argues that theoretical frameworks underpin historical interpretation and analysis, and that library history's need for interpretation "contains a demand for theory" (53). In evaluating Taylor's contribution, acknowledges that, in its attempt to make women library workers visible, Taylor's paper challenges much library historical literature in Great Britain. Notes that Taylor's paper investigates how oppressive images of female librarians developed, but states that the paper does not successfully address questions of why female library workers were oppressed and what the meanings of this oppression were. Demonstrates ways in which female library workers are reinscribed within dominant discourses within Taylor's work: by the paper's lack of recognition of the impact of varied economic positions on the category of "woman," by its acceptance of the periodization of dominant discourses, and by the paper's limited exploration of the role played by the image of the librarian-spinster. Proposes that use of a "discursive approach informed by feminist concerns may be particularly helpful in an investigation of women's position in the labor market" (55).

459. Kerslake, Evelyn. "No More the Hero: Lionel McColvin, Women Library Workers, and Impacts of Othering." ***Library History*** **17 (November 2001): 181–87.**

McColvin is regarded as a library hero for his efforts to establish librarianship as a profession with the status of others like law and medicine. Kerslake argues that he was far from a hero to female library workers. In a standard textbook and a report envisioning the future of librarianship after World War II, McColvin argued for a two-level division of library work with men holding most professional jobs and receiving larger salaries than female workers.

460. Kerslake, Evelyn, and Janine Liladhar. "'Jolly Good Reading' for Girls: Discourses of Library Work and Femininity in Career Novels." ***Women's History Review*** **8, no. 3 (1999): 489–504.**

Summarizes research on female library workers in the United Kingdom in the 1950s and the feminization of the profession as illuminated through a study of career novels from that period. The authors argue that gender-based labor market studies for the profession are insufficient and they sought other sources of data. During the 1950s, female library workers faced lower pay scales and fewer advancement opportunities, trends highlighted by formulaic career novels and their emphasis on library work for women with the desire to serve, to promote orderliness and an understanding that higher positions were off limits. Tables; bibliography.

461. Kerslake, Evelyn, and Nickianne Moody. *Gendering Library History*. Liverpool, UK: Media Critical and Creative Arts, Liverpool John Moores University and the Association for Research in Popular Fictions, 2000.

Collection of papers originally presented at an interdisciplinary conference entitled "Gendering Library History" held by the School of Media, Critical and Creative Arts, Liverpool John Moores University and the Department of Information and Library Studies, Loughborough University (United Kingdom) in May 1999. The essays explore librarianship as a cultural practice and focus on gender as a critical aspect of library work and an important determinant in the profession's development. See annotations for individual essays by Evelyn Kerslake, Nickianne Moody, Paul Sturges, Clare Beck, Jeff Schneider and Ann O'Bryan Cockerham, Chris Baggs, Mary Niles Maack, Margaret Kinnell Evans, Lindy Moore, Janine Liladhar, Val Williamson, Susie West, Avril Rolph, Alistair Black, Wren Sidhe, and Judith Bowen.

462. Kester, Norman G. "Liberating and Empowering Minds: The African/Caribbean Canadian Woman Librarian and the Development of the West Indian/Black Heritage Collection of the North York Public Library, 1980–1994." In *Untold Stories: Civil Rights, Libraries and Black Librarianship*, ed. John Mark Tucker, 167–81. Urbana-Champaign, IL: Graduate School of Library and Information Science, 1998.

Kester tells the story behind the creation of the West Indian/Black Heritage Collection at the North York Public Library in Toronto, Canada, between 1980 and 1994. For his study, Kester interviewed three Canadian librarians of note: Laurel Taylor, Rosalind Bryce (both of the North York Public Library), and Gloria Reinbergs (Toronto Public Library). He also studied reports, collection development assessments, and promotional tools such as bibliographies and bookmarks. In doing so he hoped to gain insight about not only the collection itself and its significance to the community of York but also black female librarians' ideas about and approaches to serving their respective communities through library work. Outreach to populations, advocacy for literacy services, and sponsoring relevant programs for the African/Caribbean Canadian community in York were a few of their proactive approaches to reaching their constituencies. In terms of the collection, Kester discovered that nonprint materials were as key to the quality and relevancy of the collection as printed materials because often dialect was part of the cultural connections made in using the materials. Each librarian interviewed or profiled had done very significant work in bringing the library to her community and vice versa through outreach and advocacy and, in doing so, raised the standard for contributions to the community.

463. Kneebone, John T. "Of Books, Readers, and Reading: New Directions for Virginia Library History." ***Virginia Libraries*** **45, no. 2 (1999): 16–18.**

An article about new efforts to promote research and writing about the history of libraries in Virginia. One example given of a "first-rate" library history involves the work of an early female librarian to establish the first public library in Roanoke. The author speculates about the connections between the campaign for the library and women's earlier campaigns for civic betterment in Roanoke and calls for the exploration of the political agency of women librarians in general.

464. Liladhar, Janine. "Boys Will Be . . . Playfully Antagonistic to Users?" ***Library Association Record*** **101, no. 7 (July 1999): 425.**

This is a brief report on the conference "Gendering Library History," held at Liverpool John Moores University on May 15, 1999. The conference aimed at the integration of theoretical and interdisciplinary work into library history. A paper by archaeologist Susie West argued for revising the history of eighteenth-century private libraries to incorporate women by focusing on "the interaction of the household with the house." Wren Sidhe's study of shipboard libraries examined the complex inter-relationships of masculinity, heterosexuality, and Englishness. Alastair Black developed the concept of "library boyishness" to counter earlier scholarship on library masculinities that constructed masculinity and femininity as binary opposites. Suzanne Hildenbrand delivered the keynote paper, which urged participants to move beyond writing about the history of the profession, an approach which tends to celebrate individuals and downplay conflicts. Rather, Hildenbrand stressed that library historians should view history "as a tool to assist explanation and understanding," which would permit the inclusion of material that could be damaging to individuals' reputations.

465. Liladhar, Janine, and Evelyn Kerslake. "Jilly Cooper versus the Government: Romantic Discourse of Femininity and Women's Library Employment." In *Gendering Library History*, ed. Evelyn Kerslake and Nickianne Moody, 145–62. Liverpool, England: John Moores University Association for Research in Popular Fictions: Media Critical and Creative Arts, 2000.

Liladhar and Kerslake compare and contrast the discourses in modern romance novels and in the employment and labor legislation arena to explore how each informed and impacted women's working lives. Two romantic novels and one advertisement are used to discuss the popular-culture view of working women in libraries, and discussions of key legislation such as the Equal Pay Act, Sex Discrimination Act, and other laws are used as supporting materials to contextualize the authors' arguments.

466. Maack, Mary Niles. "Documenting One Hundred Twenty Years of Writings on Women's Entry, Advancement, and Struggle for Equalization in Librarianship." *Library Quarterly* 71, no. 2 (April 2002): 241–46.

A review essay covering five major publications that constitute an ongoing bibliography on women and librarianship. The titles covered in the essay are: *The Role of Women in Librarianship, 1876 –1976*, edited by Kathleen Weibel and Kathleen M. Heim, published in 1979 by Oryx Press; *On Account of Sex: An Annotated Bibliography on the Status of Women in Librarianship, 1977–1981*, edited by Kathleen M. Heim and Katharine Phenix, published in 1984 by the American Library Association; *On Account of Sex: An Annotated Bibliography on the Status of Women in Librarianship, 1982–1986*, edited by Katharine Phenix, published in 1988 by the American Library Association; *On Account of Sex: An Annotated Bibliography on the Status of Women in Librarianship, 1987–1992*, edited by Lori A. Goetsch and Sarah B. Watstein, published in 1993 by Scarecrow Press; *On Account of Sex: An Annotated Bibliography on the Status of Women in Librarianship, 1993–1997*, edited by Betsy Kruger and Catherine A. Larson, published in 2000 by Scarecrow Press.

467. Maack, Mary Niles. "Gender, Culture, and the Transformation of American Librarianship, 1890–1920." *Libraries & Culture* 33, no. 1 (Winter 1998): 51–61.

Discusses the role of the first generation of female library school graduates in creating the ideology of public librarianship in the United States. Proposes that female librarians' gender-linked value system emphasizing altruism, advocacy, and intellectual nurturing of children and adults was influential in developing the service orientation of librarianship during a critical period of professionalization. Among the prominent female librarians of the period who were active in social reform were Mary Eileen Ahern, Gratia Countryman (called the "Jane Addams of libraries"), Grace Hebrard, and Cornelia Marvin. While female librarians of the Progressive Era typically were moderates on the issue of women's suffrage, they sought professional opportunities and often transcended stereotypes of "womanhood," even as they apparently accepted many traditional elements of gender roles. Some female librarians pursued a strategy of integration and compromise; others emphasized equality and cooperation. Mary Wright Plummer, founder of two library schools and the second female president of ALA, was considered by her colleagues to represent the best of the pioneer generation of library school women. "Viewing knowledge as power and power as empowerment, Mary Wright Plummer and the women of her generation shared equally with their male colleagues in redefining librarianship, creating a new professional paradigm that was fundamentally different from the authoritarian model" (59). Originated as a paper presented at an international conference on the history of reading and libraries, 1996, Vologda, Russia.

468. Maack, Mary Niles. "'No Philosophy Carries So Much Conviction as the Personal Life': Mary Wright Plummer as an Independent Woman." *Library Quarterly* 70, no. 1: 1–46.

Through a feminist approach to biographical study the author chronicles the life of Mary Wright Plummer (1866–1916), who directed the Pratt Institute Free Library, founded two library education programs, and was the second woman elected president of the American Library Association. The focus of the article is Plummer's efforts to construct a personal identity, and it explores three different stages of her personal and professional development: the foundation of her identity based on Quaker beliefs and practices learned in childhood; mature self-understanding, which enabled her to accept her ambition to engage fully in a work of her own; and self-actualization, which resulted in her conscious efforts to build a career strategy that allowed time for creative expression and a national leadership role in the library field.

469. Maack, Mary Niles. "Telling Lives: Women Librarians in Europe and America at the Turn of the Century." In *Gendering Library History*, ed. Evelyn Kerslake and Nickianne Moody, 57–81. Liverpool, England: John Moores University Association for Research in Popular Fictions: Media Critical and Creative Arts, 2000.

Maack profiles three women who are considered pioneers in librarianship: Mary Wright Plummer of the United States, Giulia Sacconi-Ricci of Italy, and Marie Pellechet of France. In discussing the lives and careers of each woman, Maack also presents an interesting view of the societal structures that defined women and their place at the end of the nineteenth century and how each woman succeeded in overcoming obstacles to attain an education and move forward in her profession.

470. Malone, Cheryl Knott. "Autonomy and Accommodation: Houston's Colored Carnegie Library, 1907–1922." ***Libraries & Culture*** **34, no. 2 (Spring 1999): 95–112.**

Examines the founding and development of the Colored Branch/Colored Carnegie Library of Houston, with its separate and (for a time) self-governing board of trustees, up to the disbanding of the separate board and the administration of the Colored Branch by the all-white board of the Houston Public Library. Presents the history of this library as a case study revealing typical negotiations, accommodations, and resistance of African American communities in the creation of their own institutions in a segregated society. While gender is not the principal focus of the essay, gendered aspects of the topic are discussed. Denied access to the Houston Lyceum and Carnegie Library, leaders of the African American community (in this case, mostly men) organized to create their own library service. Ernest Ollington Smith and his colleagues sought backing from prominent white men and from Julia Ideson, librarian of the Houston Lyceum and Carnegie Library; the public library board approved a small allocation if the African American community could provide suitable space for a library. The Colored Branch first opened in 1909 in rooms at the African American high school. Smith next gained approval for a separate governing board. With the support of Booker T. Washington and his native-Houstonian secretary, Emmett J. Scott, Smith and the board began a successful campaign to acquire a Carnegie Library building for the African American community. Smith presented fundraising for the site and facility as "both a project and a test of black manhood . . . something African Americans had organized, struggled for, and accomplished" (102); the building opened in 1913. Librarians hired by the board of the Colored Carnegie Library were African American women; a successful candidate's qualifications included her "freedom from family ties which would seem to assure undivided attention for the Library and her youthfulness which assures greater adaptability" (104). Following passage of a tax levee for all libraries in Houston in 1921, the city disbanded the African American library board and the library reverted to being a branch of the Houston Public Library. A Justin Winsor Prize essay; presented at the 1997 annual conference of the American Library Association.

471. Malone, Cheryl Knott. "Books for Black Children: Public Library Collections in Louisville and Nashville, 1915–1925." ***Library Quarterly*** **70, no. 2: 179–200.**

Outlines the history behind the creation of branch libraries exclusively for African Americans in Louisville and Nashville. Working as the assistant to Thomas Fountain Blue in Louisville, Rachel Davis Harris, a former teacher, was instrumental in building collections for African American youngsters, since she viewed her role as someone who not only encouraged reading but also created readers. Blue and Harris became recognized as experts on selecting and building collections for African Americans. In 1916, the Nashville Negro Public Library was opened as a branch of the Carnegie Library. Marian Hadley, an African American woman from Nashville, was sent to Louisville by librarian Margaret Kercheval to work with Blue as an apprentice in preparation for running the Nashville Negro Public Library.

472. Malone, Cheryl Knott. "Quiet Pioneers: Black Women Public Librarians in the Segregated South." ***Vitae Scholasticae*** **19 (Spring 2000): 59–76.**

Malone examines the history of black female librarians, often invisible in the literature of librarianship and education, by focusing on three librarians in the South: Rachel Davis Harris of Louisville, Bessie B. Osborne of Houston, and Marian Hadley of Nashville. Each woman began her career in the early twentieth century, participated in vocational training, and worked in segregated libraries. Other commonalities between the three librarians were their roots in the South, their library advocacy and outreach that raised them into high society, and their shared vision of the library as a way to "uplift the race."

473. Middleton, Ken. "American Women's History: A Research Guide: Librarianship." 22 April 2002. www.mtsu.edu/~kmiddlet/history/women/wh-libr.html.

Provides primary and reference sources for finding information on the history of American women in librarianship. Includes links to archival and digital collections as well as to discussion groups and associations. One collection, Kentuckiana Digital Library, has fascinating information on the "packhorse librarians," women on horseback who delivered books to rural Kentuckians in the 1930s.

474. Mielke, Andrea. ***Bennata Otten: Leiterin der Bücherhalle Lübeck 1906–1923. Eine der ersten Direktorinnen einer Öffentlichen Bibliothek in Deutschland.*** **Lübeck: Bibliothek der Hansestadt Lübeck, 2000.**

Otten, a young, inventive, and well-respected librarian of her time, educated in Berlin, laid ground for the reputation of the Lübecker Öffentliche Bücher- und Lesehalle (one of the first children's reading rooms in Germany). She was a strong advocate of open shelves, which caused a long, bitter debate not only in Lübeck but throughout Germany. Otten published some widely received books and articles but lost her last battle for a stronger, bigger public library; politically a conservative, she not only failed to introduce open shelves in Lübeck but had to give up her position altogether in 1923 in favor of a social democrat (Willy Pietsch). In 1934, she took over a firm that offered library and office furniture. Relatively little is known about her private life and her last years.

475. Moody, Nickianne. "Fashionable Design and Good Service: The Spinster Librarians at Boots Booklovers Library." In ***Gendering Library History,*** **ed. Evelyn Kerslake and Nickianne Moody, 131–44. Liverpool, England: John Moores University Association for Research in Popular Fictions: Media Critical and Creative Arts, 2000.**

Moody provides a brief history of the Boots Booklovers Libraries, a venture started by the Boots Company in Great Britain in 1898 and closed in 1966. The Booklovers Libraries were commercial ventures, located in Boots pharmacies, and sought to attract the middle and upper classes to the Boots stores by offering the library services. The Booklovers Libraries employed both men and women, but as late as the mid-1950s it was stipulated that women be unmarried. Women who held the head librarian position were well regarded in the towns in which they worked.

476. Moore, Lindy. "Women: the Invisible Library Users." In ***Gendering Library History,*** **ed. Evelyn Kerslake and Nickianne Moody, 95–130. Liverpool, England: John Moores University Association for Research in Popular Fictions: Media Critical and Creative Arts, 2000.**

Moore discusses the lack of data and historical analyses of female library users and female librarians. Examples of restrictions on library use for women in the United Kingdom and United States are presented and put into societal and educational context. The appointment of women to library staff positions, the advent of "ladies' reading tables," and reading materials most available to women are also discussed.

477. Rasmussen, Cecilia. "L.A. Then and Now: Librarian Became an Institution." ***Los Angeles Times*** **(September 12, 1999): B3.**

Pays tribute to Mary Emily Foy, Los Angeles's first female librarian from 1880 to 1884. Foy envisioned a library as more than a warehouse for books, and among her many accomplishments, she set up a cataloging system for the collection, hosted the Ladies' Reading Room, acted as referee for chess games in the Newspaper Room, and settled bets for saloon patrons downstairs, truly giving Los Angeles a "public library." Online. Available from Lexis-Nexis Universe. November 10, 2000.

478. Robbins, Louise S. *The Dismissal of Miss Ruth Brown: Civil Rights, Censorship, and the American Library*. Norman, OK: University of Oklahoma Press, 2000.

In 1950, after thirty years as the librarian of the Bartlesville, Oklahoma, Public Library, Ruth Brown was fired. Her library board had received citizen complaints that she was supplying subversive materials, a charge that was not uncommon during the hysteria of the Red Scare. Robbins suggests that Brown's dismissal was just as much a reaction against her civil rights activities in a segregated town. The book chronicles Brown's firing, looks at ALA's reaction to the case, and discusses the movie *Storm Center*, which was loosely based on the Brown episode. Reviews: Horn, Zora. "The Dismissal of Ruth Brown: Civil Rights, Censorship and the American Library." *Progressive Librarian* 18 (Summer 2001): 78.

479. Robbins, Louise S. "Fighting McCarthyism through Film: A Library Censorship Case Becomes a Storm Center." *Journal of Education for Library and Information Science* 39, no. 4 (Fall 1998): 291–311.

Examines the controversies around *Storm Center*, the only Hollywood film to challenge McCarthyism, from the film's origin in a letter to the editor of *Saturday Review* about the dismissal of public librarian Ruth W. Brown in Bartlesville, Oklahoma, to its reception by the public, librarians, and critics. Summarizes Brown's case, in which she was accused by a conservative citizens' group of circulating subversive materials, chiefly *The Nation* and *The New Republic*. Notes that the accusers were actually most disturbed by Brown's history of activism on behalf of racial equality, even though this was not the ostensible charge, and that Brown was fired despite agreeing to sign a loyalty oath. Follows the development and production of the film, especially the writers' and producers' unsuccessful efforts to forestall criticism and censorship attempts. Reviews the responses of the American Library Association and individual librarians to the film, and concludes that "those who were most intimately connected with libraries were not unanimous in their praise of the film's or their profession's virtues" (303). Compares the film's story, as finally released, with the facts of the Brown case. The film's pivotal episode came directly from the Brown case, in which a middle-aged librarian, alone and without representation, faced the powerful men of the city council and lost her job. In both film and case, a citizens' committee brought the charges to the attention of the council; in both, a group organized to reinstate the librarian and displayed a degree of feminism in the process. The film's most prominent addition was the hysterical child Freddie Slater. The film's most significant omissions are Brown's interracial activities and the strong group of Bartlesville women who worked for racial equality. Presented at the 1998 conference, Association for Library and Information Science Education.

480. Ronnie, Mary. "Library Education in New Zealand: The Role of the New Zealand Library Association." ***Australian Library Journal*** **47 (November 1998): 355–66.**

Mentions that in the 1930s New Zealand librarians' wages were based on a rate for women who were supported by their families.

481. Samek, Antonia. ***Intellectual Freedom and Social Responsibility: An Ethos of American Librarianship, 1967–1973 (American Library Association).*** **Madison, WI: University of Wisconsin, 1998.**

Samek explores the history of social responsibility activism within the American Library Association (ALA) during its peak between 1967 and 1973. She achieves this by using published and unpublished primary and secondary sources, specifically interviews with those involved in social responsibility activism and archival material from ALA's Social Responsibility Round Table, the Sanford Berman papers, and the Radical Research Center Papers. Samek also examines the idea of the library's role in culture and society by studying seminal works by Italian political and cultural theorist Antonio Gramsci, connecting his ideas of hegemony to the power struggle unfolding within ALA between 1967 and 1973. Samek also examines the idea, purpose, and librarians' use of alternative press literature, at the time an important and controversial source of different perspectives on society. Reviews: *Progressive Librarian* no. 19/20 (Spring 2002): 127–131 (reviewed by Jenna Freedman).

482. Sidhe, Wren. "Interwar Masculinities, Libraries for Sailors and Powers of Literature." ***Gendering Library History*****, ed. Evelyn Kerslake and Nickianne Moody, 222–31. Liverpool, England: John Moores University Association for Research in Popular Fictions: Media Critical and Creative Arts, 2000.**

Sidhe discusses the ways in which libraries impacted the lives of sailors during the early twentieth century. A brief history of the Seafarer's Education Service is also provided. The Service, established to promote high moral values and education in part through reading books, theorized that by reading quality literature, sailors would feel a stronger connection to their homeland and to their masculinity.

483. Smith, Rita J. "Just Who Are These Women? Louise Seaman Bechtel and Ruth Marie Baldwin." ***Journal of Youth Services in Libraries*** **11 (Winter 1998): 161–70.**

Although Louise Seaman Bechtel (1894–1985) and Ruth Marie Baldwin (1917–1990) never met, they are the primary people behind the Louise Seaman Bechtel Fellowship at the Baldwin Library of Historical Children's Literature at the University of Florida Libraries in Gainesville. The fellowship, which is awarded by ALA's Association for Library Service to Children, is funded by money from Bechtel's estate. Bechtel was a publisher of children's literature. The fellowship also recognizes the research resources gathered in children's literature by Dr. Baldwin. The article describes Bechtel's career in publishing and the genesis and progress of Dr. Baldwin's collection of children's books.

484. Stevens, Norman. "The Last Librarian." ***American Libraries*** **32, no. 9 (October 2001): 60–64.**

Set in the future, this article discusses the changes undergone by the library profession since the late nineteenth century. Describes the changes in library terminology as the roles and perceptions of libraries and librarians change. Also focuses on gender issues in librarianship and stereotypes of librarians.

485. Swaffield, Laura. "Centenary." ***Library Association Record*** **100, no. 4–12 (1988).**

To celebrate the one hundredth anniversary of its official publication, the *Record*, in 1999 the Library Association (Great Britain) created a column with historical tidbits from past issues. The countdown begins in April 1998 with a look at the 1980s and travels back in time, decade by decade, to the turn of the twentieth century and the founding of the magazine. Sprinkled among the landmarks of the profession's progress and humorous accounts of association in-fighting are numerous indications, both serious and silly, of women's status. With the running title "Centenary," each column also carries a unique title: "So Recent But So Different" (April, 205), "Sexism, Violence and the LA" (May, 239), "Enemies: Politics, Pop, Porn, Patrons" (June, 294), "The Strife-Torn Struggle for Solidarity" (July, 353),

"Oh, What a Library War!" (August, 402), "Between Carnegie and Carnage" (September, 458), "The Roaring, Rates-Pinching '20s" (October, 512), "I Wish I Had a Rose-Garden" (November, 573), "Gentlemen, Gentlemen!" (December, 629).

486. Weihs, Jean. "Remembering: It Was Not the Good Old Days." ***Technicalities*** **18, no. 7 (July 1998–31 August 1998): 1, 11–12.**

Author recalls that when she began working as a librarian, women who married would often be demoted and remain at an entry-level librarian's wages.

487. Weihs, Jean. "Remembering: It Was Not the Good Old Days Revisited." ***Technicalities*** **19, no. 5 (May 1999): 1, 9–11.**

Includes responses to an article previously written by the author, one of which describes obstacles faced by a married female librarian in the 1950s.

488. West, Susie. "Rare Books and Rare Women: Gender and Private Libraries 1660–1830." In ***Gendering Library History*****, ed. Evelyn Kerslake and Nickianne Moody, 179–95. Liverpool, England: John Moores University Association for Research in Popular Fictions: Media Critical and Creative Arts, 2000.**

This chapter examines how gender can be incorporated into the study of book collecting within the upper classes in the eighteenth century using a qualitative, interdisciplinary approach. West discusses the cultural and architectural aspects of library as space in the homes of the upper classes and also examines the history of women as book collectors.

489. Wiegand, Wayne. "This Month 93 Years Ago . . ." ***American Libraries*** **29, no. 9 (October 1998): 87.**

This article discusses the fact that Melvil Dewey was forced to resign in 1905 from his position as New York State Librarian. Dewey was accused by several well-known female librarians of behaving "improperly" toward them at the 1905 ALA Conference. Wiegand implies that Dewey's positive contributions to the profession blind the library profession from seeing his less favorable attributes.

11

Salary and Pay Equity

This chapter is related to employment issues but focuses more specifically on issues related to salary and pay equity within the field.

490. "The 1998 Salary Survey: An Overview." ***Information Outlook*** **2, no. 11 (November 1998): 16–17.**

Presents the results of the 1998 Special Libraries Association (SLA) salary survey to which 2,435 members (41 percent) responded. The median pay for information professionals in the United States is $47,000 (U.S. dollars) and in Canada it is $49,800 (Canadian dollars). The results are also reported by type of institution: corporate, federal government, state and other government, public library, academic (subject), and academic (general). Overall, the mean percent change in earnings for Canadian respondents was 4.5 percent whereas it was 5.2 percent for U.S. respondents.

491. "ARL Annual Salary Increase Outperforms Inflation." ***Library Hotline*** **31, no. 32 (12 August 2002): 1.**

Brief article highlights the results of the ARL Annual Salary Survey 2001–2002. The study shows a 4.1 percent average pay increase for women in the profession. The gender balance in librarianship is 35.4 percent male and 64.6 percent female, which is in line with the ratio for the past twenty years.

492. "Australian Pay-Equity Case Nets Librarians 25% Increase." ***Library Hotline*** **31, no. 14 (8 April 2002): 6.**

Brief article highlights the Australian ruling to increase the pay of librarians since "librarians had been underpaid because work in female-dominated professions had historically been undervalued."

493. "California Pay Equity Survey Proves Low Salary Complaints." ***Library Hotline*** **31, no. 40 (7 October 2002): 4, 6.**

Author states that the unfair compensation of librarians compared to other professions is due to the fact that women make up the majority of workers in the profession.

494. "Canada Settles Pay-Equity Battle: Government Librarians Included." ***Library Hotline*** **28, no. 44 (8 November 1999): 2.**

The Canadian government agreed to pay between CDN \$3.3 and \$3.6 billion to approximately 230,000 mostly female federal government workers. The librarians in the group are being compensated with about \$30,000 each, for having been paid less than men who work in similar professions.

495. "Guide to Analyzing Salary Inequities Published." ***Academe*** **88, no. 1 (January 2002–28 February 2002): 15–16.**

Paychecks: A Guide to Conducting Salary-Equity Studies for Higher Education Faculty, second edition, is published jointly by the United University Professions (UUP), the American Association of University Professors (AAUP), and Lois Haignere, Inc. This book helps faculty, administrators, and policy makers understand salary analyses and provides technical information needed by researchers conducting multiple-regression salary reviews. Topics include race and gender bias detection, selecting a salary-equity consultant, and ways to ensure equity in faculty salaries. Studies that reveal salary inequities are often used as a basis for making salary adjustments at colleges and universities.

496. "How Much Do We Pay Our Public Library Directors? Part I and Part II." ***Public Library Quarterly*** **19, no. 1 & 2 (2001): 47, 23.**

Part I compares the salaries of public library directors with city and county managers and public works directors and breaks it down by population served. Part II compares the salaries by region of the United States.

497. "Minneapolis PL Director Salary Increased." ***Library Journal*** **128, no. 1 (January 2003): 15.**

The Minnesota Department of Employee Relations increased the salary limit for the open Minneapolis Public Library director position after two top candidates withdrew from the search in November 2002 due to the \$120,000 salary limit. The new salary limit of \$130,000 substantially exceeds the governor's pay, which is less than \$115,288; most Minnesota public employee salaries are prohibited from exceeding 95 percent of the governor's pay.

498. "More Money, Please: Low Salaries in Nebraska." ***Nebraska Library Association Quarterly*** **28, no. 4 (Winter 1998): 22–23.**

A call to arms by a library director urging rural library workers, the majority of whom are women, to work to change their chronically underpaid status. She calls for librarians to campaign together with the Nebraska Library Association in order to rectify this situation. As of this writing some progress had been made.

499. "Pay Equity Gap Closing: SLA Report." ***American Libraries*** **30, no. 11 (December 1999): 25.**

This *AL* Brief announces the result of the SLA's 1999 salary survey. This survey reports that the median salary for women is now higher than that for male information professionals.

500. "Salaries: Outrage at Regrade Degrade: Reclassification of Government Workers Could Lead to Pay Cuts for Librarians in Great Britain." ***Library Association Record*** **102, no. 8 (August 2000): 428.**

This brief news item describes a move in some British localities to unify manual and white-collar salary scales, following a 1997 decision by the National Joint Council for Local Government Employees. All staff must undergo pay and grading reviews. In Solihull, librarians complain that up to 70 percent of them would have their salaries lowered as a result; in Coventry the outcome is similar. Labor unions have rejected the regrading and threatened an "industrial action." Only ten of four hundred-plus local councils have completed the regrading. In some locations, library assistants moved up the salary scale as a result.

501. "Salary Surveys." ***EContent*** **23, no. 6 (December 2000): 68–70.**

Reviews Internet sources of salary and wage surveys and data produced by the government, commercial publishers, trade publications, organizations, and individuals.

502. "SLA: Median Salary Tops $54,000." ***Library Journal*** **126, no. 20 (December 2001): 11.**

Results of the Special Libraries Association's 2001 annual salary survey indicate that the median pay for full-time U.S. special librarians was $54,500, a 10.9 percent increase from last year. Special librarians' earnings exceeded the median earnings of all types of librarians by more than $10,000. The mean salary for male librarians is higher than that for females ($60,766 and $58,554, respectively). The highest salary mean of $78,227 was reported for the pharmaceutical and medical chemical industry.

503. "Two Canadian PL Unions Strike for Pay, Hours Equity." *Library Hotline* 31, no. 39 (30 September 2002): 3–4.

Reports on the Saskatoon chapter of the Canadian Union of Public Employee's strike charging gender-based wage discrimination. The intent is to bring the salary levels of the predominantly female workers in line with their male counterparts.

504. "Women Gain in Pay, but 24% Gap Remains." *HRFocus* 78, no. 12 (December 2001): 12.

Brief article reporting on *Working Woman*'s 2001 salary survey, which indicates that female IT managers, professors, librarians, pharmacists, and chemists can expect to earn as much or more than their male counterparts. (See 544, *Working Woman* article by Lavagnino.)

505. Amdursky, Saul. "Money Matters: Kalamazoo PL's Innovative Link between Staff Compensation and Library Revenue Could Revolutionize Salaries." *Library Journal* 127, no. 17 (15 October 2002): 39–41.

Amdursky, Director of Kalamazoo (MI) Public Library, presents total compensation linked to revenue growth as an innovative solution to protecting salaries of public library workers and controlling costs. Total compensation that is tied to revenue growth from property taxes has the potential to increase fairness in compensation. According to this pay structure, all library employees' salaries are adjusted annually based on the same revenue-based formula for total compensation, which includes both salaries and benefits. The ratio of the overall library budget to salaries and compensation is maintained regardless of revenue growth, which protects personnel but increases the need for cost control in other areas. Drawbacks to total compensation include lower salary adjustments when benefit costs increase, staff resistance, increased demands on library directors, and limitations on the plan's applicability to libraries without an independent revenue stream. Amdursky argues that total compensation allows upper management and library boards to take responsibility for developing better salaries for library workers.

506. "Judaica Librarians' Salaries: Some Comparisons." In *Proceedings of the 33rd Annual Convention of the Association of Jewish Libraries*. Association of Jewish Libraries Conference 33rd: 1998, Philadelphia, PA, 197–202. Association of Jewish Libraries, 1999.

Further analyzes the results of the first Association of Jewish Libraries salary survey. Discusses the low salary range for AJL librarians and attributes this to the high number of women (84 percent) in Jewish libraries. Describes Judaica librarianship as a "feminized" profession and briefly describes literature examining gender discrimination.

507. "Who Earns What Today: An In-Depth Look at the First AJL Survey (1997)." In *Proceedings of the 33rd Annual Convention of the Association of Jewish Libraries.* Association of Jewish Libraries Conference 33rd: 1998, Philadelphia, PA, 203–7. Association of Jewish Libraries, 1999.

Summarizes the results of the 1997 Association of Jewish Libraries salary survey. The survey examined gender, level of education, age, location, and type of employing institution. The results show that the association principally consists of women (84.3 percent); over half of the membership works part-time (38.8 percent) or are volunteers (20.8 percent), and men (22.1 percent) are more likely to have a higher degree (e.g., a doctorate) in a subject area outside of library science than women (5.2 percent). The article also reported disparities in earnings between men and women: more men (31.5) reported earnings $50,000 or higher while only 6 percent of women reported similar earnings. A higher number of women (25 percent) make between $10,000 and $30,000 compared to men (10 percent).

508. Association of Research Libraries. "*ARL Statistics and Measurement Program: Salary Survey.*" 30 November 2001. www.arl.org/stats/salary.

Links to the entire *ARL Annual Salary Survey 2000–2001* in a PDF file as well as to selected data tables back to 1995 and 1996. Tables display data for salaries by position and experience, sex, racial/ethnic background, geographical region, size, and type of research library.

509. Berry, John N. III. "The Compensation Crisis: Librarianship's Chronic Salary Depression Threatens Its Future." *Library Journal* 125, no. 4 (15 February 2000): 100.

Suggests that higher salaries are the only solution to the shortage of librarians, focusing on the salary-related protests by both the library unions and top management at New York City's three large public library systems. Advocates for the setting of minimum salary levels by states and for increased lobbying of funding authorities by library organizations like ALA and by individuals.

510. Berry, John N. III. "Governed by Administrators: ALA Must Tackle Problem of Librarians' Salaries." *Library Journal* 125, no. 19 (15 November 2000): 6.

Berry asks why the ALA has not effectively addressed the problem of librarians' salaries and sees a connection between this issue and the domination by library administrators of the membership of the ALA Council and Executive Board. He advocates for a change in the composition of the Council, which is the policy-making body of ALA.

511. Berry, John N. III. "The Salary Effort Gets Rolling Even Though Paroxysms of Parliamentary Maneuvering Cause Delay." *Library Journal* 127, no. 12 (1 July 2002): 6.

As a key theme of the 2002 American Library Association (ALA) Annual Meeting, the pay initiative for library workers continued to gain momentum and received increased attention from librarians attending the conference. Mitch Freedman, newly elected ALA president, had made the pay initiative a campaign focus and featured it in his inaugural address. The Better Salaries and Pay Equity Task Force had been recently organized, launching its Campaign for America's Libraries before Freedman was inaugurated. Fifty-five conference attendees received advocacy training based on the Task Force's new "Advocating for Better Salaries and Pay Equity Toolkit" (www.ala.org/advocacy). Keynote speakers, filmmaker Michael Moore and author Barbara Ehrenreich, talked at length about the pay problems of librarians. In contrast, sessions of the ALA Council and Executive Board revealed the reluctance of leadership to finance the pay initiative and confusion over the governance of ALA's newly formed Allied Professional Association (ALA/APA), which caused a great deal of debate and failure to act. At issue were the new association's plans to engage in activities that benefited members instead of libraries, which would threaten ALA's tax-exempt status. Members without executive support will have to find other ways to capitalize on the momentum gathered and move the pay initiative forward.

512. Berry, John N. III. "Serve and Starve? Not Now: Don't Let Association Staff Blunt the Salary Movement." *Library Journal* 127, no. 18 (1 November 2002): 8.

Berry decries the lack of leadership from the staff at the American Library Association in support of increased salaries for library workers, despite the fact that better salaries are a major initiative of ALA President Mitch Freedman. Berry argues that members of ALA are ill served by ALA staff that resist advancing the salary movement. In particular, Berry cites the editor of *American Libraries*, who claimed that salary concerns suffer from "bad timing" in the current weak economy. Berry suggests that ALA headquarters staff are insulated from many of the costs associated with association membership and conference attendance and lack understanding of the realities facing many of their members.

513. Blessing, Laura K. "Using Statistical Techniques to Reduce Salary Inequities among Librarians at the University of Texas at Arlington." ***Library Administration and Management*** **15, no. 2 (Spring 2001): 80–84.**

Salaries of librarians and archivists at the University of Texas at Arlington were studied using multiple regression analysis. Factors such as position, rank, longevity, and performance were used to plot professional experience scores for each participant. Results of the study were used to implement new salary equity packages.

514. Brey, Carol A. "Taking Our Salary Fight to the Streets: Why We Need a New 'Campaign for America's Librarians.'" ***Library Journal*** **127, no. 7 (15 April 2002): 38–39.**

The author, a member of ALA's Better Salaries and Pay Equity Task Force, calls for a "Campaign for America's Librarians" to complement ALA's previously established "Campaign for America's Libraries." Communities have long known the value of libraries, but librarians need to advocate more strongly for themselves and their profession in order to redress their low salaries, which remain lower than those for comparable jobs in professions requiring similar qualifications and skills. ALA's salary survey for 2001 reported a mean salary of $32,981 for beginning librarians. Public librarians' salaries are the lowest, particularly in the Southwest, and a negative impact can be seen in recruitment and unfilled positions. Directly advocating for higher pay is recommended. Tools such as ALA's *Pay Equity and Action Manual for Library Workers*, job evaluation studies, partnerships with other municipal organizations and unions, and outreach to the press have proved effective at El Paso Public Library, El Paso, Texas, where the author is director of libraries.

515. Carson, Herbert C. "Placements and Salaries, 1996: Counting on Technology." In ***The Bowker Annual Library and Book Trade Almanac: Facts, Figures, and Reports*****, 356–67. New Providence, RI: R. R. Bowker, 1998.**

Data show that women continue to account for a large percent (78.2) of library school graduates. Median salaries for women have remained the same, and men still are receiving higher starting salaries, except in the Northeast. Women's average salary went up 2.1 percent in 1996.

516. Cortis, Natasha. "Pay Equity and Human Service Work: A New South Wales Case Study." *Australian Journal of Political Science* 35, no. 1 (2000): 49–62.

In a 1998 New South Wales Pay Equity Inquiry, librarians and other types of female-dominated jobs were compared to male-dominated industries and occupations with the intention of highlighting how female-dominated employment may be undervalued. In these case studies, hairdressers were compared to motor mechanics, clerical workers and child-care workers to metals tradespeople, seafood processors to general boatdock hands, and librarians to geoscientists in the public sector. These studies were useful in breaking down how remuneration was determined and highlighted the factors that deny equal earnings for men and women. It was also suggested that earnings disparities between male-dominated and female-dominated jobs are a result of the "invisibility of caring and emotional labour" that doesn't fit anywhere into the industrial notion of work.

517. Coulson, G. "Salaries, Status and Sector: Career Dilemmas and Choices Facing the New Information Professional." *Impact, the Journal of the Career Development Group* 3, no. 3 (March 2000): 42–44.

Using his own experience in job hunting as an example, Coulson found the salaries for academic library positions were not competitive with salaries in the corporate sector and surmises that this may account for why new professionals like himself are not going into academic librarianship. Academic libraries are losing the energy and drive that new professionals can bring to their institutions. Coulson recommends that academic libraries cease to be complacent with the "undervaluing" of the profession and instead market the valuable skills and qualifications needed in a professional, establish a minimum "graded" salary for positions, and limit the use of paraprofessional staff in professional positions.

518. Crane, Hilary. "Pay-Equity Ruling in Favour of Federal Government Librarians in Canada." *Feliciter* 44, no. 9 (September 1998): 23–24.

On July 29, 1998, a Canadian Human Rights Commission (CHRC) tribunal upheld a complaint by the Public Service Alliance of Canada that government employees in female-dominated categories were not receiving equal pay for work of equal value. The tribunal ordered adjustments to salaries of employees in the affected job categories, to reflect value relative to jobs performed mostly by men. The decision, the result of a fourteen-year pay equity fight, affects public servants in librarian categories and also library technicians in the clerical category. Susan Burrows, National

Library of Canada, comments that librarians have been in the forefront of the pay equity battle since 1979, when they presented a case for pay equity; the librarians' appeal prompted other complaints to the CHRC from female-dominated groups. Although the government of Canada has paid more than $850 million in equalization payments from 1990 to 1998, the unions complained to CHRC that these payments did not deal with the full scope of wage discrimination, so pay-equity negotiations continued; Burrows reports that the majority of librarians supported the decision to hold out for the whole amount. Includes a copy of a letter from Sydney Jones, president of the Canadian Library Association, to Marcel Massé, president of the Treasury Board of Canada; the letter notes that the workforce of most libraries is dominated by women and urges the Government of Canada to accept and implement the CHRC tribunal's decision.

519. DiMattia, Susan. "Canadian PL Unions on Strike: One Strike Coincides with UNET Meetings; Other Driven by Pay Equity." ***Library Journal*** **127, no. 17 (15 October 2002): 16.**

Canadian Union of Public Employees (CUPE) members in Brantford, Ontario, began a walkout on September 12, protesting the lack of regular schedules for part-time workers and seeking guarantees against outsourcing. The strike coincided with the annual meeting of the UNESCO Model Library Network (UNET) in Brantford. CUPE members in Saskatoon, Saskatchewan, walked off for three hours on September 25 after rejecting a 4 percent wage increase for each year of a two-year contract, charging gender-based wage discrimination. The union proposes a job evaluation plan to reach pay equity between jobs held predominantly by female library workers and those held predominantly by males and requiring similar qualifications.

520. Echavarria, Tami. "Pay Equity after Thirty Years." ***California Libraries*** **8, no. 6 (June 1998): 1, 10.**

In recognition of National Pay Equity Day 1998, Echavarria discusses pay equity in librarianship. Though pay equity has improved in general, she points out that pay inequality is the greatest in librarianship. The fact that librarianship is a woman-dominated profession emphasizes the importance of overcoming gender bias in our profession. Echavarria also points out that even though pay inequity is an issue for minorities in librarianship, it has not garnered the attention it deserves.

521. Eggertson, Laura. "Women Hail Victory of Pay Equity Ruling: Ottawa Owes Civil Servants $2 Billion in Back Wages." ***Toronto Star*** **(July 7, 1998): A1.**

Reports on the billions of dollars the Canadian government was ordered to pay to women in public service as back wages because they earn less than men in comparable jobs. Among the civil service jobs mentioned were librarians. See also articles on this story in the *Wall Street Journal* November 1, 1999: B13; *New York Times* November 19, 1999: A17; *Montreal Gazette* March 25, 2000: A12; *Montreal Gazette* July 20, 2000: A12. Online. Available from Lexis-Nexis Universe. August 2, 2000.

522. Flagg, Gordon. "We've Buttered Our Bread, Must We Lie in It? State of Professional Salaries." *American Libraries* 31, no. 3 (March 2000): 31.

Gordon Flagg writes an opinion article introducing the theme of the March 2000 issue on librarians' salaries. Flagg refers to James LaRue's article that suggests a direct correlation between low salaries and female professions.

523. Fox, Charlie, and Raymond Rooney. "Library Support Staff Salary Survey." *Library Mosaics* 11, no. 4 (August 2000): 8–12.

Reports data on highest and lowest salaries by type of library and geographic region but not by sex.

524. Fruin, Di, Elizabeth Fletcher, and Elizabeth Casey. *Pay Equity Case Study: Librarians and Geologists, February 1998*. Sydney, New South Wales: Office of the Director of Equal Opportunity in Public Employment, 1998.

This report compares the work and pay of librarians and geologists in New South Wales, Australia. The study was prompted by an earlier study (1991) that found that female-dominated occupations in Australia's public sector received on average only 85 percent of the pay of comparable male occupations. The present study addresses the following research questions: "Are the librarian and geoscientist professions comparable in terms of qualifications and work value? What is the remuneration at various levels of work value for each profession? What contribution might the following factors make to any differences in remuneration: working conditions, patterns of pay increases, award structures and histories, sex discrimination and market influences?" (10). Twenty typical librarian jobs in the State Library of NSW and twenty typical geologist jobs in the NSW Department of Mineral Resources were evaluated by panels of human resource practitioners using two different point factor systems: the Organisation Consulting Resources system (OCR) and the Hay system. The study confirmed that the profession of librarianship is female-dominated, while that of geologist is male-dominated. Both occupations require similar educational qualifications at the entry level and similar years of experience to advance to senior levels; however, librarians face more hurdles (in the form of merit-based competitions) to achieve the senior grades. The work value of the two professions is comparable but the pay is not. For example, senior librarians grade 2, with titles such as team leader, were given point scores equivalent to those of senior geologists. However, a senior geologist with four years of experience is paid 19.75 percent more than a senior librarian grade 2 with the same years of experience. The pay gap for jobs with equivalent work value is smaller for entry-level positions but widens for senior positions. Charts and graphs are included to illustrate the disparities.

525. Gregory, Vicki L. "Beating Inflation Now." ***Library Journal*** **124, no. 17 (15 October 1999): 36–42.**

Library Journal's forty-eighth annual Placements and Salaries Survey (1998) reports a 5.4 percent increase in average starting salaries for librarians, from $30,270 in 1997 to $31,915 in 1998. Other reported trends include: higher average starting salaries for graduates in technologically oriented jobs, slowly rising salaries for minority graduates, steady graduation rates, 93.2 percent placement in library jobs, 81.5 percent placement in full-time permanent positions, larger average salary increases for women, including a survey of female graduates in the Northeast and Southeast regions enjoying higher average starting salaries than males, and no schools reporting difficulty placing students. Graduates asked about the placement process reported employers' desire for a mix of technological and traditional library skills and cited the need for more classes in computer networking and teaching. Tables included.

526. Gregory, Vicki L. "Placement and Salaries 1998: Beating Inflation Now." In ***The Bowker Annual of Library & Book Trade Information*****, 319–31. New York: R. R. Bowker, 2000.**

Review of 1998 data shows increasing salary equity between men and women. In fact, a survey showed that 1998 female graduates in two regions had higher starting salaries than men. Women make up 79.6 percent of LIS graduates. Women's average salary rose 6 percent. Article includes data tables.

527. Gregory, Vicki L., and Kathleen de la Peña McCook. "Placement and Salaries 1997: Breaking the $30K Barrier." In ***The Bowker Annual Library and Book Trade Almanac: Facts, Figures, and Reports*****, 376–89. New Providence, RI: R. R. Bowker, 1998.**

Data show that average beginning salary for librarians is going up and for the first time was over $30,000. Women accounted for 44.46 percent of graduates. Male graduates still make about $500 per year more than their female colleagues. Tables of salary data are included.

528. Gregory, Vicki L., Kathleen de la Peña McCook, and Norman Oder. "Breaking the 30K Barrier: Salaries for Many New Librarians Finally Cross a Psychological Frontier." ***Library Journal*** **123, no. 17 (15 October 1998): 32–38.**

Library Journal's forty-seventh annual Placements and Salaries Survey (1997) reports that the average beginning salary for new graduates broke the $30K barrier at $30,270, a 2.9 percent increase over the 1996 figure of $29,480. The growing economy and increased placements in academic and special libraries are seen as possible reasons for the increase. The survey indicates several other trends, including significant salary gains for minority graduates and higher average starting salaries for technologically oriented jobs, along with the addition of several new job categories, no discernible narrowing of the gender gap for salaries, steadily growing graduation rates, and greater availability of jobs. Graduates asked about the placement process cited the importance of technological competencies in job preparation as well as traditional expertise and management skills. Tables included.

529. Gregory, Vicki L., and Sonia Ramfrez Wohlmuth. "Placement and Salaries 1999: Better Pay, More Jobs." In ***The Bowker Annual of Library & Book Trade Information*****, 322–35. New York: R. R. Bowker, 2001.**

The average salaries for women increased by 5.2 percent while those of men grew by 12 percent in 1999. Salary parity that was evidenced in 1998 studies is no longer apparent. Article includes data tables.

530. Gregory, Vicki L., and Sonia Ramirez Wohlmuth. "Better Pay, More Jobs." ***Library Journal*** **125, no. 17 (15 October 2000): 30–36.**

Library Journal's forty-ninth annual Placements and Salaries Survey (1999) reports a 6.5 percent increase in average starting salaries for librarians, from $31,915 in 1998 to $33,976 in 1999. The gender parity that emerged last year in two national regions has disappeared, with men's average starting salaries rising 12 percent and women's only 5.2 percent. Other reported trends include 92.7 percent of graduates placed in libraries, salaries rising 6.2 percent for minority graduates, public libraries showing the lowest average starting salary at $29,643, and rising placements of graduates in college and university libraries and public libraries. Graduates reporting on job preparation indicated the need for emphasis on traditional areas of librarianship as well as on technology. Tables included.

531. Hall, Philippa. "The NSW Pay Equity Inquiry: A New Approach for the New Century." *Labour & Industry* 10, no. 2 (December 1999): 33–51.

Hall reports on the New South Wales Pay Equity Inquiry conducted in 1998 to investigate how pay inequality occurs, how work has been valued and remuneration set, and how pay equity would impact the economy. The investigation was heavily based on case study comparisons of female- and male-dominated occupations, one of which involved comparing librarians to geoscientists in the public sector. The Industrial Relations Commission found that the work of librarians had initially been undervalued, and that there had been a policy of hiring women to provide cheaper labor. Librarians had fewer promotion prospects and less recognition of the value of experience than the comparison group, geoscientists. However, the IRC also found that job evaluation alone did not take all aspects of the value of work into account; there was also consideration of working conditions such as field trips, camping out, and shift work. It was stated that although there is still room for improvement, the Inquiry's use of expertise and insights and an archive of evidence, particularly in the case studies, has set the most significant new directions for seeking pay equity since its Equal Pay Case in 1972.

532. Harrison, Linda. "The Wages of the Profession . . ." *Library Association Record* 101, no. 6 (June 1999): 340.

Harrison heard a radio ad for the new government minimum wage, which featured a librarian. Although distressed by the stereotyped image of "quietly spoken, female, middle-aged, apologetic, etc.," she was more outraged by the fact that some librarians are paid below the minimum wage. Other professions, such as medicine and accounting, do not tolerate low salaries, even though more women have entered them. Further, librarians are as well educated as other professionals. She asks, "Are the universities producing too many librarians? Is the LA [Library Association] doing enough to protect its members?" Reporting that the ad urged, "Whether you are a librarian or a labourer, tell your employer about the new minimum wage," Harrison declares that "it only begs the question: 'Why the hell don't the employers know, and why can't they appreciate the work of librarians in the Information Age?'"

533. Hooper, H. "Schools Way Out of Line on Salaries and Conditions." *Library Association Record* 100, no. 1 (January 1998): 19.

The letter writer comments on the low salary scales in advertisements in Library Association (UK) periodicals and references a recent posting for a school librarian in the greater London area. The writer further notes that "librarianship is an overwhelmingly female profession and not noted for militancy, but perhaps some challenges under the Equal Pay Act with the backing of the Association could take librarianship out of the doll's house and into the real world where mortgages have to be paid, school shoes bought, cars repaired, clothes cleaned, etc." Anthony Tilke (professional advisor, Youth and School Libraries) responds by agreeing with the letter writer's points. He also reports that the LA writes to schools that advertise substandard salaries, informing them of the Association's recommended salary scales, but feedback from employers is mixed.

534. Hunter, Rosemary. *The Beauty Therapist, the Mechanic, the Geoscientist and the Librarian: Addressing Undervaluation of Women's Work*. Sydney, NSW: ATN WEXDEV, University of Technology, Sydney, 2000.

In 1999, the Australian Technology Network Women's Executive Development Program (ATN WEXDEV) sponsored a series of lectures at seven Australian universities honoring the late Claire Burton, an Australian researcher, activist, and professor. From her early work as a doctoral student at Macquarie University, Burton's work focused on women's work, subordination, and pay equity. The volume, edited by Rosemary Hunter, a colleague of Burton's, includes the text of the lectures, each focusing on issues of gender pay equity, as well as a short biography of Claire Burton, a bibliography, and a report on the events held to celebrate her life. Reviews: *Labour & Industry* 11, no. 3 (April 2001): 123–24 (reviewed by Barbara Pocock).

535. Johnson, Albie. "How Are We Doing?: Compensation for Librarians in the Fenway Library Consortium." *Technicalities* 20, no. 1 (January 2000–28 February 2000): 6–8.

This article presents the results of a salary and compensation survey of the Fenway Library Consortium. This study considered salary and benefits of 210 employees from fourteen, mostly smaller academic, libraries. Results show that there were eight female and six male directors and that women directors earned both the lowest and highest directorship salaries. The average salary for women directors was $208 less annually. The range for women directors was $50,000–$89,999 while the range for male directors was $57,500–$77,499.

536. Kolb, Deborah M., and Ann C. Schaffner. "Negotiating What You're Worth: In Feminized Profession, Librarians Need Some Tips to Help Fight Sluggish Salaries." ***Library Journal*** **126, no. 17 (15 October 2001): 52–54.**

Negotiation research suggests possible behavioral factors that may contribute to the problem of low salaries for librarians and the continuing gender gap in pay equity. Librarians seeking employment can counter these trends by adopting negotiation strategies and changing personal behavior when addressing salary and other compensation. Suggested strategies include focusing on strengths and accomplishments and considering nonfinancial rewards as part of compensation packages.

537. Kyrillidou, Martha. "Salary Trends Highlight Inequities—Old and New." ***ARL Newsletter*****, no. 208/209 (February 2000–30 April 2000).**

Highlights trends in university research librarian salaries by examining the data retrospectively. Reports that the salary gap between women and men is closing but, especially in U.S. libraries, very slowly. At the current rate it could take up to twenty years for salary inequities to disappear.

538. Kyrillidou, Martha, Julia C. Blixrud, and Jonathan Green. ***ARL Annual Salary Survey 1998–99*****. Washington, D.C.: Association of Research Libraries, 1999.**

Contains data on salary and years of experience for male and female librarians at ARL institutions for 1998–1999. For the third consecutive year, female directors are receiving higher salaries than their male counterparts. The overall average salary for women continues to lag behind the average for men, and years of experience do not fully explain the salary gap.

539. Kyrillidou, Martha, Julia C. Blixrud, and Rodriguez, Ken. ***ARL Annual Salary Survey 1997–98*****. Washington, D.C.: Association of Research Libraries, 1988.**

Contains data on salary and years of experience for male and female librarians at ARL institutions for 1997–1998. The data shows that the average salary for female directors is slightly higher than the average salary for male directors in university libraries. However, in most job categories, the average salary for men exceeds the average salary for women. Years of experience do not completely account for differences in pay between men and women.

540. Kyrillidou, Martha, and Michael O'Connor. *ARL Annual Salary Survey 1999–2000*. Washington, D.C.: Association of Research Libraries, 2000.

Contains data on salary and years of experience for male and female librarians at ARL institutions for 1999–2000. Female directors continue to receive higher salaries than male directors do. Overall salaries for women are lower in most job categories and years of experience do not account for the difference in salary between the sexes.

541. Kyrillidou, Martha, and Karen Wetzel. *ARL Annual Salary Survey 2000–2001*. Washington, D.C.: Association of Research Libraries, 2001.

Contains data on salary and years of experience for male and female librarians at ARL institutions for 2000–2001. The average salary for female directors continues to be slightly higher than the average for male directors. However, the average salary for women in most job categories lags behind the average salary for their male counterparts. Reviews earnings trends for women in the last twenty years.

542. Kyrillidou, Martha, and Mark Young. *ARL Annual Salary Survey 2001–02*. Washington, D.C.: Association of Research Libraries, 2002.

Contains data on salary and years of experience for male and female librarians at ARL institutions for 2001–2002. For the first time in five years, the average salary for male directors surpasses the average salary for female directors. The average salary for women continues to be less than the average salary men receive, and this trend suggests a persistence of the gender gap in the profession.

543. LaRue, J. "Can't Get No Satisfaction: Library Pay in the 21st Century." *American Libraries* 31, no. 3 (March 2000): 36–38.

This article traces the history of low library wages dating back to the beginning of librarianship. LaRue suggests that Melvil Dewey intentionally recruited women into the profession because of their innate sense of forming values outside of the home in a community setting. This moral nature influenced women to succumb to low wages. Though library wages continue to be low today, there are slow noticeable improvements.

544. Lavagnino, Doria. "The 2001 Salary Survey." *Working Woman* 26, no. 7 (July 2001–31 August 2001): 44–47.

Reports that the 24 percent wage gap between men's and women's salaries has barely budged in a decade. The good news, however, is that female IT managers, professors, pharmacists, chemists, and librarians can expect to earn nearly as much or more than their male counterparts. Specifically under the library science category, the mean salaries for library directors and heads of reference are now higher for women than for men, although men still earn more as heads of medical and law libraries.

545. Miller, Herbert A. "Sources of Compensation Surveys." *Journal of Business and Finance Librarianship* 4, no. 3 (1999): 15–30.

Miller provides an overview of compensation surveys from the major producers such as the Economic Research Institute (ERI) to small firms specializing in particular fields. He provides a detailed discussion of major publishers and provides a couple of bibliographies for further consultation. Miller comments on the challenges of collecting compensation surveys: the sources can be expensive, information is dated as soon as the publication is in print, and the workplace is constantly changing with the creation of new industries and jobs.

546. Moberg, David. "Bridging the Gap: Why Women Still Don't Get Equal Pay." *In These Times* 8 (January 2001): 24.

Reports that, according to *The State of Working America*, the fact that women now earn "72 cents" for every dollar earned by men, it is mostly due to falling real wages among men, rather than women's real rising wages. Discrimination is particularly evident in female-dominated jobs, such as librarians and retail clerks, where these workers are paid approximately 18 percent less than if they were employed outside the "pink ghetto." Because of this, there has been a surge of labor union organization of women workers, who make an average of 38 percent more than their nonunionized counterparts.

547. O'Connor, Michael. "ARL Librarian Salaries Rise Faster than Inflation." *ARL Newsletter*, no. 208/209 (February 2000–30 April 2000).

Based on data from the *ARL Annual Salary Survey 1999–2000*, librarians' salaries in both Canada and the United States increased at a rate higher than inflation. Salary differences by sex and race are reported as well as comparisons to full-time faculty in U.S. doctoral institutions.

548. O'Sullivan, Keith M. C., and Valerie J. Lawrence. "Even Nurses Get More." *Library Association Record* 101, no. 3 (March 1999): 150.

In this letter to the editor, two Oxford University librarians quote a salary offered in a recent *Library Record* advertisement and state that "compared to more prominent public-sector-dominated professions (even, we must say, nurses) librarians particularly are still poorly paid." They urge the Library Association to become more militant on salary issues.

549. Oder, Norman. "Librarian Salary Hearings Set in N.Y." ***Library Journal*** **125, no. 1 (January 2000): 16–20.**

The New York City Council's Committee on Parks, Recreation, Cultural Affairs & International Intergroup Relations passed a resolution to hold oversight hearings on the library's loss of staff and possible salary adjustments for librarians. Union leaders, library directors, and library staff testified to the problems with the ongoing staff deficit and its impact on library services. The library workers' union is seeking a 15 percent salary adjustment, which would cost the city $9 million. Starting librarians in New York earn $31,296, far less than those in other major cities like San Francisco or Seattle.

550. Oder, Norman. "Salary Crisis at NYC PL's Remains Unresolved." ***Library Journal*** **125, no. 16 (1 October 2000): 14.**

New York Public Library is taking the lead in negotiations to adjust salaries upward for four thousand librarians and library staff spread across the New York, Brooklyn, and Queens Borough Public Library systems. Negotiations broke down when library administrators proposed funding the increases only with a corresponding increase in the work week from thirty-five to thirty-seven and a half hours. The union plans to step up protests at library events, stating that the proposal will not help recruit or retain staff. City officials appear to be influenced by the fear that a salary increase for the library union would bolster efforts by larger city unions to request similar increases.

551. Okuda, Sachiko. "Pay Equity: What's It All Worth?" ***Feliciter*** **46, no. 6 (2000): 314–17.**

This article describes the 1999 payout settlement between the Public Service Alliance of Canada and the Canadian government over pay inequality in six of the federal civil service's top female-dominated professions, including librarianship. After fifteen years of negotiations, the retroactive payout of $3.6 million was awarded. In 1977, research started comparing the salaries of two library organizations, one of which employed mostly women and the other, mostly men. It was discovered that the men were making $3,000 more than the women.

552. PLA Committee on Recruitment of Public Librarians. "Recruitment of Public Librarians: A Report to the Executive Committee of

the Public Library Association, January 2000." ***Public Libraries*** **39, no. 3 (May 2000–30 June 2000): 168–72.**

Discusses the ability of public libraries to recruit quality candidates, focusing on salary as the main criterion. The report and recommendations of the committee are based on a year of study, surveying, and discussion. The survey indicated that low salaries are causing librarians in public libraries to seek higher-paying positions outside the field. The report summarizes places to seek quantitative library salary data and also touches on other issues in recruitment. The committee cites a need for a systematic recruitment plan from the national organizations as well as at the local level. Bibliography and the survey results are available at www.pla.org, the Public Library Association's website.

553. Quint, Barbara E. "Gender Equity in Salaries Achieved for Some Information Professionals but Not for Others." ***Information Today*** **16, no. 11 (December 1999): 60.**

1999 Annual Salary Survey of the Special Libraries Association (SLA) found that the median salaries of female information professionals equaled or surpassed those of their male counterparts. In the United States, the median full-time salary of female SLA members is $49,550 whereas it is $48,672 for their male peers. In Canada, the median salary was $52,000 for both men and women. Although this trend may signify the end of pay inequity in the library profession, the survey found that the gap in mean salaries is narrowing but has not been eliminated. The article claims that SLA is the first library professional organization to report this trend in salaries and compares its findings with surveys conducted by the Association of Research Libraries (ARL) and the American Library Association (ALA). It attributes the establishment of laws prohibiting discrimination in pay as a contributing factor.

554. Rogers, Michael, and Norman Oder. "Female Special Librarians Finally Achieve Pay Equity." ***Library Journal*** **124, no. 19 (15 November 1999): 12.**

The annual salary survey of the Special Libraries Association released in October 1999 reports that, for the first time, the median salaries of female information professionals are equal to or higher than those of their male counterparts. The median salary for female SLA members was $49,550, compared to $48,672 for male members. Male and female Canadian SLA members have equal median salaries at $52,000. Both national median salary figures reflect greater pay increases for women than for men.

555. Seaman, Scott, Nancy Carter, Carol Krismann, and David Fagerstrom. "Market Equity Tempered by Career Merit: A Case Study." *Journal of Academic Librarianship* 26, no. 4 (July 2000): 225–32.

This article reports the method used to realize market equity for librarians at the University of Colorado, Boulder. Authors report that most studies in this area are gender-based and conclude that while females dominate the profession, they continue to be paid and valued less. This case study employs merit-based analysis, not gender, in order to achieve market parity for librarians.

556. St. Lifer, Evan, and Michael Rogers. "Women Directors at Research Libraries Earn More than Men." *Library Journal* 123, no. 6 (15 April 1998): 14.

This brief news article highlights several points from the Association of Research Libraries (ARL) Annual Salary Survey 1997–1998. Female research library directors earned slightly higher salaries than their male counterparts for the second year in a row. However, men surpass women in most ARL job categories, with women's earnings averaging 93 percent of men's. Minorities are reported to earn about 4.5 percent less than their white counterparts. The median annual pay for university research librarians in FY 1997/1998 reached $44,435; nonuniversity research librarians' median pay reached $55,055.

557. Terrell, Tom. "Salaries Rebound, Women Break Out: Pay and Job Variety Both Increase in Spite of a Tough Economy." *Library Journal* 127, no. 17 (15 October 2002): 30–36.

Library Journal's 2001 Placements and Salaries survey reports on the status of 2001 graduates from ALA-accredited library and information science schools. Graduates reported increased salaries and opportunities in traditional and new library positions. The average starting pay for 2001 graduates is $36,818, a 5.49 percent increase over the 2002 average of $34,871. Average salaries increased 5.98 percent for men and 5.37 percent for women. Men make $2000 more than women in average starting salaries, but women are getting higher pay than men at the high ends of pay scales. Additional salary data include breakdowns by location, gender, minority status, job assignment, and institution type. Placements in college and university libraries were down from 2000, as were those in school libraries; public library placements increased slightly. Graduates commented on the importance of "people skills" and strategic planning abilities for successful placement and stressed the need for preparation in budgeting, management, and technology issues. Includes tables.

558. Terrell, Tom, and Vicki L. Gregory. "Placement and Salaries 2000: Plenty of Jobs, Salaries Flat." In *The Bowker Annual of Library & Book Trade Information*, 382–95. New York: R. R. Bowker, 2002.

In 2000, the average salary for women increased by 3.78 percent, a significant difference from the .57 percent increase in men's salaries. Men continue to have salaries 5 percent higher than those of women. Women's salaries in special libraries are higher then those of their male coworkers. In high-tech jobs, men's salaries decreased by 4.4 percent while those of women increased 4.5 percent, a major shift from the previous year. Article includes data tables.

559. Terrell, Tom, and Vicki L. Gregory. "Plenty of Jobs, Salaries Flat: Library Pay Is Not Immune to the National Slowdown." *Library Journal* 126, no. 17 (15 October 2001): 34–40.

Library Journal's fiftieth annual Placements and Salaries Survey (2000) reports a smaller increase in average starting pay for librarians than in the past two years, in which salary increases outpaced inflation. The average salary is now $34,871, a mere 2.3 percent increase over the 1999 average of $33,976. For minority graduates, salaries rose 11 percent; the average salary for women rose 3.18 percent in 2000 while that for men increased only .57 percent. Placement in the high-tech "other" job-type category dropped, with a slowdown in the rise of men's salaries in this area that did not affect the overall disparity between men and women. An increasing number of graduates accepted positions with vendors, which offer the highest average starting salary of $42,250, itself a 14 percent increase over the 1999 average. Graduates reporting on job preparation stressed technology skills accompanied by teamwork and communication skills, along with the key areas of cataloging and collection development. Tables included.

560. Titus, Elizabeth A. "A Recommended Methodology for Determining the Disparity Between Women's Salary Levels and Those of Men in the Librarian Professorate in an Academic Library Setting." In *Advances in Library Administration and Organization*, ed. Edward D. Garten and Delmus E. Williams, 123–73. Vol. 18. 2001. Greenwich, CT: JAI Press.

This study builds on a methodology developed by E. L. Scott in 1977 for identifying and measuring sex discrimination in faculty salaries. Titus reviews the theoretical and research literature on gender-based wage gaps and discusses the utility of multivariate regression analysis. She then applies Scott's original methodology and four variants of it to academic librarians with faculty status at selected public universities in Illinois. All five statistical models reveal salary disparities when (a) men are compared to women and (b) white men are compared to women and minorities, although the size of the negative residuals differs depending on which variables are included. (The independent variables in the study are year of birth, year of highest degree, highest degree level, level of position, rank held, and years of professional library experience.) Titus subjects the data to additional statistical tests to determine the strongest predictive variables: year of birth, rank held, and level of position. She reports that the most precise findings result when men are compared to women, since grouping women and minorities together obscures the gender dispersion. She concludes that Scott's methodology, with recommended modifications, can be used to identify cases of pay inequity among the librarian professoriate and that "any library could easily gather the data and do the procedures cost effectively." She suggests that further research is needed to understand why "gender-based wage disparities exist even in a female-dominated profession where the females . . . participate in setting salary increases" through peer review processes.

561. Titus, Elizabeth A. "A Recommended Methodology for Determining the Disparity between Women's Salary Levels and Those of Men in the Librarian Professorate in an Academic Library Setting." Ph.D. diss., Northern Illinois University, 1998.

Uses a methodology widely used in academe, the Scott (1977) study, to determine whether a similar recommended methodology could be developed to determine the disparity in salary levels between men and women in the librarian professorate in an academic library environment. Gathers data from the five largest public, state-supported academic libraries in Illinois and tests this information using a multivariate linear regression technique. Tests five predictor models for two comparison groups and performs two types of analyses: a negative residual analysis and an empirical analysis. The findings suggest the possibility for creating a recommended methodology for determining the disparity between women's salary levels and those of men in the librarian professorate. Further suggests that gender-based wage disparities persist, despite the active participation of women in the salary recommendation process and despite the dominance of women as members of the professional group being studied. Determines that both the female-dominated group as a whole and females within the same female-dominated group may be experiencing gender-based wage discrimination.

562. Turner, Anne M. "California Makes the Case for Pay Equity." *Library Journal* 127, no. 17 (15 October 2002): 42–44.

A study by the California Library Association (CLA) compared compensation of public library workers to those doing similar work in other public agencies and found a pattern of inequitable pay. The data was gathered by CLA members, who reported on typical positions in their libraries and compared them to similar positions in other departments. The job summaries were cross-checked with specifications for city and county jobs and included social workers, fleet maintenance managers, building clerks, and parks and recreation personnel. Job comparisons at all levels revealed significant differences between library and nonlibrary salaries. The smallest salary disparity of $2,940 exists for entry-level professional staff and the greatest disparity of more than $11,000 exists between top salaries for library directors and nonlibrary executives. Additional comparisons break down differences between jobs at various levels. Factors identified as contributing to the disparity include gender-based wage discrimination, a lack of accurate human resources standards for job classification, comparison, and compensation, weak union representation, and passivity on the part of library workers. Includes tables.

563. Wetzel, Karen A. "ARL Salary Survey 2000–2001 Released." ***ARL Newsletter*, no. 214 (February 2001): 9.**

Summarizes the 2000–2001 ARL Annual Salary Survey. Table shows average salaries for men and women, minority men and women, average years of experience, and number of positions filled. Also reports data on library directors.

564. Young, Mark. "ARL Salary Survey Highlights." ***ARL Newsletter*, no. 221 (April 2002).**

Highlights trends in the 2000–2001 salary survey. One trend that remains constant is that average salaries for men surpass those of women in the majority of job categories (fifteen out of twenty-seven). This cannot be explained completely by differences in years of experience. Women average more years of experience in every category in which they average higher pay, but there are several categories in which women average more experience but lower salaries.

12

Sexual Discrimination and Harassment

This chapter includes publications that focus on discrimination and harassment.

565. Blessinger, Kelly D. "Problem Patrons: All Shapes and Sizes." ***The Reference Librarian*****, no. 75/76 (2002): 3–10.**

This short article identifies several types of problem behavior by library patrons. A 1992 case of sexual harassment against a female librarian at the Freeport (Illinois) Public Library is recounted. The harasser was barred from the library but sued to regain access, citing denial of his First Amendment rights. The court ruled that the library could not bar the harasser and had to pay his legal fees; the librarian resigned. The article also alludes to the discomfort caused to female library employees by patrons viewing Internet pornography and notes that "people have been charged with harassment for far less." Also published in *Helping the Difficult Library Patron: New Approaches to Examining and Resolving a Long-Standing and Ongoing Problem*, ed. Kwasi Sarkodie-Mensah, 3–10 (New York: Haworth Press, 2002).

566. Borin, Jacqueline. "E-Problems, E-Solutions: Electronic Reference and the Problem Patron in the Academic Library." ***The Reference Librarian*****, no. 75/76 (2002): 149–61.**

Borin discusses several types of problem patron behavior associated with new technologies such as the Internet and cell phones. In the brief section titled "Pornography," she addresses the hostile work environment that may be created when library users access and display graphic sexual websites.

Library policies that explicitly address sexual harassment are recommended, and Appalachian State University Library's policy is quoted. Also published in *Helping the Difficult Library Patron: New Approaches to Examining and Resolving a Long-Standing and Ongoing Problem*, ed. Kwasi Sarkodie-Mensah, 149–61 (New York: Haworth Press, 2002).

567. Bunton, Anne. "Economic Views of Gender Discrimination in Labor Markets (bibliographical essay)." ***Choice*** **35, no. 7 (March 1998): 1141–52.**

This bibliographic essay discusses literature and a few websites that focus on "women's experience with discrimination within labor markets" (1141). Due to the vastness of the literature on the subject, the essay includes mostly works that would be useful for undergraduate students and excludes works in the Marxist tradition. Throughout the twentieth century, women's experience in the labor force has been marked by unequal employment opportunities, workplace segregation, lower wages or earnings, and lack of access to higher or specialized education. Various theories have examined gender discrimination in the workforce, from the early advocates of women's rights (Mary Wollstonecraft, John Stuart Mill, and Charlotte Perkins Gilman) to theorists using existing models (neoclassical, institutional, feminist, etc.) to examine the condition of women in the work force. The essay concludes with key Internet sites, listservs, and electronic forums. References.

568. Chattoo, Calmer D. "The Problem Patron: Is There One in Your Library?" ***The Reference Librarian*****, no. 75/76 (2002): 11–22.**

Chattoo offers several definitions for, and typologies of, problem patrons in libraries, including visual, verbal, and physical harassment. Also published in *Helping the Difficult Library Patron: New Approaches to Examining and Resolving a Long-Standing and Ongoing Problem*, ed. By Kwasi Sarkodie-Mensah, 11–22 (New York: Haworth Press, 2002).

569. Reynolds, Nigel, and Amit Roy. "Sculpture's Breasts Put Women Off Lunch." ***Daily Telegraph (London)*** **(21 January 2000): 13.**

Article reports that the British Library will remove a sculpture of a naked woman with prominent breasts from the staff canteen, after sixty women librarians and curators petitioned the library's chief executive. The petition stated that the sculpture grossly distorted the female body, that it was sexist, offensive, put the women "off their food," and encouraged men to make lewd remarks. Dhruva Mistry, the artist, said that the women were probably just "jealous of his well-endowed woman." The sculpture was donated to the library anonymously, and when it is removed from the canteen, it will likely be placed in one of the library's public areas.

570. Ritchie, S. "2000 and Beyond: Is Sex in Libraries Still an Issue?" *Impact, the Journal of the Career Development Group* 3, no. 5 (May 2000): 66–69.

Ritchie provides background on the founding of Women in Libraries (WiL) in 1979 and discusses the group's efforts to address gender inequalities and pay inequities in the library profession in the United Kingdom. In the last two decades, more women are in senior management positions, and their earning potential is higher than it was for their predecessors. Pursuing a career became more acceptable for women in the 1980s, and they made gains in achieving middle management positions. By the 1990s, a sufficient pool of qualified women was in the profession, and they have gradually begun to move to higher posts. However, men still account for a disproportionate number of senior managers. In 1998, 38 percent of women in public libraries were in top-level posts compared to 62 percent of men. The percentages for academic libraries are nearly the same (39 percent women, 61 percent men). The biggest barriers for women achieving employment or managerial positions are the number of jobs with flexible work schedules and lack of opportunities to work at home.

571. Ritchie, S. "2000 to 1: A Sex Oddity." *Impact, the Journal of the Career Development Group* 3, no. 5 (May 2000): 69–73.

Reprint of a 1979 article that presented the results of a small pilot study of librarians in English public libraries show 106 men in senior posts and only two women. Survey findings describe qualifications, career length, and aspirations of English librarians. Suggests that odds against a woman reaching level 1 are 2000 to 1. (The article was previously published in *Assistant Librarian* 72, no. 3 [March 1979]: 38–41, and this reprinted abstract can be found in Kathleen Heim and Katharine Phenix, *On Account of Sex: An Annotated Bibliography on the Status of Women in Librarianship 1977–1981* [Chicago: American Library Association, 1984].)

13

Women Librarians as Authors

This chapter encompasses issues related to the writing, publishing, and scholarly communication of women in the field and includes studies of authorship patterns, productivity trends, and authorship profiles, for example.

572. Atinmo, M. I., and S. W. Jimba. "Gender and Authorship Patterns in an African Librarianship Journal, 1991–1997." ***Library Review*** **51, no. 8/9 (2002): 458–63.**

The *African Journal of Library, Archives and Information Science* (AJLAIS) was launched in 1991 as a medium for researchers in Africa in librarianship, archives, information science and other related information fields for disseminating their research findings. At the time the journal was launched (1991), there was no continental journal for disseminating research findings; rather, research findings by African researchers were scattered in moribund national journals in Africa or those published outside the continent. In this article, the authors subjected the journal to analysis by gender, collaboration, and institutional affiliation. They studied 95 research articles contributed by 118 authors and concluded that there is a need to encourage female publication output in all sectors of librarianship and information science in Africa.

573. Bahr, Alice Harrison, and Mickey Zemon. "Collaborative Authorship in the Journal Literature: Perspectives for Academic Librarians Who Wish to Publish." ***College and Research Libraries*** **61, no. 5 (September 2000): 410–18.**

In examining authorship collaboration among academic librarians, the article notes that women are more likely to collaborate with men, men collaborate less than women, and men are more likely to write with women than with other men while the opposite holds true for women.

574. Bahr, Alice Harrison, and Mickey Zemon. "An Analysis of Articles by College Librarians." *College and Research Libraries* 59, no. 5 (September 1998): 422–32.

Presents publishing trends of college librarians and related characteristics. The literature from *College and Research Libraries* and *Journal of Academic Librarianship* was examined from several perspectives, including gender. Women and men published about the same number of articles, despite the fact that there are more women librarians in the profession.

575. Conkling, Diedre. "Dead Links." *Library Journal* 126, no. 20 (1 December 2001): 8.

Conkling responds to Blaise Cronin's "Amazons R Us" (*LJ* 126, no. 17, 2001: 54), reporting that the literature in question, by Sarah Pritchard and Roma Harris, was dated and hard to find online. Cronin's 1995 article, "Shibboleth and Substance in North American Library and Information Science Education" (*Libri* 45, no. 1, 1995: 45–63), stated many of the arguments included in the later *LJ* article. The original article received thoughtful criticism by John Buschman in his "A Blaise with Indignation," from *Progressive Librarian* 10, no.11 (Winter 1995/1996, www.libr.org/PL/10-11_Editorial.html).

576. Cronin, Blaise. "Amazons R Us: Feminist Ideology and Librarianship." *Library Journal* 126, no. 17 (15 October 2001): 54.

Questions the rigor of scholarship investigating the relation between gender and librarianship. Cronin finds an uncritical acceptance of feminist and constructivist ideologies in the writings of Roma Harris and Sarah Pritchard in particular. He suggests that such scholarship is at odds with the reality of librarianship as presented in the professional literature and as experienced by practicing librarians.

577. Cronin, Blaise. *Pulp Friction*. Lanham, MD: Scarecrow Press, 2003.

Included in this compilation of Cronin's *Library Journal* columns are a reprint of his "Amazons R Us" (October 15, 2001) column in which he dismisses the work of feminist scholar/librarians Roma Harris, Hope Olson, and Sarah Pritchard as "speculation masking as scholarship." In response to letters to the editor, Cronin also wrote a short column, which *LJ* declined to print but which is included in this collection, called "Angry Amazons," in which he dismisses most of the responses to his first column as "ad hominem invective." Cronin's "Amazons R Us" column sparked a lengthy discussion on FEMINIST, the listserv of the ALA Feminist Task Force.

578. DeCandido, Grace A. "Cronin's Screed." ***Library Journal*** **126, no. 20 (1 December 2001): 8.**

Responding to Blaise Cronin's "Amazons R Us" (*LJ* 126, no. 17, 2001: 54), DeCandido points to the correct source of a misquotation by Cronin and defends the quality of work by two authors he attacked, Karen G. Schneider and Sarah Pritchard. DeCandido is former editor-in-chief of the ceased *Wilson Library Bulletin*, which published some of the scholarship in question.

579. Gordon, Rachel Singer. "A Feminist Columnist." ***Library Journal*** **127, no. 1 (1 January 2002): 10.**

Gordon responds to Blaise Cronin's "Amazons R Us" (*LJ* 126, no. 17, 2001: 54) and reports that Camille Paglia, whom Cronin calls "redoubtable," identifies herself as an "Amazon feminist." Gordon calls Cronin "reactionary" and suggests that *Library Journal* recruit one of the many feminist scholars maligned by him as a regular columnist.

580. Joswick, Kathleen E. "Article Publication Patterns of Academic Librarians: An Illinois Case Study." ***College and Research Libraries*** **60, no. 4 (July 1999): 340–49.**

Study discusses publishing trends of Illinois librarians in college and research libraries. Data on author gender, collaboration, and numbers of articles are presented. Illinois female librarians are publishing at a rate that is representative of their population in librarianship, unlike women in the field at large. They are also more likely to publish collaboratively.

581. Lipetz, B. A. "Aspects of JASIS Authorship through Five Decades." ***Journal of the American Society for Information Science*** **50, no. 11 (September 1999): 994–1003.**

In 1999, the Journal of the American Society for Information Science (JASIS) celebrated fifty years of publication. It is, by many measures, one of the most important and respected literature sources in the field of information science. In this article, Lipetz studies the publication by examining one volume from each decade and analyzing the data on author's affiliation, gender, and country. Also noted were data on length, content, and "colonicity" of the title, as well as the extent of citing and self-citing in the paper. The percentage of authors who are female had grown (from 20.6 percent in 1955 to 33.8 percent in 1995) but is higher in many related journals than it is in JASIS. Librarian authors (academic or not) grew from 5.9 percent (1955) to 13.8 percent (1995).

582. Schneider, Karen. "Lurching Out of Context." *Library Journal* 126, no. 20 (1 December 2001): 8.

Schneider responds to Blaise Cronin's "Amazons R Us" (*LJ* 126, no. 17, 2001: 54), in which, she claims, a quote from her, "Amazons with laptops," is used out of context and without attribution. Schneider calls the Cronin article an "incoherent assault on women in librarianship."

583. Schulman, Patricia Glass. "Could It Be Sexism?" *Library Journal* 126, no. 20 (1 December 2001): 8.

Schulman responds to Blaise Cronin's "Amazons R Us" (*LJ* 126, no. 17, 2001: 54) and suggests that his attacks on feminism and scholarship about women in librarianship are both groundless and sexist.

584. Wright, Joyce C. "Black Librarians as Creative Writers." In *Handbook of Black Librarianship*, 2nd Edition, ed. E. J. Josey and Marva DeLoach. Lanham, MD: Scarecrow Press, 2000.

Wright conducted interviews and biographical research to write this chapter on black librarians who are also creative writers. Her essays focus not only on her subjects' biographies and publications but also how their writing is impacted by their librarianship, and vice versa. Those profiled include Joyce Cooper Arkhurst, Augusta Braxton Baker, Margaret Perry, Elizabeth Fitzgerald Howard, Sharon Bell Mathis, Audre Geraldine Lorde, Dudley Randall, Anne Spencer, Charlemae Hill Rollins, Ann Allen Shockley, Alice Faye Duncan, Sundaira Morninghouse, Leslie Morgan Collins, Arna Bontemps, Oliver Austin Kirkpatrick (John Canoe), and Vaunda Micheax Nelson.

Author Index

Note: All numbers refer to entries, not pages.

Geographical Index

Note: All numbers refer to entries, not pages.

Subject Index

Note: All numbers refer to entries, not pages.

About the Editors and Contributors

Stephanie Atkins is the assistant circulation and bookstacks librarian at the University of Illinois at Urbana-Champaign Library. She earned her MSLIS from the University of Illinois at Urbana-Champaign in 1999. Her research interests include personnel training, collection management, and project management in libraries.

Stephanie Davis-Kahl is currently the visiting information services librarian at the Ames Library at Illinois Wesleyan University. Previously, she was the research librarian for education and outreach at the University of California Irvine Libraries. Her research interests include the library's contribution to the value and impact of information literacy outreach, creativity in librarianship, and uses of popular culture in information literacy. Stephanie holds a master's degree in library and information science from the University of Illinois at Urbana-Champaign. In her free time, Stephanie enjoys movies, shoe shopping, cooking (mainly desserts), and knitting.

Betty Evans is an assistant professor of library science and reference librarian at Southwest Missouri State University in Springfield. In addition to her reference department responsibilities, she teaches the beginning library science course as well as library instruction for individual classes. Betty's research interests include literacy and the promotion of leisure reading to college students and providing library services in the distance learning environment.

Jennifer Evans has undergraduate degrees in history and women's studies. A librarian since 1997, she has experience in special collections in academic, public, and independent research library settings, including positions at the University of Washington and the Folger Shakespeare Library in Washington, DC. She lives in Seattle, Washington.

Angi Faiks is associate director and collection management team leader of the DeWitt Wallace Library at Macalester College in St. Paul, Minnesota. Angi oversees the serials, acquisitions, cataloging, and collection development operations. She received her master's degree in library science from the University of Illinois.

Dolores Fidishun is head librarian at Penn State Great Valley School of Graduate Professional Studies in Malvern, Pennsylvania. In this position she supervises the library and instructional design departments. Her areas of research include adults and computer training, women and computing, the library/computer center interface, adult education and libraries, and instructional design and technology. She holds an Ed.D. in leadership in higher education and an M.Ed. in adult education from Widener University. Her MSLS is from Drexel University. She also holds a BS in library education from Kutztown University.

Kelly Hovendick is a reference librarian and the subject specialist for sociology and women's studies at the E. S. Bird Library at Syracuse University. Prior to her current position, she was the social sciences librarian at University of Missouri, in Kansas City. She received her master's in information resources and library science from the University of Arizona in 1999.

Betsy Kruger is coordinator of central public services and an associate professor of library administration at the University of Illinois at Urbana-Champaign Library. She earned her master's in library science in 1985 at the University of Chicago.

Catherine A. Larson is associate director of the Artificial Intelligence Lab, in the Management Information Systems department at the University of Arizona. Prior to her present position, she was data services librarian at the University of Arizona Library and had previously held a variety of positions in academic libraries. She received her master's degree in library and information science from the University of Illinois at Urbana-Champaign in 1986.

Helga Luedke is a librarian at Stadtbücherei Frankfurt am Main—die Medienzentrale in Germany.

Rosemary McAndrew, assistant professor/librarian at the Community College of Philadelphia, is responsible for leadership for and management of library instruction. Rosemary is a graduate of the Institute for Information Literacy's immersion program and currently serves on the ACRL Standards & Accreditation Committee. She received her MLS degree from Drexel University and is a master's candidate in the English department of Rutgers University.

Laura Micham is the director of the Sallie Bingham Center for Women's History and Culture, part of Duke University's Rare Book, Manuscript, and Special Collections Library. The Sallie Bingham Center is charged to acquire, preserve, and provide access to published and unpublished (personal papers and organizational records) materials that reflect the public and private lives of women past and present. Laura's recent projects include organizing a symposium on abortion to celebrate the fifteenth anniversary of the Sallie Bingham Center, commemorate the thirtieth anniversary of Roe v. Wade, and promote the Bingham Center's collections documenting the history of abortion. Laura's research interests include the archivist as activist, feminist pedagogy, and the women's health movement.

Carolynne Myall, head of collection services at Eastern Washington University, is active in the Association for Library Collections & Technical Services and the Washington Library Association. She coedited *Portraits in Cataloging and Classification* (Haworth, 1998), edited *Alki: The Washington Library Association Journal* (1998–2002), and has contributed to library journals and reference works.

Hope A. Olson is a professor in the School of Information Studies at the University of Wisconsin, Milwaukee. She received a Ph.D. from the University of Wisconsin, Madison, School of Library and Information Studies in 1996, an MLS from the University of Toronto in 1974, and a BA from Gustavus Adolphus College, St. Peter, Minnesota, in 1972. Her research interests include classification theory; classification and culture; organization of information; feminist, poststructural, and postcolonial perspectives; and bias in subject access standards.

G. Margaret Porter is a librarian in the reference department of the Theodore M. Hesburgh Library, University of Notre Dame. She has served as the subject liaison for the gender studies program since its inception in 1989. In addition to gender studies, she also manages collections in American studies, African American studies, film, television, and theater, and journalism. Her special interests include collection building for interdisciplinary areas, library instruction methods in interdisciplinary studies, and increasing diversity in academic/research libraries.

Bernice Redfern is a reference and instruction librarian at the Martin Luther King Jr. Library at San Jose State University and serves as a liaison to the departments of anthropology, sociology, and social sciences.

Melanie Remy is the instructional services coordinator for the information services division at the University of Southern California.

Amber Ritchie is a graduate student at the School of Library and Information Studies at the University of Alberta.

Sandy River is an architecture and humanities librarian at the Texas Tech University Libraries. She serves as liaison to and selector for the TTU women's studies program.

Ryan Roberts earned his M.S. and C.A.S. in library and information science from the University of Illinois at Urbana-Champaign and, since 2000, has worked as a faculty librarian at Lincoln Land Community College. He maintains the official websites for British authors Julian Barnes (www.julianbarnes.com) and Ian McEwan (www.ianmcewan.com) and is editorial assistant for the London publisher *Between the Lines*. He is currently compiling a bibliography of the works of Julian Barnes.

Susan E. Searing is an associate professor of library administration at the University of Illinois, Urbana-Champaign, where she is in charge of the Library & Information Science Library. She previously worked as the associate director for public services at the University of Wisconsin, Madison, Library, as the women's studies librarian for the multi-campus University of Wisconsin system, and as a reference librarian at Yale University. She coteaches a course at UIUC on "Race, Gender, and Information Technology." In 1992 she was honored with the ALA Equality Award. In 2000, she was the first recipient of the ACRL Women's Studies Section Award for Career Achievement in Women's Studies Librarianship.